Thinking Continental

Thinking

UNIVERSITY OF NEBRASKA PRESS | LINCOLN AND LONDON

Continental

Writing the Planet
One Place at a Time

Edited by Tom Lynch,
    Susan Naramore Maher,
Drucilla Wall,
    and O. Alan Weltzien

Poetry in "Return to Finland, Robert Creeley, Continental Drift" is from *Selected Poems of Robert Creeley, 1945–2005*, by Robert Creeley, edited by Benjamin Friedlander. © 2008 by the Regents of the University of California. Published by the University of California Press. Used with permission. Lines of poetry in "Pathways of the Yellowstone" from Gary Holthaus's *Circling Back* (Salt Lake City: Peregrine Smith, 1984) are use with permission from the author. Lines of poetry in "Life on the Western Edge of It All: Conceptions of Place in Tess Gallagher's Lough Arrow Poems" are from Tess Gallagher's "Oliver," in *Narrative* (Spring 2016), www.narrativemagazine.com/issues/spring-2016/poetry/oliver-tess-gallagher and from *Midnight Lantern: New and Selected Poems* (Minneapolis: Graywolf Press, 2011) are used with permission from the author.

Library of Congress Control Number: 2016054692

Set in ITC New Baskerville by Rachel Gould.

Contents

PART 2 | *Watershed Ways*

Introduction

An Alignment of Stones

TOM LYNCH, SUSAN NARAMORE MAHER,
DRUCILLA WALL, AND O. ALAN WELTZIEN

In his book *Staying Put: Making a Home in a Restless World* (1994) Scott Russell Sanders argues passionately that people should find a congenial place to live and then root themselves deeply into it, resisting the blandishments and professional allure of constant mobility. He argues that such an approach is best for both human communities and the natural world. Wendell Berry has made a similar proposition for decades throughout his vast corpus of volumes. While many readers have been inspired by such arguments, and certainly there is much to recommend them, the perspective offered by Sanders and Berry has also been criticized. Their "staying put" ethos, the argument goes, is a potentially provincial and narrow privileging of local knowledge and identity over the more global, cosmopolitan, or planetary perspectives that represent the world we really live in and the scale of the environmental threats we really face. The "staying put" arguments are sometimes portrayed, whether fairly or not, as a kind of nostalgic retreat from the complexities of an increasingly globalized planet.

This dichotomy is well represented by the title of Ursula Heise's book *Sense of Place and Sense of Planet: The Environmental Imagination of the Global* (2008). Heise decries the essentialism that often limits discussions of place and argues that "remaining in one place for many decades, taking care of a house or farm, intimately knowing the local environment, cultivating local relationships, being as self-sufficient as possible, resisting new technologies that do not improve human life spiritually as well as materially are options no longer available to many."[1] The consumer economy reshapes landscapes across the planet, she argues, creating "nonplaces," "geographies of nowhere."[2] Moreover, cosmopolitan allegiances pull against local affinities, place-based identity. "In a context of rapidly increasing connections around the globe," Heise puts forward, "what is crucial for ecological awareness and environmental ethics is arguably not so much a sense of place as a sense of planet." Networks—"political, economic, technological, social, ecological"—link the many scales of life lived, from the local out into the world.[3] Heise's book is an insightful corrective to a sometimes fetishized and uncritical worship of the local. As she wryly notes with her opening reference to the *Hitchhiker's Guide to the Galaxy*, what is "local" is simply a matter of perspective.[4] Indeed, astronomers speak of a local group of galaxies.

It's perhaps not a coincidence that the proponents of localism are more likely to be North Americans—from the United States or Canada—whereas the skeptics of localism tend to be, like Heise, more internationally inflected. Sanders, Berry, and others of the localist persuasion are responding to specific North American circumstances. In nations composed to a large degree of settler colonial immigrants, and in which people move from place to place with remarkable ease, it makes sense to see many social and environmental problems as products of hypermobility and a lack of rootedness and loyalty to place. There's a strong logic at work here. But such a perspective makes less sense in, say, Europe, where many people have lived hundreds of generations in the same small region and where a sense of distinctive place-based identity and belonging to the soil has as often bred discord as harmony. For people whose ancestry in a place might go back to the Bronze Age but who are now daily battered by a deterritorializing array of globally deployed forces, the staying put argument might well seem obtuse.

In the critical move to simplify and establish easy dichotomies such as these, however, people commonly exaggerate differences and ignore complexity. Though it has become a critical commonplace to denounce binary thinking, such thinking permeates the discussion, obscuring the many ways, for example, Heise expresses sympathy for rooted local knowledge and Sanders acknowledges the need for global awareness. "We can live wisely in our chosen place," Sanders avers, "only if we recognize its connections to the rest of the planet." Such recognition is hard won. "The challenge," he explains, "is to see one's region as a focus of processes that extend over the earth and out to the edges of the universe." Each place, in his assessment, "is only one of an infinite number of places where the powers of nature show forth."[5] Mitch Thomashow's book *Bringing the Biosphere Home* makes a comparable argument. Thomashow links backyard to biosphere and shows how knowledge of planetary ecological processes informs one's local awareness and, crucially, vice versa. His phrase *cosmopolitan bioregionalism* may seem an oxymoron to those who prefer to think in binaries, but it makes perfect sense if one understands the essential interconnectedness of local and planetary. Heise's comparable term, *eco-cosmopolitanism*, approaches the same insight from a different direction. If we think of the "cosmo" in both formulations to mean not simply the urban, with which it is often conflated, but the planetary (and in some senses, after all, the *cosmic*), then the distinction between Heise's "planet" and Thomashow's "biosphere" seems more a matter of emphasis than kind; and though one might be identified as a bioregional localist and the other a cosmopolitan globalist, in fact their commonalities outweigh their differences.

Yet even here we must be cautious. Cosmopolitanism has its own limitations. It tends to presume that what works for the metropolis works as well for the provinces and that the values and interests of an educated and much-traveled elite (such as most of the authors and readers of this book) can represent the values and interests of all. It's no surprise that Berry has challenged the popular bumper sticker slogan "Think Global Act Local." He argues that not only is it not desirable to think globally but it is not even possible; it is a dangerous illusion.[6] For Berry global thinking relies on a level of abstraction that is anathema and represents more the cause than the solution to our planetary environmental crises. We can never know enough to think globally, he cautions, and it is a caution we would do well to heed.

But in general the argument of this volume is that such dichotomies—local-global, cosmopolitan-provincial, place-planet— are misleading. If it doesn't quite adopt Berry's utter skepticism, it is nevertheless suspicious of the many kinds of abstractions that often pass for global thinking. Separating place from planet, it suggests, is a bit like separating organ from body. It can be done, but the consequences are rarely beneficial.

In regard to terminology we are inclined to advocate the distinction bioregionalist Peter Berg has proposed between the "global" and the "planetary." Pairing nation-states with the term *globe* and bioregions with the term *planet,* Berg distinguishes between globalism and what he refers to as "planetarianism." "Planetarians . . . are people who view themselves from within the biosphere," he proposes, "rather than from the top of it, extend importance beyond the human species to include other life and the processes by which all life continues. The planet is organismic," he offers, "and expresses itself through diversity." He argues that "we are in the midst of a crucial struggle between globalist and planetarian interests regarding our ongoing mutual inhabitation of this planet." Berg sees "globalists" as allied with "trans-national corporations" in a process of "taking away the potential for planetary/regional consciousness."[7]

We think this is a useful distinction, to align *global* with the transnational political and corporate systems engaged in a process commonly referred to as globalization, and to use *planetary* to refer to biospheric, multicultural, and eco-centered interrelationships that often form the core of resistance to globalization. Such a distinction has more recently been advocated by Paul Gilroy in *Postcolonial Melancholia.* Responding to very different circumstances (racial politics in the British Isles), Gilroy proposes to pair the idea of the local not with the global but, like Berg before him, with "the idea of planetarity." "I have opted for this concept," he argues, "rather than the more familiar notion of 'globalization' because those regularly confused terms, 'planetary' and 'global'—which do point to some of the same varieties of social phenomena—resonate quite differently. The planetary suggests both contingency and movement. It specifies a smaller scale than the global, which transmits all the triumphalism and complacency of ever-expanding imperial universals."[8]

In one formulation in which he seeks to merge the local with the planetary, Berg proposes a sequence of nested scales from "bioregion to continent to planet," offering the continent as the mediating nexus between one's local bioregion and the planet's biosphere.[9] Hence, we propose, "thinking continental" could be construed to mean the capacity to think between scales, to connect the local with the planetary. Such is the aim of this volume.

In the last decade environmentally focused writers and scholars across disciplines have placed greater emphasis on examining the Anthropocene, discerning Critical Zone science, chronicling political ecologies, and articulating the concept of a global or planetary citizenship. The aftermath of colonialism and settler colonialism, the continuation of extractive industrial practices, the reality of weapons of mass destruction and climate change, have added urgency to the art and science of landscape writing. How the local and planetary interconnect or act disparately, how discrete microclimates relate to the larger biome, how human communities tie into the fabric of all life, have made "writing for an endangered world" (one of Lawrence Buell's titles) pressing and fraught. Reckoning with macrospace—the larger matrix of biome, region, continent, hemisphere, ocean—has become necessary as humanity grapples with extreme weather, deforestation, industrial agriculture, species decline, and topocide. The "glocal" perspective continually widens out from one's chosen landscape and continually returns to it; it best enables us, for example, to imagine and act upon the accumulating evidence of climate change, wherein extreme weather "events" and patterns constitute a shifting, new norm. Concepts such as bioregionalism, geo-engineering, disaster risk reduction, ecological humanities, and the like have energized environmental studies in the twenty-first century. The authors of *Sustaining Earth's Critical Zone* argue that alternations "in land use and climate are forcing rapid and profound changes in the continental surface that require an unprecedented intensity and scale of scientific observation."[10]

These challenges also require the keen insights not only of scientists but of poets, humanists, and social scientists as well. Among the false dichotomies this volume seeks to challenge is the one between the sciences and the humanities. The complications of history—natural and cultural—in Buell's assessment have put humans in a world where "environmental connectedness requires acts of imagination not at one stage alone but three: in the bonding, in the telling, in the understanding."[11] Imagination remains a potent force in assessing and reconfiguring the landscapes around us, the social constructions we have inherited. This volume braids together these various theoretical and academic approaches with strands of more personal narrative and poetry, seeking to provide one model of how our imaginations can encompass the planetary while also being true to the experiences of our own bodies in our own life places.

We have clustered the essays into three sections. Each section title reflects a common texture or condition pervading those particular essays. The first section, "Ground Truths," contains essays preoccupied with landscapes or landforms. The second, "Watershed Ways," features essays focusing upon bodies of water, whether rivers, lakes, or saltwater coastlines. The third, "Planetary Currents," includes essays overtly concerned with ways in which international or intercontinental forces shape particular contemporary local economic conditions or conceptions of identity as well as the planetary exchange of literary texts, their writers, and their influences.

Opening "Ground Truths," Elizabeth Dodd's "A World of Islands" provides a lyrical meditation on island biodiversity by way of her visit to New Zealand's Maud Island, a sanctuary for highly endangered species located between New Zealand's north and south islands. Flightless birds such as the kakapo, the world's largest parrot, struggle for survival on this island strictly controlled by New Zealand's Department of Conservation and under constant threat of invasions by mice, rats, and stoats. Her essay meditates on the tangle between indigenous and exotic species in the spirit of David Quammen's *The Song of the Dodo*, which she cites near the end of her piece.

O. Alan Weltzien's "Three Stations along the Ring of Fire," a wide canvas, focuses upon the world's largest chain of volcanoes and earthquake hotspots, of which New Zealand forms a corner. Organized around a triptych of famous volcanoes he climbed—Washington's Mount Rainier, Japan's Mount Fuji, and Ecuador's Chimborazo—he speculates about both the felt sense of connection and disconnection along the ring that girdles the Pacific Ocean. He concludes that this macroregion challenges and disputes any experience of unity because its size defies our ability to imaginatively close the circle.

Geologist Harmon Maher, in "The Deepest Layer," oscillates between the two research areas that have defined his career: the central Great Plains of North America and Svalbard, an archipelago north of Norway. Maher uses the metaphor of layers, or strata, to explain his search for the novel, when he "see[s] the edge of understanding," and his appreciation of landscape aesthetics. To underline his celebration of beauty in geology, he includes ten photographs that, with his graceful expository captions, point us back to his title and provide the aesthetic answer to its implicit question.

Nessa Cronin's "Ground Truths: Deep Mapping Communities in the West of Ireland" embraces deep mapping in validating community mapping projects. Cronin chronicles the work of the x-po Mapping Group in Kilnaboy Parish, County Clare, as a prototype of a more "creative process of place making." The result of this particular mapping of the invisible landscape (Kent Ryden's title) is a vertical and horizontal map neither fixed nor complete, an open-ended work in progress. From the "The Full Story? Tracing Kilnaboy Townlands" exhibit, Cronin concludes that *place*—this rural place or any other—always includes attachment, detachment, and mobility.

The next pair of essays, by two Italian scholars, zero in on a pair of specific Italian landscapes not that far from one another. Fabiana Dimpflmeier's essay, "Where Narratives Met: Microplace and Macrospace in Early Fascist Primary School Textbooks and the Case of Eugenio Cirese's *Gente buona*," studies a crucial 1925 text that documents a revitalized regionalism that in turn sponsored a revitalized nationalism. *Gente buona*, both "a primary school textbook dedicated to the Molise region" (on the Adriatic) and an "anthology of literary texts," illustrated a new interest in dialects and so-called regional primitivism. This new validation of a local landscape extols, above all, the Molise population's "relationship to the land." National identity, in her argument, depends upon specific local ground truths.

Andrea Benassi's essay, "Imagining the Memory of the Earth: Geo-

Site and the Aesthetic of the Anthropocene," defines the concept of "geo-heritage park" through a case study of Gypsum Mountain Park in Italy's Romagna region. Benassi argues for "geo-heritage as a public space." Under the sign of the Anthropocene, he construes two definitions of the same landscape: one as a product of "deep global time" and the other as an extractive site according to traditions of farming and gypsum mining. Focusing upon Tiberius's Cave near Mount Tondo, he sees contrary traditions of use by miners, scientists, and cavers, just as the cave area includes both a natural system of cavities and passageways and a contrary linear system denoted by mineshafts and tunnels. The essay cautions against risks to the karst system and microclimate from continued gypsum mining.

"Ground Truths" closes with Jess Allen and Bronwyn Preece's "Cacophonous Silence (The Sound of Falling Wildly): A Transnational Experiment in Ecological Performance Poiesis." This "collaborative composition" by two performance artists, one from central Wales and the other from coastal British Columbia, spins off the familiar koan-like question concerning the sound of a tree falling in the forest. By their own account a "reflexive-poetic reading of the multi-month transnational performance," which is "not necessarily linear," the piece is multi-textual, a braid of poetry and commentary in several fonts that invites readers "to fall" and embrace uncertainty. They claim falling serves as "a performative device for eco-activist performance." Their work includes a video performance available on the internet and suggests that thinking continental, and indeed *trans*continental, may require experimental and hybrid forms of artistic production.

The anthology's second section, "Watershed Ways," features six distinct locations along rivers or lakes, seashores, and one sea. It opens with Tom Lynch's "Braided Channels of Watershed Consciousness: Loren Eiseley's 'The Flow of the River' and the Platte Basin Timelapse Project." Lynch closely reads one of Eiseley's most famous essays, "The Flow of the River," and pairs it with the Platte Basin Timelapse Project, created by two Nebraska photographers. Over forty remote cameras (shooting every thirty seconds) dispersed across the 90,000 square-mile basin enable online viewers to experience both the river's flow and unity. This paired example of "watershed consciousness" enables the process of "narrative re-inhabitation."

Brendan Galvin's "Plovers, Great Blues, Horned Owls: A Poet's Ecotone," written in the tradition of Thoreauvian close observation, records and lyrically celebrates his walk of decades along a salt marsh and beach located on upper Cape Cod Bay. Galvin embodies the wisdom of local knowledge because "this one place, occupying maybe a square mile, is endless." Though he claims himself an amateur birder, Galvin records and extols nuanced changes in migratory bird populations and fisheries. His ecotone blending salt water, dunes, marsh, and woodland includes chapters from the modern human history of the Little Pamet River.

Susan Naramore Maher's "Superior: Reimagining the Interior of a Continent" opens and closes at Hawk Ridge Bird Observatory, above the north shore of Lake Superior. The many strands of "Gitchee Gumee," Duluth, and North Woods history she gathers illustrate her theme of "this grand exchange," wherein "itinerancy is a defining aspect of Superior's shores." This meditation upon seasonal change highlights "ice-out," spring fishery runs, and the geologic, trapping, and shipping histories of this interior region bordered by a lake larger than our imagining. It spans Ojibwe and Dakota occupancy and her own migration to this region several years ago. Maher gracefully demonstrates the process of residency, of dwelling in a place characterized by migration.

Migration poses the central issue in Bernard Quetchenbach's "Pathways of the Yellowstone," a Rocky Mountains counterpart to Maher's paean. His opening provides an overture of histories of migration. Quetchenbach uses a German biological term, *Zugunruhe*, "the characteristic urge that spurs migration," as a lens through which to examine patterns of motion through the Yellowstone Park and river valley, both sites of "crossing paths." He traces bird, pronghorn, buffalo, Native American, and nineteenth-century "westering" migrations, nodding ultimately at the railroad and Billings, Montana's largest city, and he closes with his own migration back to this region, where he had earlier worked for four years.

Rick Van Noy's "The Proximity of Far Away: Climate Change

Comes to the Alligator" shifts the focus and uses North Carolina's Alligator River National Wildlife Refuge to unpack the paradox of his title—the governing paradox of climate change. In the context of ocean warming Van Noy assesses the psychology of climate change deniers as he interviews local officials regarding, and himself experiences, dramatic shifts in a key shoreline ecotone. In this "frontline community" tree mortality spikes because of salination, and the piping plover serves as a "dying canary in a very dangerous coal mine." Van Noy argues that to save this refuge, we must invoke "that protective instinct" and tell stories that "should involve how climate change affects something very near and dear to each of us."

Mary Swander's essay, "What You Take from the Sea," shows this Iowa writer in temporary residence in her mother's home country in Connemara, on Ireland's western tip. In her Claddaghduff cottage she witnesses the community's timeless response to the drowning of two local fishermen in a currach and compares their response to playwright John Millington Synge's tight, classical tragedy, *Riders to the Sea*. Swander experiences anew Synge's play through the funeral masses and burials of these two men in St. Brendan's Cemetery on Omey Island, where many ancestors of her own are also buried. Her elegiac essay highlights a community's dependence upon the seas and the constant dangers inherent in that dependency.

Finally, Emilio Cocco's "Recontinentalizing Europe: Terrestrial Conversion and Symbolic Exchange at Europe's Mediterranean Frontier" urges a fundamental perspectival shift, from landmasses to the seas, because oceans constitute "the primary *medium* of a globalized society." Cocco borrows from border studies an emphasis upon "social and material exchanges between the seas and the land" in lobbying for "alternative, post-terrestrial macro-spatial ideas" for Europe. He calls upon scholars to reconceive Europe from its changing "social-material edges" and reconnect the Mediterranean Sea "with a macro-spatial European representation in which the sea is mostly absent." His advocacy of "material and imaginary 'terrestrial conversions' of watery spaces" seems prescient in the twenty-first century.

Part 3, "Planetary Currents," explicitly stresses a primary theme of this collection, the chronic interpenetration of the planetary with the local. Nancy S. Cook's "The Lariat and the GPS: Cowboys, Cattle Ranching, and Global Agricultural Practices" advocates a new kind of ranching story that accurately reflects twenty-first-century macroregional realities defined by a range of international trade agreements and corporations. She argues that too much nineteenth- and twentieth-century literature involving ranching celebrates the lore of cowboy and microregion despite the long history of hybridity and adaptation. Her essay insists upon a stronger alignment and assessment of the "rhetorics of ranching cultures" in terms of the "rhetorics of macroregions."

Drucilla Wall's "Life on the Western Edge of It All: Conceptions of Place in Tess Gallagher's Lough Arrow Poems" begins with Wall's close observation and love of this western Ireland site in County Sligo and then moves fluidly in and out of American poet Tess Gallagher's poetry set in this place. Gallagher, a (U.S.) Pacific Northwest native, has for decades compared two Wests in her work, the American and the Irish, which enables Wall to find unlikely resemblances, identifying these Wests as similar climatic and mythological regions that embrace, even insist upon, a unity of all living processes, including death. Wall's celebration of "westness" as ecotone and liminal zone again attests to the presence of the planetary in the local.

In Eamonn Wall's "Return to Finland, Robert Creeley, Continental Drift" the celebrated Irish American poet takes stock of his "multiple sense of belonging," his feeling of being "at home on two continents." Back in Helsinki with his new American citizenship, he's mistaken for Irish even as he studies poet Robert Creeley's unhappy residency in Helsinki (1989) in terms of Creeley's return visit (1996). By way of Creeley and his own experience, Wall argues that "writing is local and continental rather than national."

And finally, Joel Weishaus's piece, "Excerpts from COSMOGRA- PHY: Re-Minding Our Place in the Universe," assumes a wide-angle, global-cosmic perspective. He first describes his "five-year Digital Literary Project that reflects the universe archetypally." As a journal, it features "the trope of invagination," a species of footnote commentary that itself constitutes one genre among many. Weishaus's "project" includes seven planets, sun, moon, and "Incognita," "a body . . . encircling Earth in pre-Copernican orbit"—a whimsical glance back to geocentrism. Like an intriguing appetizer, the "excerpts" include three numbered sections from sun, moon, and Saturn, respectively.

Serving as a form of word-music and an invitation to further contemplation, at the end of each of the book's three sections we provide a grouping of poems to crown the concepts of the vast, expansive, and intimately complex interconnectedness of our continents. The poets engage history, science, nature, migration, eco-consciousness, and, of course, the inevitable mysteries of the human heart. Thirty-nine poems in all, they resonate among themselves and with the prose essays around them to enhance the reader's experience of the book as a whole. Like jewels catching the light unexpectedly, the poems draw the mind's eye into experiences both familiar and strange.

Among the thirty-one distinguished poets are five U.S. state poets laureate: Walter Bargen and Aliki Barnstone of Missouri, Kimberly Blaeser of Wisconsin, Twyla M. Hansen of Nebraska, and Alberto Ríos of Arizona. In addition, Indigenous poets Alice Azure, Kimberly Blaeser, Heid E. Erdrich, and Linda Hogan add deeper dimensions to the poetic conversation. Irish and Irish American voices, including Michael S. Begnal, David Brannan, Tony Curtis, Greg Delanty, Susan Millar Dumars, Tess Gallagher, Michael Heffernan, Barry Johnston, Joan McBreen, Daniel Tobin, and Colm Tóibín, offer an international, transatlantic, and immigrant perspective. And a sprinkling of American poets with hybrid identities and the accompanying intriguing points of view further highlight how we interact with the natural world in both local and global ways. They include David Brannan, Christine Casson, Kelly Cherry, Dawn Dupler, Ann Fisher-Wirth, Brendan Galvin, Major Jackson, William Logan, David Lloyd, Marjorie Saiser, Katherine Soniat, Pamela Uschuk, and O. Alan Weltzien. These poets have collectively authored dozens of books of poetry, essays, translations, and scholarly works as well as hundreds of individual pieces contributed to the best anthologies, collections, literary journals, and online publications, not to men-tion the many awards and honors they have accumulated with nearly embarrassing frequency.

The three sections of poetry are designed to hold an intuitive progression of ideas and emotions that resonate with each other and with the essays. The intriguing, and often unexpected, range of imagery, sound, rhythm, form, and argument suggests varied and meaningful ways for readers to grapple with and engage the many-layered sense of place that shapes each of us, as we move into our shared future of contested interactions with both the natural world and built environments in the simultaneous interconnection of local experience and global beingness that can be called "writing the planet one place at a time." These carefully chosen and sequenced poems look deeply into complex and elusive experience, leaving the reader fortified and ready for further thought and endeavor.

Bringing together the distinctive imaginations and voices of these various scholars, writers, and poets across landscapes, experiences, disciplines, and genres is the central project of *Thinking Continental.* From their locations on continental river systems, isolated islands, oceanic shores, on the North American grasslands, the Italian mountains, the Irish coastline, or the forests of British Columbia, contributors to this collection wrestle with the complexities of a place-based writing that wants to speak to larger realities, greater connections, and global currents.

In the Gleninagh Valley, tucked deep inside the complexly folded landscape of the Twelve Ben mountains of Ireland's Connemara region, Tim Robinson lay on a sunny slope sipping coffee with his hiking companion. As he watched the inevitable sheep grazing across the valley, his eyes were arrested by "a row of little bumps on the profile of a low ridge a few hundred yards away. Something regular, it seemed, something organized, contrasting with the sprawling topography of the bog; evidently worth investigating." Roused from repose, he crossed the boggy landscape and was climbing the glacial moraine that transects the valley when he noticed that "there on the crest of the ridge was a line of six boulders; roundish, sack-shaped, glacial boulders of quartzite. There was no doubt about which way the line pointed; the largest—it was only waist-high—being at one end, and distinguished from the rest by the streaks of white quartz in it." "I knew enough," he remarks in "Through Prehistoric Eyes," "to recognize this as a Bronze Age site."[12] Later he mentioned the stone arrangement to an archaeologist friend, who was inspired to visit the site. Pondering the stone alignment with a trained eye, the archaeologist "noted that they do not just point vaguely at the mountains, they point precisely at the col, the high pass between two peaks, above the precipice. And, revisiting the site on midwinter's eve, he observed that the sun sets neatly into that cleft in the horizon, when viewed from the alignment."[13]

With his voracious fractal curiosity, Robinson traces the implications of this discovery, noting that "the mountains themselves are 460 million years old, and the moraine was built ten or fifteen thousand years ago, but it was in the Bronze Age, say four thousand years ago, that this focusing of the terrain into a landscape took place—an event of a new sort, an act characteristic and perhaps definitive of humanity of all times and all places."[14] Robinson considers the ancient origin of the rocks, the tectonic forces that raised the mountains, the subsequent erosion and patient glaciation that carved the valley, the casual tumbling of the boulders onto the valley floor, and the eventual arrangement of those boulders to mark the seasonal dance of the Earth and sun by a long-vanished Bronze Age people, who, by doing so, transformed terrain into landscape, abstract space into meaningful place. And then, of course, the casual notice of these boulders thousands of years later by a passerby who sought to understand their meaning and so brought them back into the fold of human awareness, thereby restoring their role as mediators between human and cosmos. Robinson emphasizes that "this site marks the intersection of an astronomical constant with a constant of human spatial awareness; it is in itself ceremonious, observant of the geometry of humanity and the heavens."[15]

In describing the stones of Gleninagh Valley, Robinson shows how intense concentration on the local, the very here and the very now, can set in motion a chain of connections and associations that generate an understanding of place extending deep into time and distant into space. Every place, however nondescript and seemingly secluded and provincial, is marked with the traces of the entire planet's becoming. Like those Bronze Age people who aligned these stones, we just need to be observant, open to possibilities, and so be able to synchronize our own embodied and local awareness with the larger passage of our home planet through space and across time.

Such is the ambition of this volume.

NOTES

1. Heise, *Sense of Place and Sense of Planet*, 53–54.
2. See John Tomlinson's argument on "nonplaces" in *Globalization and Culture* and James Howard Kunstler's characterization of the homogenizing forces of the modern economy in *The Geography of Nowhere.*
3. Heise, *Sense of Place and Sense of Planet*, 55.
4. Heise, *Sense of Place and Sense of Planet*, 3.
5. Sanders, *Staying Put*, xvi.
6. Berry, "Futility of Global Thinking."
7. Berg, *Biosphere and the Bioregion*, 42–43.
8. Gilroy, *Postcolonial Melancholia*, xv.
9. Berg, *Biosphere and the Bioregion*, 27.
10. Banwart et al., *Sustaining Earth's Critical Zone*, 3.
11. Buell, *Writing for an Endangered World*, 17.
12. Robinson, "Through Prehistoric Eyes," 200.
13. Robinson, "Through Prehistoric Eyes," 201.
14. Robinson, "Through Prehistoric Eyes," 205.
15. Robinson, "Through Prehistoric Eyes," 203.

BIBLIOGRAPHY

Banwart, S. A., J. Chorover, J. Gaillardet, D. Sparks, T. White, S. Anderson, A. Aufdenkampe, S. Bernasconi, S. Brantley, O. Chadwick, C. Duffy, M. Goldhaber, K. Lenhart, N. P. Nikolaidis, and K. V. Ragnarsdottir. *Sustaining Earth's Critical Zone: Basic Science and Interdisciplinary Solutions for Global Challenges.* Sheffield: University of Sheffield Press, 2013.
Berg, Peter. *The Biosphere and the Bioregion: Essential Writings of Peter Berg.* Edited by Cheryll Glotfelty and Eve Quesnel. New York: Routledge, 2015.
Berry, Wendell. "The Futility of Global Thinking." *Harper's*, September 1989, 16–22.
Buell, Lawrence. *Writing for an Endangered World: Literature, Culture, and Environment in the U.S. and Beyond.* Cambridge MA: Belknap, 2001.

Gilroy, Paul. *Postcolonial Melancholia.* New York: Columbia University Press, 2005.

Heise, Ursula K. *Sense of Place and Sense of Planet: The Environmental Imagination of the Global.* Oxford: Oxford University Press, 2008.

Kunstler, James Howard. *The Geography of Nowhere: The Rise and Decline of America's Man-Made Landscape.* New York: Touchstone, 1993.

Robinson, Tim. "Through Prehistoric Eyes." *Setting Foot on the Shores of Connemara and Other Writings.* Dublin: Lilliput Press, 1997.

Sanders, Scott Russell. *Staying Put: Making a Home in a Restless World.* Boston: Beacon, 1993.

Tomlinson, John. *Globalization and Culture.* Chicago: University of Chicago Press, 1999.

Thinking Continental

PART 1 | *Ground Truths*

A World of Islands

ELIZABETH DODD

The problem with Deep Time is figuring how to figure it. In animations of old Pangaea, the Northern Hemisphere slides away to its separate destiny and leaves behind Gondwanaland, still dedicated to continuity, a continent for how-many-millions-of-years before India speedboats north to pry the Himalayas skyward as it rams the Eurasian coast. Here's a depicted globe, arrows like an acupuncturist's needles bristling in the ocean's skin. Here's a Mercator Projection like the maps pulled down against cement block walls from fifth grade at East Elementary or rolled out on the living room floor. Maybe it's the latter, since the corners seem dim and poorly focused, the overhead light fixture reaching only so far.

The major players are all drawn in bold black lines: South America, Africa, India, Australia. Antarctica lurks on the horizon, and I want to make some touch-screen move to shift perspective, pulling the brown-or-white border to the center screen. New Zealand is always way off in the margin, unrecognizable. In contrast to Africa's confident outline, these islands seem like a series of botched attempts to draw the inner ear: the hammer, anvil, and stirrup are all shaken loose from their proper positions and left in a pile where the artist grew tired of this science fair project and went out for a nice walk. While the story of the mammals-that-became-us continues with Africa front and center, New Zealand's drama carries on so nearly offstage it's almost like a deliberate sleight-of-hand, everyone who wants to cuddle the baby gorillas or even the koalas distracted while, a tiny island world on two tectonic plates, New Zealand stretches its changing body and the moas rise to browse the austral bush.

Here's a clock face with the ages of the Earth arrayed like hours around the analog rim. The lifeless world appears as noon-to-three; the next six hours are cryptozoic meditation while the planet learns to breathe. Carbon dioxide in, oxygen out. At ten forty-five life climbs out on the land to sun itself and test the metamorphosed air. I keep staring at Australia, the modern continent with Tasmania like a corner broken off and Asia splayed along the planet's upper left. *Where is New Zealand?* That part of the planet is shaded dark, like the polar circles, and if I bring my nose to the page, the book directly under the desk lamp where I've worked all morning, I can nearly convince myself I see a pale smudge. It's the way we imagine the unconscious, floating somewhere in our oceanic selves, and god only knows what pilgrimages might take us there.

Divarication from the source: ancestors of the ratites, giant flightless birds, walked across Antarctica (deciduous then, despite long winter darkness within the polar circle). What was that like, un-iced, unfrozen, cycling through the never-dark of polar summer and, on the flip side, a mild never-light? When I visited the Rio Negro in Brazil, each rotation of the Earth split time into equal parts: by six thirty every evening, the sun fell straight down, fast, into a sweltering tropical night, frogs hollering from the flooded treetops, Orion standing on his head in the sky above. At dawn howler monkeys and a clatter of parakeets. Once I saw a rhea in a wet meadow near the Amazon's delta. I saw it in full sun.

Rhea, emu, ostrich, cassowary, kiwi. Strong legged, thick boned, wings no more than window dressing, denim watch pockets that never hold a pocket watch. Gondwana birds. Moa: Diornis. Euryapteryx. Anomalopteryx. Pachyornis. Emeus. Megalapteryx. *Where is New Zealand?*

On the map Maud Island looks like one of the pair of abstract stingray earrings my partner, Dave, gave me one year so I could keep a glint of sunlit water on my body after a week at the beach. Thimble-tiny in the filigree of sea-circled hilltops in Marlborough Sound, at the top of New Zealand's South Island, the island offers refuge to a few of the species disappearing from the archipelago continent. Like much of the country, Maud Island was turned to agriculture ("hill farms," we'd call them in Appalachia, where I grew up) by the end of the nineteenth century. Sheep, goats, I don't know what else. Then in the 1970s the government acquired the property as a scientific research station and a wildlife preserve. Only 5 percent of its native forest—"bush," the New Zealanders say—still plunges roots into the island's abrupt slopes. But protected now, the bush is growing back.

Somehow this thumbprint hilltop had, through three centuries since Europeans first arrived, escaped the scourge of mice. The rats-stoats-weasels triumvirate of New Zealand bird death has been absent for decades now, banished when the preserve was opened. Australian possums, if they were ever here, are gone as well. None of these mammals was indigenous; they'd all arrived with Europeans, hundreds of years after the Polynesians' dogs and rats gave the first interruption to the geologic epochs—seven of them—where birds evolved without mammals in the shadows to shape quick, evasive lives. Insular, as if afloat, a raft without wolves, coyotes, lions, deer. Without rats. Without, mostly, us.

Now endemic geckos cluster in old concrete structures in the woods' returning shade. At night little blue penguins return from the day's fishing and seem to limp along the slippery streambed to nesting boxes set out for them on a hillside trail. "Fairy penguins," they're also called, but their ungainly gait uphill makes them look more like harbor seals auditioning for the role of Sisyphus in a comedy film. Brought back from another island, a population of endangered weta—crickets that grow as big as mice—are doing well. A pair of takahe, dark-feathered and scarlet-billed gallinules the size of a large rooster—of which only two hundred or so exist in the world— are raising supremely ugly chicks in the pasture slopes remaining from the island's days of farmland. Just a few dozen sheep still stand around in a general posture of dull resentment in their fenced-in paddock near the manager's house.

The island, once a defensive lookout against Axis invasion during World War II, was considered safe enough to become a breeding center for the world's largest parrot, the kakapo, a creature brought as close to extinction as North America's whooping crane or California condor. I've seen condors in the range of their reintroduction, like data spots plotted on a closely watched map: on the Grand Canyon's south rim, where young from the captive breeding program are introduced, still in cages, to the adults already free; one bird soared beside the highway in southern Utah; one perched along the Bright Angel trail. I've seen whooping cranes a thousand miles apart: in the washed-out light of the Texas coast; in New Mexico's Bosque del Apache, in water glistening beneath the breath of autumn-yellow cottonwoods; in Kansas and Nebraska, glimpsed in brief, migratory stops; in Wisconsin, where chicks are hand-raised by puppets, each bird precious in the tally of a population trying to lift high enough to cast a shadow beneath transcontinental flight.

But the kakapo, like the takahe, like the kiwi, like the moa laid low by Maori hunters in just a few generations—all these birds are flightless. Nocturnal, slow moving, kakapo are so poorly equipped to contend with predatory mammals that they never think to flee. They freeze. Even their shadows, in starlight, disappear as they stand still as tree ferns when they think that they've been seen.

I've heard recordings of their calls: in mating season the males send out low, rhythmic booms like wind across a giant bottle, like a bass note setting a tempo for a melody not yet arrived. Or the females—what's called their "song" is a rasping scrape of sound, a chicken doing an imitation of fingernails on a blackboard. They could raise a din of noise or fall as silent as my own computer once the recorded track is done.

On January 17, 1770, in the eastern reaches of the Marlborough Sound, Joseph Banks distracted himself from ruminations on the diet of the Maori, about which he'd been obsessing ever since learning that sometimes the flesh of enemies "killd in war" was cooked and eaten. Traveling with Captain James Cook on the *Endeavor*, he was the expedition's botanist and a kind of impromptu anthropologist, negotiator, and general science officer. He tried to pay attention to everything. Having not only seen the bones of the consumed but learned from the very mouths of the men who'd eaten their defeated enemies about this custom, Banks was feeling grim. The voyagers called that part of Marlborough Sound "Cannibal Bay," at the northeastern fringe of water and land.

But he recorded gamely in his journal,

This morn I was awakd by the singing of the birds ashore from whence we are distant not a quarter of a mile, the numbers of them were certainly very great who seemd to strain their throats with emulation perhaps; their voices were certainly the most melodious wild musick I have ever heard, almost imitating small bells but with the most tuneable silver sound imaginable to which maybe the distance was no small addition. On enquiring of our people I was told that they had observed them ever since we have been here, and that they begin to sing at about 1 or 2 in the morn and continue till sunrise, after which they are silent all day like our nightingales.[1]

What he heard were korimako, bellbirds, a kind of honeyeater whose songs seem to trace invisible archways, latticing the shadows with the clarity of their calls. But bellbirds also help to fill in the forest around themselves: they are the main pollinator for mistletoe, for example, as they gather the blossoms' nectar. And they're part of the linguistic imagination of the place: *Ka rite ki te kopara e ko nei I te ata—like the bellbird singing in the morning*, says a Maori simile.

The editor of Banks's journals lamented in a footnote, "But alas! That chorus of melodious wild music is no longer heard where he heard it."[2] And true enough, by 1962, the time of republication, the korimako had undergone a sharp decline, like so many other endemic species, and was gone from the South Island.

The screeching and booming of the kakapo disappeared from Marlborough Sound by 1897. Coastal areas, quickly stripped of forests and vulnerable to the rapid spread of pests around both farms and marinas, had never been a stronghold for those birds. But when the government acquired all of Maud "for the preservation of wildlife," almost immediately the no-longer-wild lives began arriving.

The idea of island sanctuaries was first tested—to failure—in the late nineteenth century, when a man named Richard Henry became the first caretaker of Resolution Island, eighty steep-sloped square miles ringed in seawater, with a view of the mainland's snowcapped peaks in Fiordland. He trapped and moved 474 birds from the mainland, mostly kakapo and kiwi, but the isolating moat of ocean wasn't wide enough. Sometime in the 1880s, stoats had been imported to the mainland from Europe to control New Zealand's rampant rabbits, also imported, and the animals managed to swim through Dusky Sound. Swift, bounding footprints on the shore, a sharp-toothed sudden ripple, seize, and strike. Feathers the color of moss, a last scatter of beak and bones, and the painstakingly curated kakapo were gone. However, Henry had also relocated a few to Little Barrier Island and Kapiti Island. Some of the birds on Kapiti held out until the 1930s, and that fact suggested the approach was worth trying again, coupled with active pest control.

Year after year conservationists combed the isolated mountains of Fiordland, searching for birds. They camped in the rainy mountain bush, slept in wet tents throughout cold spring and chilly summer, hiking into stony valleys, all of them almost impossibly steep. As desperation grew, a winter expedition set out to Stewart Island in the Foveaux Strait—which had been a holdout for the birds despite the rural farmers' cats—the far southern point where the geologic clasp with Antarctica had at last let go. The party found and captured sixty-five birds.

Facing a severe genetic bottleneck, a breeding cycle highly dependent on the variability of native food, and a constant threat of ordinary disease or accident, the recovery effort of the 1980s developed an intensely coordinated choreography. Managers, hoping the males would go through their own complex dancing and displays and convince females to mate, loaded the birds into carriers and whisked them by plane from one location to another as the trees in far-flung locations ripened their unpredictable crops. If that went well, volunteer nest minders arrived to crouch nearby all night to protect eggs or chicks while the solitary females left to forage. At their lowest ebb the kakapo numbered fewer than ninety birds. And of those only a handful were females, who might or might not be fertile.

After transglobal correspondence and phone calls over a series of weeks, I received permission to visit Maud and to stay overnight at the Department of Conservation's bunkhouse. I could bring three members of my family too. Chris Birmingham, the sanctuary manager, would greet our party, take us on a tour, and let us spend time ranging through regenerating forest and a few slopes still in pasture from the decades of farming. The visit was approved at various levels throughout the Department of Conservation, a sprawling agency still sorting out new chains of command after a national reorganization. "I'm not sure who's in that office now," I was told more than once. "Let me get back to you."

Three months before our planned arrival, I received a new email from Chris. Across centuries Maud Island had remained mouse free. Other mammalian pests had arrived but were then eliminated, including a few litters of stoats when resolute females, already pregnant, swam from the mainland to give birth. But now that isolation had been breached.

"We have detected an incursion of mice on Maud in the last fortnight, which is devastating news in more ways than one," he wrote. Our final preparations took on a much more somber mood.

I booked a water taxi to reach the island, chosen from a select list of approved operators. Before departure we'd have to undergo quarantine-inspection at the station in Havelock. We'd need to arrive a full hour early; screening the gear necessary for an overnight trip would be a very involved affair, removing all suspect plant matter as well as any stowaway creatures. I agonized about this, worrying delay might mean we'd miss our boat and anxious not to bring problems to the staff who'd given us both permission and the promise of their time. I carefully pulled grass seeds from the leather ankles of our boots, pried dirt from the tread, cleaned the soles with bleach and water. Maybe we'd be good to go.

The inspector in Havelock was a gentle man with thin legs, sturdy shoes, and an ample torso. His name was Robin, and the spindly legged New Zealand robin could have been his namesake. A volunteer, he lived just three houses away and walked up the road to meet us. Handshakes all around—my partner, Dave; my brother, Hudson; his wife, Dawn. Then Robin unlocked the door, and we entered a large room lined with stainless steel countertops, a formidable array of cleaning supplies, and cubbies in the wall for what we'd leave behind. Our own packs were forbidden; we'd be issued waterproof daypacks and large plastic storage crates for food, bedding, clothing—everything for our twenty-four hours on an island with wildly endangered species.

We were deputized to prescreen our own gear: remove sleeping bags from stuff sacks, check the zippers, check the bags. We pulled both sleeves and pockets in our raincoats inside out like paupers in a Chaplin film. Robin carried a little whisk broom to brush away whatever might cling to the corners. Food must be scrutinized—anything could have crept into boxes or open bags. Robin fretted about the recent discovery on Maud. He couldn't imagine how rodents might have passed through his inspection, and by then neither could we. He was a good man, and thorough. But he had other stories, more cheerful than mousy. A rural kid who came for a school trip showed up in shoes "with a good two inches of cow shit." One group arrived with a huge bucket of cherries from their orchard; Robin checked every single one and found a worm.

When it came to my boots, I stood beside him proudly. "You've done a pretty good job," he offered. But my exhaustive work had really been just a warm-up. Now out came the orthotics: a little flour of plant parts had been ground beneath each heel. The insoles were two foot-cushioning honeycombs that still held seeds. With a metal pick that looked like a dental tool, he pried them, one by one, into a plastic tub.

In all our biosecurity check took ninety minutes.

If Maud is unmistakably an island, that's not true for much of the land in Marlborough Sound. On the map the forms look feathered, crenelated, and you have to work to trace them out: which are peninsulas and which—no, not that one—are real islands? Hills reach like fluttering seaweed toward the unseen distance of the Tasman Sea. They gesture through time, too, back to the end of the Oligocene, an age of higher oceans. The peaks of the Southern Alps would have poked through the rising sea, while the finger lands of Marlborough Sound might have slipped entirely underwater. Deep Time, again, and a controversy among geologists—was New

Zealand totally submerged back in the proto-Pacific, the sea called "Panthalassa"? The Lord Howe Ridge, the Campbell Plateau, the Chatham Rise—names from today's nautical charts are tethered to land that, during the separation from Australia, stretched into thin shelves of continental crust, submerged by the widening Pacific. The ocean rose and fell; isolate, still pole bound, Antarctica began to sheath itself in ice. I love to think of the accreted sediment of ages and epochs, the lift and swell and crest and trough, as if time, light like, is both particle and wave, traveling through water, rock, and air, the sound of it, the touch of it. Here. Now.

At Maud Island's tiny dock, Chris Birmingham greeted us with firm efficiency. He slapped a wet mat on the dock; it oozed and dripped with the disinfectant Trigene. We wiped our shoes across it as if we all had come slathered with those two inches of cow shit. I'd been reading about the fungal infection killing frogs from within their own skin and realized that not only would we be walking among painfully rare birds—the little family group of takahe, the solitary kakapo—we'd also stand in the same damp woods where shiveringly rare frogs would be blinking in the shadows. Those 310 hectares are home to the *pakeka*, a frog found nowhere else in all New Zealand and, therefore, nowhere else in all the world.

Maud Island frogs are tiny, silent, and each tadpole swims only in the isolating pool of its own egg, never in the pulsing schools that clot in frog ponds elsewhere in the world. They seem almost like anti-frogs. Their ancestry traces back to Pangaea itself, before Laurasia's long, slow rending from the south. Two hundred live on the island; a similar number have been relocated elsewhere to help avoid a sudden die-off of the whole population. Biosecurity; Trigene; kindly Robin—how tenuous the efforts seemed, against the tsunami threat of biologic inundation.

I've had plenty of encounters with frogs, but only some have pressed themselves deeply into memory. Once a tree frog the same pale gray as the siding on the house hunkered in motionless verticality on a chilly Kansas morning. I cupped it in my hands and breathed on it, feeling the tiny, weightless feet suddenly push against my palms as it tried to enter the warm cave of my open mouth.

Once, bicycling in southeast Ohio's hills, I stopped in the shade where the road dipped into poachy ground. The sound of spring peepers dizzied me with delight, and I remembered their cacophony years later when my aunt in eastern Oklahoma held the phone up to the woods on her back deck.

"What is that sound?" she asked me. "Frogs," I said.

And she recalled that phone call, too, when I stood beside her as she lay dying in April, the frog songs outside tying us both to that moment we'd shared through old-fashioned landlines from three hundred miles apart. I think that now the sound of frogs will always seem to me elegiac, a wave of open fricatives against impending silence.

Maud Island's research station perches halfway up the island's slope: two large bunkrooms; an office; a great room for cooking, dining, and lounging on cast-off, synthetic-upholstered furniture when the rain sheets impressively down. But first we headed to another quarantine room, where our crates were reinspected for stowaways. Chris introduced us to the only other occupant at the station, a student with a wispy beard and a distracted air, and then he sped away for an errand of some kind while we unloaded. Chris and his wife, another wildlife ecologist, had a baby only a few months old, so their lives were fragmented into unpredictable parcels. But he returned as clouds rolled in to give us the promised walking tour.

It was misting when we passed the old ammunition shelter along the track. All the more reason to step up, into the concrete cave that held the occasional penguin egg—look, said Chris, here's one that's a dud. We paused, sniffed the twentieth-century scent of old concrete, and held our cellphones, flashlight mode, into the dark. Weta clustered together like daddy longlegs in the high corners. Lifted from a snarl of bent legs, a weta will crawl from your shoulder to the top of your head if you let it, and I did, its feet tickling my skin with movement that felt both sweet and creepy until, at the upper axis of my head's imperfect globe, it stopped.

We never saw the kakapo. "Night parrot" in Maori, "owl-like" in

Linnean Latin, the lone bird on Maud was named Sirocco, and he was tricked out with a radio collar to eavesdrop on his wanderings. Chris checked his whereabouts throughout the afternoon and said Sirocco wasn't being friendly. True enough, he stayed well away from the research station and the trails where we walked at night, spotting constellations of glowworms all along the bank and those penguins slumping their way uphill. Back in the bunkhouse I lay awake awhile, listening for the squeak of mice, the screech of the kakapo. Neither: just the thrum of rain again, rain drumming on the roof, and a little later the sound of human snoring. I thought about rats and stoats and wondered: If I'd plunged from the island into the sound, swum hard, could I have made it to the mainland, crawled out, gasping with cold, to stand on the deforested slope? Maybe. Maybe not. If we'd had a week, not just a night, could we have headed out beneath clear skies, listening for the kakapo? In an online recording, researchers play back the sound of another bird's booming, amplified in the dark beneath tree ferns and rimu. Outraged, the real bird flaps his wings—you can hear the feathers, whap whap whap whap—and screams like a screech owl, finishing with a plaintive whine. He doesn't know that he's the only living bird that's there.

Back home with maps and books, I fill the rooms with music, Miles Davis's *Pangaea*. Sometimes it's just the CD player in my study, quietly murmuring from its place on the bookcase. Sometimes it's the full stereo system downstairs, in what realtors call the open floor plan, wireless speakers calling to one another from one room to another. It's still a real CD player, though, so there's a pause when one disc is finished, just before another starts. Today it's Miles Davis.

"This open-ended music gives you the impression it could go on forever," say the liner notes, and I think it's true.[3] Two winds, two guitars, two percussionists. This sonic mirroring surrounds a single bass; it's rhythm-centric, it's tectonic. Trumpet and organ, sax and flute: sounds lift and curl like life itself, melodic forays into the circumambient tempo, the wah-wah pedal molding phrases into long-necked calls. Sit between speakers for the track "Gondwana," and the small-percussion ticks and thumps all bounce against each other and against the wall above your head. The trumpet's silent till five minutes in.

Lie down on the rug and close your eyes. Is that a xylophone? A wood block? Insects, finches? The music rifts and collides, falls into silence. For now you are the center of the world's drifting ages. Breeze unwinding from the ceiling fan rustles pages where you set down your book. *Glossopteris*, an ancient fern-ish plant that grew 230 million years ago. The rise of southern beech trees, *Nothofagus*. Fusion jazz, synthesized, electrified, but in the music Miles is breaking up. Pain-gouged by sickle-cell, a disintegrating hip.

And there's the track "Zimbabwe," squawking and bubbling trumpet flares, electric like the spin of Google Earth as you slide perspective to the south. Guitar hits growl like great cats just before they leap into speed. Look at the map of Africa, Mozambique wasp-waisted between Zimbabwe and the sea, Madagascar hanging like a giant offshore storm. Pull up Antarctica to the center of the flattened globe. The Dismal Mountains might have snugged against what's now the city of Maputo. One hundred and thirty million years ago, the first irruptive fissures in the supercontinent; fifty million later and the separation left each landmass to its own biogeographic course.

"I expect you can see where we're headed," writes David Quammen in *The Song of the Dodo*. "We're headed toward understanding the whole planet as a world of islands."[4] Then: "I never end songs; they just keep going on."[5] The next day we rejoined the water taxi, tooling back to the mainland—the South Island—through the labyrinth of Marlborough Sound.

NOTES

1. Banks, *Endeavor Journal,* 455.
2. Banks, *Endeavor Journal,* 456 n. 1.
3. Whitehead, liner notes to *Pangaea by Miles Davis.*
4. Quammen, *Song of the Dodo,* 130.
5. Davis, with Troupe, *Miles,* 329.

BIBLIOGRAPHY

Banks, Joseph. *The Endeavor Journal of Joseph Banks 1768–1771*. Vol. 1. Edited by J. C. Beaglehole. Sydney: Angus & Robertson, 1962.

Davis, Miles, with Quincey Troupe. *Miles: The Autobiography*. New York: Simon & Schuster, 1989.

Quammen, David. *The Song of the Dodo: Island Biogeography in an Age of Extinctions*. New York: Scribner, 1966.

Whitehead, Kevin. Liner notes. *Pangaea by Miles Davis*. CD. Columbia/Legacy Records, 1975.

Three Stations along the Ring of Fire

O. ALAN WELTZIEN

When I climb Washington's Mount Rainier under a clear sky, I begin to see how it crowns a "long stately procession" running roughly north-south.[1] I study Glacier Peak and Mount Baker to the north—volcanoes I have also known all my life. Rising higher on Rainier, I gaze south and pick out, as I expect to, Mount St. Helens, Mount Adams, and in Oregon, Mount Hood and Mount Jefferson. But I cannot see central Oregon's volcanoes from Rainier, let alone northern California's magnificent Mount Shasta, which I later climbed. Even from commercial flights from the right window seat, the simultaneous unity of Cascadian volcanoes eludes me. Further, I can't sense the "procession" as only one link in the many-linked Ring of Fire curving thousands of miles beyond one's visual field. It's far too big to see. Yet I could imagine what I could not see.

Geologists know and easily explain the Pacific Ring of Fire according to the rub of lithospheric plates (those plates from Earth's upper mantle or crust that slide across a deeper mantle), yet its size exceeds our common political or cultural understanding. After all, it traces a fiery circumference around the world's largest ocean. It represents a misshapen horseshoe, oriented more northwest-southeast than north-south, its respective tines—New Zealand and Tierra del Fuego (Argentina and Chile)—pointing toward Antarctica with its many volcanoes such as Mount Erebus and Ross Island. The Ring includes 452 volcanoes and is "home to approximately 75% of the world's active volcanoes," according to popular website sources. Additionally, "approximately 90% of the world's earthquakes occur along the Ring of Fire."[2]

Humanity has long drawn space and time transects across this gigantic, irregular curve. The equator and the international date line, respectively, loosely crosshatch the horseshoe. The former divides hemispheres (just as the Pacific Ocean, along with the Atlantic, separates hemispheres); the division of time (the date line) further subdivides the spatial divisions engendered by the equator and the Pacific Ocean, respectively. Of course these artificial quadrants mask the geological story of unity represented by historic Gondwanaland as well as the visual unity of the Pacific Ocean girded by volcanoes, a unity repeatedly testified to by astronauts in orbit. The ocean's unity represents the earth's, as Soviet/Russian cosmonaut Alexei Leonov, the first man to spacewalk, verified: "The Earth was small, light blue, and so touchingly alone. . . . The Earth was absolutely round. I believe I never knew what the word round meant until I saw Earth from space."[3] Individual, regional, and nation-state self-images and definitions rarely embrace this macrospace of salt water rimmed by lava and active seismic zones. A red horseshoe enfolding our vastest blue space, the Ring of Fire as a macroregion defies our everyday imagination, despite the infrequent but disastrous felt experience, and extraordinary physics, of swift sound waves, tsunamis—one of the signal heartbeats of this giant horseshoe. Let alone earthquakes. More than one geologist believes it should be called the Ring of Subduction Zones, Earth's largest "place."

The Ring of Fire and the Pacific Ocean take so long to transit (even in a 747, it takes more than fourteen hours to travel from Los Angeles to Sydney) that they elude conception as a unity. Yet the unpredictable processes of subduction, as ocean plates pile against and slide under land plates, resulting in eruption or earthquake or both, remind us of a unified entity, a macroregion antecedent to human jurisdictions characterized by language or political borders, let alone climate or time zones. John Calderazzo's *Rising Fire: Volcanoes and Our Inner Lives* probes some of the ways in which people in Indonesia, the Philippines, Japan, Ecuador, or Chile live by and with volcanoes. In many cases systems of explanation (from the mythic and folkloric to the scientific) and accommodation demonstrate common values and behaviors. After all, many of us feel deep attraction to volcanoes because of their palpable connection with the earth's interior and some desired affinity between that and our own interior, as though macrocosm (Gaea) references microcosm (our individual lives).[4] In many Indigenous regions particular volcanoes are *storied*, personified as beings, which tradition animates and reifies in all their awe.

Within the Ring of Fire tomorrow meets today just as East blurs with West. These traditional human systems of categorization lose their currency within its huge space. Rather, geology bounds and unifies it through this distended bead of volcanoes. The fiery perimeter encircles the earth's largest watery mass and least-populated space. Yet along some strands of the Ring, such as Indonesia, the Philippines, Japan, and Central America, dense populations crowd the bases and slopes of many active volcanoes.

To probe the diverse meanings of volcanoes in our inner lives is to accept citizenship in a transpacific region bounded by volcanoes. I have sought this citizenship—imagined a kinship, as a middle-aged white American, with a macroregion that transcends time zones and hemispheres—through three volcano climbs that I fancifully call stations along the Ring of Fire. But rather than any Via Dolorosa, I regarded these climbs as strenuous acts of prayer in the Zen Buddhist tradition of walking meditation celebrated by Gary Snyder.[5] They represent but three pauses among the hundreds that unify this incomplete circle—what we call today and tomorrow, west and east and north and south, a distended map with curving lines.

To map these stations, I borrow a second, rich metaphor from Christian art history. In my personal triptych, the central panel, wider than the framing panels only because of my lifelong knowledge, displays Washington State's Mount Rainier. The left panel features Japan's Fujisan and the right Ecuador's Chimborazo, or "Chimbo." The triptych spans about half the Ring, and from each panel shines a high, rounded dome: snowpeaks that have long visually dominated their respective physical and human landscapes. Of course a triptych's serenity belies the Ring's fire. Volcanic eruptions from the Ring make international news. On September 27, 2014, Japan's Mount Ontake, second only to Fuji, blew up, killing fifty-seven hikers (ironically, the same death count as from the May 18, 1980, Mount St. Helens's eruption). And in April 2015 Calbuco, in southern Chile, erupted three times in a week.

A triptych, though, suggests the right spiritual relation—a habit of passive or active (i.e., walking) veneration or pilgrimage—intuited by many in the presence of volcanoes. In a rough sense these snow-peak panels mirror one another, as within them stratovolcanic facts meet human aspiration. The triptych serves as an altar to a macroregion exceedingly difficult to grasp. Such peaks—snowy, rocky, forested, or some combination—thickly bead the ring. Certainly these particular domes, and many other volcanic peaks, have pulled me obsessively to them since adolescence.

I

I cannot remember not gazing upon Mount Rainier, arguably North America's dominant volcano because, as a Puget Sound native, I grew up in its shadow. Always a mountain fanatic, though a mediocre climber at best, I hiked ever higher in the Cascades, which are dominated by a string of volcanoes stretching from British Columbia to Northern California. Mount Rainier, the most glaciated mountain in the United States' Lower 48 states, also looms as the steepest as defined by "prominence."[6] After all, it rises almost three miles about forty-five miles east of Puget Sound. I know from hiking and climbing that Rainier becomes far larger once one steps around or up it. Rainier inspired the United States' fifth national park (1899), the first centered on a volcano. And for many in the Northwest it exerts a steady gravitational attraction. Rainier has figured as a market brand for generations, and in several recent decades its shape graced Washington State license plates.

I wrote about my Mount Rainier climb, which occurred my forty-first summer, many years ago; more recently, I have tried to take the measure of Rainier and the other volcanoes in terms of regional identity.[7] Looking far back, I see that my day hikes on its west and north flanks prepared me for a climb that felt in one sense like a homecoming. Since then I have tried to understand its spell, particularly as I've lived far from its sightlines for more than three decades. In the process I've studied Nisqually and Yakama attitudes toward "Tahoma," the preferred native name, as of course their length of habitation near it vastly exceeds the relatively recent white presence.

For the Nisqually *Ta-co-bet* signifies "the place where waters begin,"

or "nourishing breasts," because not only the Nisqually and Puyal-
lup Rivers but many drainages flow in all directions from Rainier.
"Ta-co-bet" represents the home of both "Sagale Tyee, the Creator,
the Great One," but also angry "spirits of the mountain." Given
the inherent dangers from volcanoes and Rainier's well-known sta-
tus as one of the most dangerous on the continent, this tradition
of ambivalence seems prescient.[8] Rainier poses particular dangers
from lahars: fast-moving flows composed of rock debris, rock, and
pyroclastic (i.e., erupted) material that course down valleys. Cecelia
Svinth Carpenter, author of *Where the Waters Begin: The Traditional
Nisqually Indian History of Mount Rainier*, explains that "Indian peo-
ple do not desire to trespass on the holy land that lies above." They
consider tree line to be "the sacred demarcation line that encircles
the entire mountain."[9] Natives by and large kept their distance;
however, in the past 150 years whites have increasingly reversed
this habit as they recreate near and on the volcano.[10] Particularly
during summer season, crowd conditions exist on Mount Rainier
National Park's roads and the volcano's standard climbing routes.[11]

Certainly Rainier has attracted artists and writers for a long time.
Early in the twentieth century, Northwest art photographer Imogene
Cunningham famously posed nudes in Rainier's alpine parks with
part of the dome as backdrop. Poets Marianne Moore and Denise
Levertov wrote specifically about Rainier in the early and late twen-
tieth century, respectively.[12] Northwest novelists Tom Robbins and
Jim Lynch both memorably cite Rainier.[13] Gary Snyder, speaking of
Mount St. Helens specifically but of the Northwest volcanoes gener-
ally, captures their ambiance with Himalayan imagery: "West Coast
snowpeaks are too much! They are too far above the surrounding
lands. There is a break between. They are in a different world . . .
the big snowpeaks pierce the realm of clouds and cranes, rest in
the zone of five-colored banners and writhing crackling dragons in
veils of ragged mist and frost-crystals, into a pure transparency of
blue."[14] When I first read this verse paragraph from "The Climb"
a decade ago, it rang a bell inside me. It still rings. Though I've
never seen prayer banners or wheels fluttering on an approach or
route, these volcanoes indisputably belong to "a different world."

Like many, I climb as a pilgrim stepping upward temporarily into this other world.

As I climbed Rainier, I imagined a geographical homecoming, and I knew what to expect glancing 100–150 miles north and south. I also pretended what I couldn't see beyond those limits. In my poem "The Snowpeaks" I bridge that gap:

> snow pearls rise
> north-south pendant, tiny
> arc in the girdling
> Pacific rim fire.

When I finally stood atop Rainier's Columbia Crest (the highest point along the inner rim), I consummated a long, always elusive love affair, yet a gap remained. "The Snowpeaks" concludes,

> they exist apart—
> we so want
> to be
> part of them.[15]

I always have wanted to be part of them, particularly since I aimed directly for Rainier when walking to junior high school in a Bellevue, Washington, before skyscrapers. In the summers of adolescence and early adulthood, I kept drawing nearer, hiking onto snowfields and beyond glacial moraines, discovering each day a different fore-grounded mountain. It's no accident that the ninety-mile trail ringing Rainier is known as the Wonderland Trail.

The more I studied the history of Rainier, a sacred place for Natives and, with different consequences, for whites, the more I realized I hiked and climbed as part of a long procession. During the evening at Camp Schurman, on that long June evening in 1993, I gazed across decades as I pored over features of southern Puget Sound and Lake Washington. I fancifully located the home where I grew up, reversing the perspective of childhood. The only Washingtonian in our party of four, I kept trying to connect the dots between past and present. On the Emmons-Winthrop route (the northeast side) we started up late, after dawn, but climbed quickly. I wanted to stay atop Columbia Crest for awhile, though I had no interest in spending the night as John Muir had, alternately hot and frozen. A framed photo on my office desk shows me with my tongue obtruding in the upper right corner of my mouth. Stretching behind me, several snowpeaks rise to the south.

That north-south line of Cascadian snowpeaks—my inheritance—dominates, for some, the regional geography and imagination. While I'd read about the Pacific Rim of Fire in classes and studied maps—I'm a map geek—I didn't understand, through my body, what it meant until a pair of more recent trips involving 2 prominent volcanoes among those 452. I traveled far west on the Ring and then far south.

II

Our older son started studying Japanese his senior year in college and hasn't stopped. In 2012 he'd arranged to work for an organic farmer in northern Hokkaido for three months, after which I visited for half a month. I'd already told him Mount Fuji, or honorific "Fujisan," had to be in the plans. He and his girlfriend, who grew up in Tokyo, had already climbed it an earlier summer, via the oldest standard route, the Yoshida-guchi (northern) route above Lake Kawaguchiko. He told me one Fujiyama (Mount Fuji) proverb. There are two kinds of fools: the man who has never climbed Fuji and he who climbs a second time. Alec risked foolishness for me. We devised a new saying: It is easier to climb Mount Fuji than to see it. Most visible in January, when its white skirts adorn travel posters and digital sites, in the rainy season and summer heat it stays occluded. We never saw it except in its middle girth, under our boots.

Volcanoes thickly stud the Japanese archipelago; almost three quarters of the country is classified as mountainous, and it counts either 109 or 118 volcanoes, depending upon the website you consult. Approximately 10 percent of the world's active volcanoes pimple this link of the Ring of Fire. In Japan you can hardly avoid volcanoes unless you stay in Tokyo or other big cities. Most do. Centerpiece of the Fuji-Hakone-Izu National Park, Fuji's symmetric cone towers far higher than any other volcano. For millennia Mount Fuji signifies the home of several deities, among them Sengen, the "Goddess of Fuji," whose temple was on the summit.[16] Folklore links it to the tenth-century "Tale of the Bamboo Cutter," and according to Henry D. Smith, "Mt. Fuji was seen as the source for the secret of immortality, a tradition that was at the heart of [Katsushika] Hokusai's own obsession with the mountain."[17]

During the Edo Period (1603–1868) "Fujiko" represented the cult of Mount Fuji worship. In the nineteenth century artist Hokusai created Japan's most famous woodblock print series, known as the *Thirty-Six Views of Mount Fuji*, which document Fuji's dominance in the popular imagination.[18] A laminate copy of Hokusai's second print in the series, "Red Fuji," adorns my desk. The "Official Web Site for Mt. Fuji Climbing" states that this mountain, a geologic synecdoche for Japan, has long been designated "a Special Place of Scenic Beauty." On June 22, 2013, nearly one year after our climb, Fuji was officially declared a UNESCO World Heritage Site. Fuji has long been the most crowded volcano, particularly during the "official climbing season," usually the two months or more beginning July 1. The earlier Fujiko pilgrimage tradition has turned international, as foreigners constitute over one-third of the climbers, who now number upward of a half-million in that season. The longest queues occur in mid-August, during Obon Week, one of Japan's primary holiday seasons.[19] This hadj, like the one to Mecca, features streams of pilgrims.

Oregon State University's Volcano World website states that *Fuji* probably derives from *Huchi* or *Fuchi*, the Aino Goddess of Fire. Gary Snyder explains that in Buddhist iconography Fudō Myō-ō (Immovable Wisdom King), "an ally of mountain ascetics," "is almost comically ferocious-looking with a blind eye and a fang, seated on a slab of rock and enveloped in flames."[20] When I've seen images of Fudo, I laugh at his staged ferocity. I figured I would find neither Huchi nor Fudō on Fuji. I also suspected I would find few traces of mountain asceticism, given the elaborate infrastructure of cabled paths and huts on Fuji's routes. Contrary to the fourteen stations of the Via Dolorosa, there are ten stations on Fuji and each route (road end) begins at station 5 (with station 10 on the crater). A tight numerical sequence.

I had long known that Fuji stood as the world's most climbed volcano but thought we might beat the crowds by climbing the night of June 30 (the official season beginning at midnight). Fuji entails a night climb because the purpose—true with many volcanoes on and off the Ring—is to see the rising sun (the Japanese flag) from the summit. I had tried to prepare myself for masses on the mountain, more than Rainier, though I didn't know what to expect.

I never saw Fuji from any distance, including Gotemba, the town east of the mountain from which we took the special bus to the Subashiri trailhead (2,000 m), in misty forest. We'd opted to climb via the eastside route. A pair of shop clerks offered us cups of mushroom tea. I'd already survived a mild typhoon in Kyoto and a day's downpour near Ise. The mist increased along with my anxiety as the light failed. A young fit Brit, Colin Buck, had joined us. We started hiking at 8:15 p.m., winding in and out of gnarled trees the first kilometer or two. We saw occasional clusters of headlamps elsewhere above tree line, when I finally saw Fuji's moderate-angle slopes with fingers of snowfields. Lights blazed at the huts of stations 7 and 8: odd brilliant clusters below the upper cloud ceiling. After Alec weathered a brief bout of altitude sickness at station 8, we plodded upward in fresh rain, weaving in and out of a sinuous caterpillar of teenagers dressed in identical yellow rain gear. Neither Alec nor I wore rain pants, as I'd neglected to pack them, nor did we own pack covers. I hadn't transported my trekking poles either.

Alec had promised noodle shops at the summit; apparently a post office operates there too. Such amenities distance Sengen, Huchi, and Fudō and give the lie to mountain ascetics. At the crater rim you walk up stone steps under a tori gate. It was just after 3:00 a.m., and we had over an hour to await a dawn we would not see. I started to shake in the buffeting rain, all thoughts of a leisurely crater walk—the *Ohachi-meguri*, a four-kilometer walk that rises to eight points, including Kengamine, the highpoint—washed away. No lighted shops penetrated the driving dark. In the wet I felt more deprived than pampered. After a few minutes we stumbled down the cabled track, my glasses blurred.

Back at station 8 about 4:30 a.m., those gathered suddenly froze, mid-gesture, as a pale lemon sun, swathed in cloud, emerged for a few seconds between cloud layers. Before I could position my camera for some shots, it slid upward behind the curtains. As we descended and warmed up, our sweaty, wet clothes ripened. We didn't see clear sun for days.

After Fuji we indulged ourselves with *onsen* and lavish meals at a Lake Kawaguchiko resort. My poetry book, *The Snowpeaks*, closes with "36 Views of Mt. Fuji," in four parts, that distill the climb and parody the notion of views and vision.[21] On that first morning of the official climbing season, we shared the route and summit with scattered others but not many. Though I sensed no Fujiko reverence, my wet skin and insufficient packing inadvertently made me a mountain ascetic.

The left panel of my triptych, with shapely Fuji, displays a beauty I never saw.

III

About a year after Japan two doctor friends, both far better mountaineers than I, invited me to join them for a Chimborazo climb in January 2014. Both Dan and Scott had white-watered in Ecuador's "Amazonas" before, and Scott had reached the 18,000-foot level on Chimbo nearly twenty years earlier, before his party had to turn back. Flying into Quito with Dan from Houston, I flew into a new continent. We would spend several days acclimatizing, which included hiking a pair of volcanoes, Pichincha and Iliniza Norte. If we made it, I would ascend above six thousand meters (19,685 ft.) for the first time.

Though Ecuador does not boast the number of volcanoes Japan does, a couple dozen crown the Cordillera, Chimbo highest among them. I didn't understand the Indigenous lore surrounding it before my arrival, but I knew one unusual fact about it as well as the tales of two nineteenth-century Europeans who are associated with it. The odd fact about Chimbo lured me fiercely: because of Earth's shape (oblate spheroid), with its equatorial girth bulging like too many aging men, from the summit of Chimbo one stands farther from Earth's center and closer to the sun than any other point on Earth. Chimbo is over seven thousand feet farther from Earth's center than Mount Everest's summit and about 2.4 kilometers higher.[22] I loved the notion of standing higher than Everest's summit, closer to the sun.

In the nineteenth century, when European mountaineering developed as a sport heavily influenced by the Romantic ethos of "mountain glory,"[23] many Europeans, knowing next to nothing about the Himalayas, thought Chimbo was the world's highest mountain. The brilliant German scientist and polymath Alexander von Humboldt tried to climb it, reaching the 18,300-foot level June 23, 1802, before turning back. Many artists and writers evoked Humboldt's valiant attempt.[24] Seventy-eight years later Edward Whymper, the most famous Victorian alpinist, who in 1865 led the first ascent of the Matterhorn, reached Chimbo's highest summit on January 4, 1880. He and his party, having spent over a month approaching Chimbo from sea level at Guayaquil, went on to summit six other volcanoes, then climbed Chimbo a second time from another route. He chronicled his adventures a few years later in *Travels amongst the Great Andes of the Equator* (1892).

Senor M. Cruz, handsome aged proprietor of the Estrella del Chimborazo, our backcountry lodge, has spent a half-century climbing Chimbo and exploring Whymper's original route. We fingered old black-and-white photos of some of Whymper's camps below snow level. In fact, on our practice climb on Chimbo, we followed that route to the 5,800-meter level, just below a band of unstable rock. Though it was socked in and snowing lightly, indirect sunlight burned my neck and hands. We descended to the climbing hut, the Refugio Whymper, built in 1980, which serves as base (5,000 meters, or 16,400 ft.) for the "Rota Normal," or standard route we would follow.

Several theories about its name exist, according to Wikipedia. In the local Jivaro language, it means "Icethrone of God"; in Quichua *Urcurazu* means "Mountain of Ice." Indigenes for centuries have construed bulky Chimbo as masculine: "Taita" (Father) Chimborazo, paired with Mama Tungurahua, an active volcano that periodically smokes and belches only fifty-four miles directly east. Prevailing easterly winds deposit ash upon Chimbo's glaciers and snowfields, changing their buildup-melt cycle and hastening their recession. This woman continually irritates her man.

We three had a narrow time window for the climb, and the unsettled weather, with broad cloud banks swathing the peaks, discouraged me. Fresh snow had kept us off the top of Iliniza Norte. A large party of Austrians, also staying at the lodge, had been turned back two nights in a row. On Chimbo, as with Tanzania's Kilimanjaro, one does not enter the national park, let alone tackle the mountain, without a guide. This is a fairly new policy: as recently as the 1990s, various foreigners died on Chimbo's slopes. In fact, at the road end one begins the climb walking past the *cemetario*—a not uncommon memento mori.

On a late Friday afternoon, at precisely the right time, the clouds lifted, and we three pilgrims stood and stared for over half an hour, cameras clicking, until the light faded beyond alpenglow.[25] With this omen lifting our hearts, we began climbing just after 10:00 p.m. A waxing moon, over half, lit our steady progress. Gaspar, our handsome head guide, short-roped me; his assistant, Roberto from Bolivia, short-roped Scott and Dan. I blew like a draft horse but kept chunking, and we reached Veintimilla summit (second highest) soon after 5:00 a.m. Gaspar later told us that most climbers stop there, rather than slipping down to a slight saddle, then plodding to the Whymper summit, highest of Chimbo's five peaks. In the maze of nieves penitentes I reached the saddle but felt too tired to plunge farther. The pink world spread before us, including Cotopaxi and other *volcanes*. On the descent we saw, for the first time, the route we'd climbed, and by that afternoon we gorged ourselves in the resort town of Banos, just north of smoking Tungurahua.

In Ecuador's Valle Central I watched and walked a vertical landscape, where these big peaks spread higher than the U.S. Rockies and Mount Rainier. I finally met a mountain that dwarfs Rainier. Ecuador's Cordillera forms a particularly high link in the Ring, yet the Ring rises to its highest point farther south. In my triptych's right panel, Taita Chimbo bursts the frame, its five-peak ridge barely contained.

IV

Climbing three volcanoes separated by thousands of miles, I found morning sun, clouds and rain, then half-moon, stars, and rosy dawn. From three continents, over a span of twenty-one years, I've painted a snowy triptych, one among countless possible that invoke the Pacific Ring of Fire. The details of each well-known peak and profile vary, but each panel shines as a member of a chain so distended that we cannot picture it any more than we can picture Gondwanaland, some primal unity of continent(s). My transpacific citizenship feels hard won: though I touched the swollen horseshoe in three spots, for most of us it curves beyond our vision. Its shape exceeds our grasp. Yet the endless diversity of Indonesia, the Kamchatka Peninsula, the Aleutians, Central America, and Bolivia fades before the dominating presence of linked volcanoes. The fact that people so insistently *story*—personify, deify—"their" nearby volcanoes suggests a yearning for connection. And in other respects the rumblings of volcanoes (or earthquakes) palpably connect us to the earth's interior and terrify—or console—us regarding our own instability or transience. This macroregion returns us to our own region, above all our own body. The dance of large with small scale extends indefinitely.

NOTES

1. McConnell, "Cascade Range," 79.
2. "What and Where Is the Ring of Fire?"
3. New Mexico Museum of Space History.
4. Typical of this vein in the United States is Timothy Egan's comment about Mount Rainier: "What we don't see is the hellfire below, yet we want some intimacy with it, sensing in the ticking of the earth's heart something greater than the pulse of our own lives." *Good Rain*, 148.
5. Snyder, "Blue Mountains Constantly Walking."
6. *Prominence* means "the elevation of a summit relative to the highest point to which one must descend before reascending to a higher summit" (Maizlish, "Welcome to Peaklist"). Rainier, at 14,410 feet elevation, commands a 13,197 feet prominence, over 3,000 feet more than the next mountain.

7. Weltzien, "On Tahoma." See also my cultural history of the Pacific Northwest volcanoes, *Exceptional Mountains.*

8. By the late twentieth century Rainier's dangers due to lahars and high-speed mudflows were well documented, given population growth of well over 100,000 directly onto historic floodplains to the west and northwest.

9. Carpenter, *Where the Waters Begin*, 4, 21, 24.

10. The Indian guides who assisted during the initial ascents of both Mount Rainier and Mount Baker did not climb, though climber and historian Fred Beckey asserts, "Indians made some ascents and demonstrated that they had experience climbing mountains." *Range of Glaciers*, 14.

11. My book *Exceptional Mountains* assesses these conditions in depth. Mount Rainier has long ranked as Washington's number one tourist attraction.

12. See Moore's "An Octopus" (1924) and Levertov's triptych, "Settling In," Against Intrusion," and "Open Secret" (1992).

13. Robbins, in the "report" of Marx Marvelous (*Another Roadside Attraction*, 133); and Lynch, in the climax of his recent *Truth like the Sun.*

14. Snyder, *Danger on Peaks*, 7.

15. Weltzien, *Snowpeaks*, 49–50.

16. Much of this information is easily accessible via the Department of Geosciences at Oregon State University's Volcano World website. Also check out the Smithsonian Institution's Global Volcanism Program."

17. Smith, *Hokusai*, 10.

18. Driven in part by its popularity, Hokusai went on to create *One Hundred Views of Mount Fuji*; another ukiyo-e painter, Hiroshige, also created a *Thirty-Six Views of Mount Fuji* series.

19. The Japan-Guide.com website explains "Obon" as an "annual Buddhist event for commemorating one's ancestors."

20. Snyder, "Blue Mountains Constantly Walking," 203.

21. Weltzien, "The Snowpeaks," *Snowpeaks*, 79–92.

22. "Mount Chimborazo."

23. The phrase is the title of Marjorie Hope Nicolson's pioneering history of mountaineering, *Mountain Gloom, Mountain Glory* (1959), developed from the Romantic aesthetic of Burkean sublimity.

24. See Lubich, "Fascinating Voids."

25. I wrote a suite of Ecuador poems, two of which, "Andean Omen" (about this illuminated hour) and "Penitentes" (about the summit experience), were published in the *Sewanee Review.*

BIBLIOGRAPHY

Beckey, Fred. *Range of Glaciers: The Exploration and Survey of the Northern Cascade Range.* Seattle: University of Washington Press, 2003.

Calderazzo, John. *Rising Fire: Volcanoes and Our Inner Lives.* Guilford CT: Lyons Press, 2004.

Carpenter, Cecelia Svinth. *Where the Waters Begin: The Traditional Nisqually Indian History of Mount Rainier.* Seattle: Northwest Interpretive Association, 1994.

"Chimborazo." *Wikipedia.* Last modified June 18, 2016. Accessed July 1, 2016. https://en.wikipedia.org/wiki/Chimborazo.

Council for the Promotion of the Proper Use of Mt. Fuji. "Official Web Site for Mt. Fuji Climbing." Accessed July 1, 2016. http://www.fujisan-climb.jp/en/.

Department of Geosciences Oregon State University. Volcano World. Accessed July 1, 2016. http://www.volcano.oregonstate.edu.

Egan, Timothy. *The Good Rain: Across Time and Terrain in the Pacific Northwest.* New York: Vintage, 1990.

Levertov, Denise. "Settling," "Against Intrusion," and "Open Secret." *Evening Train.* New York: New Directions, 1992.

Lubich, Oliver. "Fascinating Voids: Alexander von Humboldt and the Myth of Chimborazo." In *Heights of Reflection: Mountains in the German Imagination from the Middle Ages to the Twenty-First Century,* edited by Sean Ireton and Caroline Schaumann, 153–75. Rochester NY: Camden House, 2012.

Lynch, Jim. *Truth like the Sun.* New York: Knopf, 2012.

Maizlish, Aaron. "Welcome to Peaklist." Last modified winter 2011. Accessed July 1, 2016. http://www.peaklist.org.

McConnell, Grant. "The Cascade Range." In *The Cascades: Mountains of the Pacific Northwest,* edited by Roderick Peattie, 65–96. New York: Vanguard Press, 1949.

Moore, Marianne. "An Octopus." In *The Poems of Marianne Moore,* edited by Grace Schulman. New York: Viking, 2003.

"Mount Chimborazo." *Unreal Facts.* Accessed July 1, 2016. http://unrealfacts .com/mount-chimborazo-is-the-closest-to-the-moon-so-the-worlds-highest -point-is-not-everest/.

New Mexico Museum of Space History. *International Space Hall of Fame.* "Alexei A. Leonov." Accessed July 1, 2016. http://www.nmspacemuseum .org /halloffame/detail.php?id=17.

Nicolson, Marjorie Hope. *Mountain Gloom, Mountain Glory: The Development of the Aesthetics of the Infinite.* 1959. Reprint, Seattle: University of Washington Press, 1997.

"Obon." Japan-Guide.com. Accessed July 1, 2016. http://www.japan-guide .com/e/e2286.html.

Robbins, Tom. *Another Roadside Attraction.* 1971. Reprint, New York: Bantam, 1990.

Smith, Henry P. *Hokusai: One Hundred Views of Mt. Fuji.* New York: George Braziller, 1988.

Smithsonian Institution. Global Volcanism Program. Accessed July 1, 2016. http://www.volcano.si.edu/volcano.cfm.

Snyder, Gary. "Blue Mountains Constantly Walking." *The Practice of the Wild*, 104–23. Berkeley: Counterpoint, 1990.

———. *Danger on Peaks*. Washington DC: Counterpoint, 2004.

Weltzien, O. Alan. "Andean Omen" and "Penitentes." *Sewanee Review* 123, no. 3 (Summer 2015): 383–85.

———. *Exceptional Mountains: A Cultural History of the Pacific Northwest Volcanoes*. Lincoln: University of Nebraska Press, 2016.

———. "On Tahoma." *Climbing Art* 27 (1994): 53–62.

———. *The Snowpeaks*. Kanona NY: Foothills Publishing, 2013.

"What and Where Is the Ring of Fire?" *World Atlas*. Last modified September 29, 2015. Accessed July 1, 2016. http://www. worldatlas.com/aatlas/infopage/ringfire.htm.

Whymper, Edward. *Travels amongst the Great Andes of the Equator*. Berkeley: University of California Press, 1892.

1. Sea, land, and sky intertwined in Svalbard, Norway—clouds fueled by the sun, linked to falling snow and then flowing glaciers, carving mountains and transporting water and minerals to a vacillating shoreline and sea that alternately claims and gives up a ceaselessly changing landscape that is "ridiculously and insanely beautiful." James Balog's *Chasing Ice*. Courtesy of Harmon Maher.

The Deepest Layer

HARMON MAHER

As an academic geologist, I have two disparate research homes, two favorite places to play—an Arctic archipelago known as Svalbard and the badlands in the central Great Plains—and this has been by choice. Start at the top of mainland Norway, travel northward across North Atlantic waters to roughly 78 degrees latitude, with northern Greenland to the west, and there lies a cluster of Arctic islands— Edgeøya, Nordauslandet, Prins Karls Foreland, Spitsbergen, Kong Karls Land, and many others. Analogously, scattered through the Great Plains are geologic oases, badland outcrops within grassland seas—Castle Rock, Scott's Bluff, Toadstool Geologic Park, Badlands National Park, and Slim Buttes. Many of my summers have been some odd mix of the crispy badlands and soggy Arctic. Why have I connected deeply with these two particular areas? Why does anyone come to love their special bit of the earth? Here are some thoughts—take what you will and ignore the rest.

Layered thinking comes naturally to a geologist for good reason. Layering is fundamental to the earth, part of its essential fabric: sedimentary layers, metamorphic layering, concordant and discordant layers, tilted and overturned layers. The stratigraphic code provides rules for naming layers, members within formations within groups, the local place-name geography the geologist must learn to navigate in an area. In Spitsbergen the Voringen Member within the Kapp Starostin Formation, within the Templefjorden Group, places one at a distinctive limestone layer up to several meters thick and full of shell fossils.[1] Each layer is a tapestry within itself, containing some curious record of past shifting landscapes, sometimes broken and contorted or even truncated. Beyond sedimentary strata there are also layers of atmosphere, hydrosphere, soil, crust, mantle, and core. Layering reflects two basic and pervasive universal organizing forces—gravity and time. Layering can illuminate the fabric of

2. View of a layered sky and earth in Badlands National Park. Each reddish horizon in the strata is a paleosoil, a time of relative surface stability during which sediment was transformed into rusty soil, where atmospheric oxygen became bound as mineral matter. Between are lighter layers where floodplain and channel sediments accumulated. The repeated banding begs further inquiry and may reflect climate fluctuations, as earth and sky are connected. Hidden in the layers is a small fault, but it is the sky that catches the eye and provides drama here. Countless such storms have contributed to the formation of each paleosoil. Courtesy of Harmon Maher.

much more than the physical earth. Layers of personal history and of the mind—conscious, subconscious, and primeval, with literally one mantling the other. Layers of memories with gaps, distortions, changes, not unlike rock strata with unconformities, folds, and metamorphism. Probe beneath the veneer of a first answer to why the connection between an individual and a particular place, and there is more—layers within the layered pages of this document.

My initial response to "Why Svalbard?" is well rehearsed, truthful, and perhaps expected. This continental corner of the Barents Shelf has an outlandish geodiversity, and consequently there is much excellent science to be done there. That geodiversity includes four major mountain-building episodes, all the common rock types and some quite exotic ones, and fossiliferous strata cumulatively miles thick that span some 800 million years of life. These fossil landscapes are embedded in a dynamic Arctic and alpine terrain full of glaciers, permafrost, large braided rivers, raised beaches, and patterned ground. Svalbard's peripatetic geologic history includes previous and much older glaciations, braided river systems with dank coal-forming swamps, hot and low-latitude tidal flats where seawater evaporated to form salts, open marine seas plied by large toothy reptilians, deltas and shorelines building out into the sea, and much more. On a larger scale Svalbard was tectonically assembled from distant scattered exotic pieces, some of which lack solid continental credentials. Because of glaciation, exposures are spectacular—ridges miles long and recently disinterred valley walls thousands of feet high revealing layered cross sections. A thin and spotty veneer of rock-clinging lichen, tundra vegetation, and nascent soil occurs, but mostly the rock is naked here, unadorned compared to more verdant areas southward. Not surprisingly, Svalbard is crawling with geologists from around the world.

The Great Plains are different, the geodiversity notably less than Svalbard's. Sediments and sedimentary rocks dominate, and it is an excellent place to study rivers, dunes, loess, and an array of fossil mammals enclosed in Rocky Mountain detritus. However, my particular geologic niche is in earth movements and deformation. More than 1.5 billion years ago, the Great Plains saw plenty of such geologic excitement, but those rocks and features are mostly deeply buried. Since that time the plains have been a semi-stable continental cratonic core—only *semi*-stable because, geologically, something is always going on. A midcontinental belly scar known as the Keweenawan rift started in the interior of the North American craton circa a billion years ago, leaving behind frozen lava flows along Lake Superior's shores and a solidified magma chamber upon which the city of Duluth now sits. But rifting waned and died, never growing to oceanic basin status, and the tectonic scar now extends under younger strata in Iowa, into the southeastern corner of Nebraska, reaching into Kansas. Several times in the long subsequent continental interior somnolence, the rift zone roots shifted and faulted the overlying, younger strata. Yet one must know where to go to see the faults—they are small, subtle. Small earthquakes occur along the scar as part of the Humboldt fault zone in Nebraska—not tectonically dead but definitely sleepy.

It was the desire to introduce students to the research enterprise that motivated my initial investment in Great Plains geology. I found

3. Cedar Pass area in Badlands National Park, where the volcanic ash-rich debris sourced to the west accumulated as the Brule and Sharps Formation, now sculpted by wind and water to form a maze of topography and a three-dimensional geologic playground. Courtesy of Harmon Maher.

certain aspects of the geology relatively unexplored, and unanticipated and interesting deeper questions emerged that brought me back for more. As it happens, sediments settling down to become sedimentary rocks can be a bit internally restless. Even without an external tectonic driver, faulting and fracturing can occur, and internal juices can move around to form veins and intrusions of sediment known as clastic dikes. This fruitful and novel research path was unanticipated, an initial diversion that became a focus, but was not in the least way fated. This geologic flyover country has been a very rewarding place to work because it has been somewhat overlooked by others.

For different reasons both areas provide ample opportunities for geologic investigations, but this initial answer is clearly incomplete. There are plenty of similar opportunities elsewhere. Why these specific localities for me? Numerous considerations are dissuasive. Svalbard is logistically challenging and expensive. Helicopter time can cost in excess of five thousand dollars an hour, and chartering expedition boats is also expensive. Field conditions are challenging and even deadly for the unprepared or uninitiated. After falling overboard without a survival suit, one has three to five minutes before fading into an unconsciousness that swiftly becomes permanent. More time is often spent getting to an outcrop than working on it, and there are troublesome inhabitants. One summer a polar bear nesting for days near excellent shore outcrops prevented us from getting some crucial samples and observations. The badlands have their comparable if not greater dangers. A rattlesnake bite and a mountain lion sighting have made me rethink a preference for solo fieldwork. Further deterrents include lightning, hail, and gully washers stemming from thunderstorms, mud gumbos of unbelievable slipperiness and stickiness that can mire any vehicle, temperatures soaring well above 100 degrees, and relentless and infernal winds. Certainly plenty of geologic science can be conducted where challenges are fewer.

So, why return again and again instead of seeking more pleasant pastures elsewhere? To answer one question with another, why read a book or watch a movie or reflect upon a painting a second time and then yet again? A simple but powerful reason is that upon return one can "see" things unnoticed before. Standing before a familiar outcrop noticing geologic features and patterns that I did not see before is a source of astonishment and delight. Seeing is a complicated act, involving detecting patterns and giving them meaning. When in the field with students just starting to acquire their geologic vision, I must remember that they literally do not see what I do. The difference is dramatic, not trivial. The obvious unconformity is unseen because it has not yet been extracted as a distinct feature apart from the rest, has not yet been named, has not been given meaning. It is a great joy to help others see more deeply, to bear witness as the earth comes alive for them. So, a simple but powerful reason to return is to have the opportunity to see more deeply and completely and to learn more.

Seeing more deeply is related to a prize that many seek. Science is about pushing the boundaries, discovering novelty. Novelty can be deeply pleasing, or disturbing, but it is strongly sought. On the surface it seems counterintuitive to return to a place to find novelty instead of looking in new places. Yet the more times you return, the more deeply you see, the more likely you are to be able to find what no one else has found, to see what others have overlooked. This discovery can then be reported to others so that they can also

4. (top) Reva Gap area of Slim Buttes in northwest South Dakota. Lower layers are tilted to the right but are overlain by horizontal layers above (at the very cliff tops). The contact between is an angular unconformity, marking a period when the lower layers were tilted and partially eroded away before deposition resumed and the overlying layers formed. A trained eye will also find a geologic fault. What caused such features to form in a stable continental interior preserved in geologically young strata is debated, at the shore of the known and the unknown, part of the lure of this place for the geologist. Excellent outcrops provide the opportunity to see more deeply. Wildlife, including mountain lions, forests to hike through in the grassy Great Plains, and colorful and dramatic rock formations provide additional allure. Courtesy of Harmon Maher.

5. (bottom) Relentlessly gray, barren, and desolate, what more can be seen in this Svalbard image? Hummocky piles of rock debris on either side of the valley are lateral moraines, which used to rest on a large glacier that has retreated out of view to the left. Talus collects as an apron at the foot of cliffs as freeze-thaw pries apart the rocks that the ice is not done with yet, one rock type tearing apart another (ice qualifies as a mineral and in aggregate as a rock). The taller mountain to the left and across the glacial moraines in the foreground is Cheopsfjellet (959 m high). On its left flank a snow chute traces a major tectonic contact, the Billefjorden fault, with dark metamorphic basement rocks on the left side and light gray carboniferous sedimentary strata on the right. Geologic features and exposures such as these make geologists salivate with anticipation. Courtesy of Harmon Maher.

see more deeply if they wish. So, with Svalbard and the Great Plains I have come to know the rocks and the geologic history deeply enough that I can see the edge of understanding, recognizing novelty and research opportunities unseen by others. This process is self-perpetuating as answers prograde the known into the unknown, leading to new questions. Understanding that the architecture of a younger mountain belt in Svalbard was strongly influenced by an older architecture ignites a new project on that older architecture, and so on. Uncovering one layer reveals another below. This obsessive search for the novel seems essential to the creative process. Arguably, what scientists, writers of fiction, or artists do differs, but all are fundamentally rooted in uncovering novelty. Different artists have recognizable styles, themes, and periods, which experts can see in the artist's work. They too return to where they have been before, looking for the shores of novelty between the known and unknown.

For me there is an additional factor in the bonding with place. I find Svalbard extraordinarily beautiful, not all the time and everywhere, but at intersections of place and moments, absolutely sublime and transcendent. To capture this quality with a photograph provides me deep pleasure and a sense of accomplishment. Our ability to capture beauty and much else in this way strikes me as being as great an advance as the printing press. Response to an image is often more primal than a response to words. Seeing is learned much earlier, part of a deeper substratum. Inspect most geologists' cameras at the end of the season, and many images therein would not be for scientific documentation purposes but attempts to capture a moment of beauty. This beauty may be difficult to capture with words. Climbing above the clouds in Svalbard to a world of light and blue sky with sharp rocky ridges swaddled in a gauzy and stretching whiteness is a sublime moment of beauty, as is hearing Gershwin's *Rhapsody in Blue* played well, but what those moments share, what common trait makes them both beautiful, is beyond me. Yet this intangible is one of the deeper layers connecting person to place, is worthy of further consideration.

What contributes to the beauty of a landscape? Someone is probably writing software with algorithms that recognize (and even

6. Telephoto image of a Dutch sailing boat in front of a calving glacier in Woodfjorden, Spitsbergen. The boat provides scale here, which can be difficult to discern both in the Arctic and the Great Plains badlands, both places generally devoid of human markers of size. Even in this image, scale is hard to discern—the ice cliffs to the left are taller than the high mast on this boat. In turn the scenery helps scale the human, providing a reminder of unknown immensities and vast realms of novelty. Changing scales helps one to see to greater depths. Courtesy of Harmon Maher.

generate) landscapes humans will statistically find more beautiful. People prefer images with bodies of water (hence the lovely fountains all over the world). Water in a myriad of forms is bountiful in Svalbard, but the badlands are iconically dry sorts of places. The rules are complex—a lot of if-then-else statements in those algorithms. Novelty can contribute to beauty, and here the exotic and remote Arctic also has an advantage in being relatively unknown by many because of discomforts and dangers that coax many to go elsewhere or to not return. The same can be said for the badlands.

Image novelty can also arise from momentary juxtaposition of different elements. Take any striking landscape, add a rainbow, and the ooh and aah meter spikes upward. If one were using a point system, animals or people silhouetted on a ridge contribute additional beauty points. Shafts of sunlight highlighting a breaching whale surrounded by wheeling birds (with a calving glacier as background)—now we are talking. Beauty is proverbially fleeting. Many opportunities have been lost in the time it takes to get the camera out, as the lighting changes or a particular constellation of features changes.

One of my favorite Svalbard images (not one that I photographed) is of a dog and polar bear facing each other with outstretched heads, noses just touching. Juxtaposed elements can change the image from static to pregnant with story—the tentative approach of bear and dog culminating in ending up nose to nose and the question of what happened afterward. In my experience Svalbard and the badlands have been particularly rich in such transitory juxtapositions. Simply wander and wait, and beauty will happen.

For me the contrast of these two landscapes, the wet and cold Arctic and the hot and dry badlands, also introduces a synergy of tension, each place increasing the exotic character and beauty of the other. Different algorithms might attempt to capture the beauty of the Great Plains landscape: endless expanses of undulating grass stretching to a far-off horizon, embellished perhaps by a colorful sunset, some cattle, a lone windmill, a windowless one-room school, the ruins of an old homestead, a small church or graveyard alone on the prairie, a carpet of sandhill flowers in bloom against a blue sky, ridges of intricately banded rock layers, dark towering thunderheads and lightning, horses running through the grass with flowing manes and tails, a silhouetted rider, or a herd of buffalo covered in snow.

I am amazed by the power of beauty, the extremes some will undertake for a fleeting glimpse or to possess or create a bit of it. Examples abound: a strenuous and even dangerous climb for a mountaintop view, extravagant sums paid for works of art, decades spent working on finding an elegant proof for a mathematical premise that few others can really appreciate. As a particularly strong proponent that beauty is to be found in nature, John Muir wrote: "When we contemplate the whole globe as one great dewdrop, striped and dotted with continents and islands, flying through space with other stars all singing and shining together as one, the whole universe appears as an infinite storm of beauty."[2] It is that "infinite storm of beauty" that resonates with me. Muir's legacy is magnificent. His long rambling and fearless forays into the natural world, oblivious to physical discomfort, with minimal trappings, and often alone, set him apart. He is, to me, a fascinating figure, a crazed religious and ecstatic mystic who turned to nature as his drug of insight, with a fierce love of life fed by a torrent of deeply perceived beauty.

7. Monument Rocks in west-central Kansas. A caprock layer at the top is harder to erode and protects softer underlying chalks from erosion from above. But freeze thaw and the winds attack from the side and undercut until the overlying material falls away, resulting in cliffs. One simple caprock layer makes the difference. With time the cliffs retreat as the rock is weathered, blown away, or transformed into soil. In this way the shorelines of these erosional islands retreat before an advancing sea of grass, and eventually the grass will transgress their eroded roots. All is ephemeral, even these rocky formations—dust in the wind. The Niobrara chalks that form the cliffs are full of marine fossils and once were the oozy bottom of a sea that stretched midcontinent from Kansas to the Arctic Ocean basin of the time. Courtesy of Harmon Maher.

Muir also found the sacred in nature, and while not spiritually dogmatic, he encouraged others to do the same. He wished Yosemite to be preserved for future generations as the most monumental of cathedrals, necessary for spiritual health. Yet more was at play than just the desire to seek beauty and the sacred. Well versed in botany, his readings are littered with references to specific plant species and the ecological roles they played. He was drawn to the Sierra Nevada Mountains as a soul-sustaining place of great natural beauty, but he also laid the groundwork for understanding how glaciation contributed to that beauty. His expeditions to Alaska were guided by the desire to see and learn more about glaciers, and his writings were full of astute observations. Such an intertwined intellectual-emotional connection with place also resonates. For some, understanding science destroys the beauty. My experience is the opposite—it uncovers, expands, and reveals the deeper beauty.

Beauty and the sacred are linked for many. One early morning, standing alone on the edge of a cliff at Sheep Mountain Table, in the South Unit of Badlands National Park, with low wispy clouds rising

8. View of the edge of Sheep Mountain Table with morning's fog wetting a grassland seated in the layered debris of the Black Hills. Here the thin veneer of life appears fragile, retreating before advancing erosion uncovers the underlying barrens. Yet within the disinterred are remnants of the soils that supported much older grasslands, along with river channels and the bones of exotic grazers and predators—all reminders of life's tremendous tenacity. Courtesy of Harmon Maher.

and dissipating toward the sun, intricately carved badlands below, and gauzy green grasslands lit by shafts of sunlight and the Black Hills beyond, with a screaming raptor's echoing call, the moment seeped inward and instilled an irrational desire to leap and soar despite knowledge of certain mortal plummet. Undoubtedly primed by the knowledge that this place was sacred to the Lakota, I could connect what I was feeling with the word *sacred*. I still can't say what *sacred* means, and I don't care to try, but it was a good experience.

What links person to place? What is described here is complicated and messy, which to me is an indication of being on the right track. Serendipity and even accident provide opportunities through life's course. The choice of what particular opportunity to seize upon is forged both by individual nature and nurture. Subsequent immersion through returning again and again leads to discovery of novelty, beauty, meaning, and perhaps even the sacred. A landscape that draws together like-minded people with shared passions cements connection and creates a sense of community. What emerges from this mix can be an absolutely glorious mess.

Some argue persuasively for the particular beauty, worthiness, and significance of their place of choice. Some places have more

9. (*top*) August 25, 2015, and the sun is setting for the first time in months over momentarily peaceful Storfjorden waters between Spitsbergen and Edgeøya, a reminder of the dark, cold winter to come. The yearly rhythm of summer light and polar darkness promises future continuity, but what is missing from this image is sea ice. In these waters diminishing sea ice over recent times speaks to change and global disequilibrium. Courtesy of Harmon Maher.

10. (*bottom*) Oscar II Land from over Isfjorden on a flight into Longyearbyen, February 29, 2009, a time when the sun is just returning to parts of Svalbard as the long polar night comes to an end. In this Arctic realm there is maximal seasonality and transformation because in the dark winter, rivers and much else are frozen in place, while in the summer muddy torrents of water and debris mobilize. Somewhat ironically, it is easiest to traverse the landscape (if one is properly equipped) when it is frozen, but many fewer people do. Svalbard veterans consider this the time of the year when Svalbard is at its most beautiful. Courtesy of Harmon Maher.

champions than others, yet is there a natural landscape so bleak and unappealing that no one has become bound to it? Is there one unique match for a given individual? Would a John Muir born in India still not find an equivalent of Yosemite somewhere in the Himalayas? I have little doubt for me that if it wasn't Svalbard or the badlands, it would be some other place of wilderness. There are plenty of other places in the world to satisfy a primal urge to know and to care, and for each, deeper layers will always remain to plumb in an unending quest. I get a kick out of the thought that infinitesimally small bits of the universe, you and I and others, have evolved the audacity to try to find meaning and beauty in our world. This inner drive is cause for optimism. Having traveled from symbiotic slime to consciousness, we are irrevocably bound to nature, and there is so much more out there to see and know in this inexhaustible and infinite storm of beauty.

NOTES

1. The guide to this stratigraphic world is the large format and 318-page-long *Lithostratigraphic Lexicon of Svalbard*, ed. Winfried Dallmann (Tromsø, Norway: Norsk Polarinstitutt, 1999).
2. John Muir, *Travels in Alaska* (New York: Houghton & Mifflin), 5.

Deep Mapping Communities in the West of Ireland

NESSA CRONIN

In a packed community hall in the West of Ireland a man starts to sing the opening lines of the *sean-nós* song "An Caiptín Máilleach" to a hushed audience. The song is about a well-known folk figure, Seoirse Ó Máille / George O'Malley, from Ballynakill. His smuggling exploits and the folk narratives associated with him are well-known to many there, but perhaps not all of them know the words of the song. As the singer closes his eyes and moves into the second verse, there is a slight falter and then a *lán stad,* a full stop. Silence. He has momentarily forgotten the words; he opens his eyes and is about to start over so that he can sing it right through by heart from the beginning when a figure sitting nearby offers the absentee line as a vocal gift. He looks down, smiles, and with a brief nod of acknowledgment continues with the song in its totality. The singer was Mícheál Ó Cúaig, a renowned exponent of the Gaelic Irish *sean-nós* song tradition from Carna in Connemara, and his offstage prompter from the wings, the English mapmaker and writer Tim Robinson.[1] Mícheál continues amid applause from the audience that fades as his voice gets stronger and the words of "An Caiptín Máilleach" fill the hall.[2]

This performance, and the setting in which it took place, demonstrates some of the ways people recognize and value the importance of place-based arts practice and historical tradition in Ireland, with the regional styles of the *sean-nós* song tradition expressing one such relationship between place, language, culture, and identity. Questions such as how, where, and why songs are sung (and stories told and remembered) are very often predicated in Ireland by a very culturally specific relationship to place and placemaking. The modest proffering of a line of an Irish language song from a Cambridge-trained mathematician to a celebrated Irish singer indicates how precious and precarious history and its memory making can be. But it also indicates how, for some traditions to survive, one must remain open to aides-mémoire from unusual and unexpected sources—whether textual, material, oral, or virtual. The separate categories of knowledge and information come in various shapes and forms, and so, as Robinson has observed, for certain histories to survive and for new ones to be written, we must remain open to alternative possibilities and sources that may emerge from new communities and technologies in the future.[3]

GROUND TRUTHING

In recent years my own engagement with people and places associated with the West of Ireland has shifted from investigations into the history of cartography and its colonial legacies to more contemporary concerns about how people inhabit their "home-places" and indeed how communities both inherit and create their cartography of belonging through everyday social and cultural practices.[4] Community mapping is an act of expressing and making tangible that which is tacit and often remains intangible, inaudible, and invisible to people "outside" of the immediate community or locale. While such work may appear to be "just" an expression of a local community mapping exercise, it may also incorporate strands of the global, whether through the expression of shared concerns about the environmental degradation of local water systems or mapping projects that acknowledge migrant spaces (whether "old" or "new") within existing local communities. And so, as Ursula K. Heise has emphasized, a sense of place is always already very much shaped by a "sense of planet," and often in surprisingly different and unexpected ways.[5]

One thing that all community mapping projects that I've been involved with have shared is an absolute excitement the participants have with the idea and practice of mapping—whether it's searching antique maps for evidence of ancient land boundaries or the act of creating a new map of their parish or suburb to proudly display in the local hall or on a web page for all to see. What continues to astonish and inspire, however, is the wealth of expert knowledge that resides outside the walls of the academy among people who would not usually call themselves cartographers or historians but are very often recognized by their peers as individuals who have a "natural inclination" for such matters. Such individuals have a lifetime of knowledge to impart to the page and very often feel the need to commit it to some form of permanent archive so that the knowledge can be retained and added to by future generations. The legacies of individuals, families, and communities are afforded a place in community mapping projects that weave the histories of collective and personal landscapes onto a map they fully recognize as being their own and of their own making. Such public mappings are (more often than not) an open-ended testament to an attempt to dignify the past while bearing witness to a present through the lens of place for a particular community.

Knowledge pathways in community-based mapping are not unidirectional. Time and again I am happily challenged by fellow mappers that what may make sense in the classroom does not always make sense "on the ground." Community mappers demand that the practice should inform the theory as much as the other way around, and if a certain term or method fails in the field, it fails for a good reason; it just doesn't fit (point noted and end of fieldwork lesson). Community mapping therefore offers different kinds of knowledges and different registers of "fact-finding" and "truth making." One form of this endeavor is through what geographers and geospatial technicians call "ground truthing." In this usage ground truthing is a scientific methodology in which data sets concerning a particular place are collated and verified based on geographical information gathered either by being remotely sensed or mathematically calculated in the field. This kind of ground truthing offers certain kinds of truths, but it can leave others out in the cold. Australian-based writer and artist Paul Carter has written about the need to rethink our idea of ground truthing and to shift away from its more technical, Geographical Information Systems (GIS) usage, in which it operates as an "instrumentalist discourse of resource management."[6] The creation of real-time dashboards of interfaces between people and place (e.g., live traffic on Google Maps extracted from mobile phone data) and other forms of geospatial information reduces place-based knowledge to a certain kind of unit that can be monetized, tweeted, and traded. In this knowledge economy certain kinds of landscapes, spaces, and places are more desirable than others. Through his own work on public space design and community renewal in Australia, Carter argues that a different form of engagement with place can allow for different kinds of ground truths to be spoken, translated, and understood. In this sense ground truthing as a practice is less about scientific data collection and verification (even though the production of "raw," quantifiable data has a function as one kind of truth formation) and is arguably more concerned with the creative process of placemaking that allows for a more open and nuanced way in which people actually live, move, and inhabit place. Such creative geographies, particularly when employed in tandem with community mapping, can allow for other kinds of truths to be articulated and mapped. Global Positioning Systems (GPS) is one kind of epistemic peg with which we tether ourselves to space, but there are other kinds of navigational systems that we employ consciously and unconsciously every day that influence the way we position ourselves within our communities and in the world. This shift from coordinates of positioning to coordinates of performance, from the technical to the tacit, are offered here through some reflections on deep mappings and creative practices associated with the making of place in the West of Ireland today.

X-PO COMMUNITY MAPPING PROJECT, KILNABOY, COUNTY CLARE

One man whose profession and private life embodied both the GPS of a vertical relationship to place and a horizontal relationship to the world was Mattie Rynne, a postmaster who lived and worked in the post office of Kilnaboy, County Clare, in the West of Ireland. Mattie was known for his discretion (an important attribute for a postmaster in any rural community), so much so that when he passed away, items that were found in his home showed that he had a very different life and world outside that of the official world of the post. His collection of books and audiotapes in the post office, which was also his home of almost seventy years, showed that he was an avid learner of languages, he listened to the BBC World Service on his radio, and his library showed a man of many interests and of wide-ranging reading and intellect. His home subsequently became a local community hub known as the X-PO (playing on the idea of it being formerly a post office, now re-created as a community meeting and exposition space), which was set up as a public art project by artist and local resident Deirdre O'Mahony in 2006.[7] Mattie's world was one that had deep-rooted connections to the area but was also a world that existed as an outpost for communications from all over the globe—particularly for Irish emigrants abroad and their families at home. Through the stewardship of O'Mahony, the X-PO is now home to four distinct but related archives that offer us a glimpse of a deep "insider" view of the world of Kilnaboy and modern rural Ireland: the personal archive of postmaster Mattie Rynne; the photographic archives (over twenty-seven thousand photographs taken over a quarter-century) of Kilnaboy resident Peter Rees; the anthropological work of the local Rinnamona Research Group revisiting the controversial 1930s study by Conrad M. Arensberg and Solon T. Kimball of the area; and finally the cartographic work of the X-PO Mapping Group.

Through a friend and colleague I was invited to become part of the X-PO Mapping Group to help with their tracing, naming, and mapping of every house and ruin in the parish of Kilnaboy, a project that had already been operating successfully for over four years when I joined them in 2011. The group then consisted (and consists today) of an all-male group of individuals who held an avid interest in the history, heritage, and geography of the local area and region: Brendan Beakey, John Kelleher, Francis Whelan, and Seán Whelan. The four men still meet on a regular basis (after dinner every Tuesday night) in the X-PO to continue their research and mappings of Kilnaboy. The group has traced the history of human occupancy present on maps, in documents, and in the ruined houses, or "cabhails," of Kilnaboy Parish and have exhibited this research regularly both to their own community and farther afield. By comparing "official" narratives of occupancy with informal records (oral and written), they have made visible, audible, and tangible many forgotten geographies and histories of the parish. I remember driving down from Galway for my first meeting with them on a Tuesday evening in the winter and thinking to myself what could I possibly offer that they hadn't already amply covered in their four years of research on the area. From my previous discussions with Deirdre about their work, I was already well acquainted with the expertise and knowledge that they already held and was unsure about what I could offer by way of assistance. Before I stepped across the threshold of the x-po that evening, in the hour and a half I was in the car driving south to Clare, I had decided that for the first few meetings I would just sit and listen, drink tea, and learn all I could about the work and (equally importantly to my mind) grow to understand the men who were undertaking such a task. And so after our first introduction by Deirdre (I think I registered an almost imperceptible surprise that I was younger than they had anticipated), I was gently quizzed about my name (Cronin, a surname in Ireland strongly associated with Cork), my Munster credentials (where *exactly* in Cork was I from, this question immediately followed by one asking where my parents are from), and what might I be able to offer to them by way of help with the project. I subsequently positioned myself as their assistant researcher on the project, as it was clear from the outset that they held the expertise and knowledge, and what I might be able to offer could come in the form of access to institutional sources (difficult to access archives, copies of old maps, funding support for their projected future exhibition) and wider considerations and ideas about how to process and hone the research into some kind of manageable form.

The methodology of the group involved the exhaustive research of census data, taxation and land registry records, archives from the Irish Folklore Collection, local historical accounts of events and oral testimonies they had collected or found, place-name translations, and a forensic examination of various editions of Ordnance Survey maps of the area from the 1840s to the present day that would leave many historical geographers in the shade. The idea was not just to mathematically pinpoint houses and features of the parish but to give an account of the homes and particularly the people who lived, and continue to live, in them. From the outset they stressed to me that they did not see this as a purely historical exercise—a map to honor some distant past—but rather, they regarded it as a map of the present informed by the past and were particularly concerned with including recently returned emigrants and newcomers to the area as well. The map of Kilnaboy therefore had a double function in offering a geography of emigrant Ireland that stretched from a parish in the West of Ireland to places in America that formed part of the imagined geography of the Irish diaspora. Their map stretched wide in terms of geographical reference (by acknowledging Kilnaboy emigrants in Britain and America) and also in terms of the past, in that they had a particular interest in locating the derelict dwellings (*cabhails*) of local people during and after the Great Irish Famine of the 1840s, an event that disproportionately devastated the western seaboard in terms of depopulation through disease, death, and emigration. They put received wisdom through the local information mill to see what matched up and could be verified and confirmed as being true on the ground. Such ground truthings also morphed from verification of facts to accurate mappings of places to the incorporation of material that would be seen as being "supplementary" in a traditional cartographic sense. The incorporation of photographs from the Rees archive and other sources (diaries, letters, postcards, journals, oral testimony, and notes scribbled on paper) into the final exhibition of their work highlighted the point that for the x-po Mapping Group creating this map of their home parish was not just a scientific exercise in ever-increasing geographical accuracy but constituted alternative ways of viewing the parish, from the different perspectives of time, place, and person. Such various (and variable) ground truthings offered both method and material for their own deep mapping of place.

DEEP MAPPING PRACTICES

As my work with the group developed and we discussed what the nature of their exhibition would be, I came to recognize that this was, in every sense of the phrase, a deep mapping project of great depth, breadth, and integrity. The term *deep mapping* has been long associated in the North American context with literary geographies of place, written either as ethnographic studies or first-person narrative scholarship, and are often associated with Native and Indigenous place-based traditions and celebrations of place. In the British, and more recently Irish, context, deep mapping is associated with visual arts, performance, and community-based arts practice. Cartographic historian Denis Wood registers his unease with the increasing application of the term *deep mapping* to projects and practices that don't seem to actually "map" anything in the sense of creating actual maps. He writes: "Well, obviously I'm just trying to figure out why they call it deep mapping, when mapping isn't what they are about, at all. They're storytellers mostly, which is great, but mostly they're not mappers. I'm talking about almost all of them, from William Least Heat-Moon to the most recent anthology of work on spatial narratives."[8] From his perspective the term *spatial narratives* (as usually they are literary-based narratives that deal with the creation of space) seems to be more fitting than the broader term and practice of deep mapping. What Woods misses here, however, is that spatial narratives tend to move horizontally, incorporating an expanding and contracting spatial register as they proceed, but do not tend necessarily to map vertically *down*, or *deeply*. This is what narrative expressions of deep mapping perform: in terms of being both a horizontal encompassing of "surface" place and a vertical drop into different kinds of deep time, intersecting transverse layers of history, culture, and place. This intricate layering of spatial narratives of place is, for Susan Naramore Maher, a hallmark of narrative forms of deep mapping. As Maher argues, "What distinguishes the deep map form from other place-based essays is its insistence on capturing a plethora of interconnected stories from a particular location, a distinctive place, and framing the landscape within this indeterminate complexity."[9] We also, however, need to consider different traditions that have emerged in deep mapping practices in recent times due to different disciplinary formations and the intersection between public geographies and arts-based practice in

Britain and Ireland in recent years. In the Irish context in particular, through the cross-fertilization of ideas and cross-hatching of methods in the areas of cultural geography, art and performance, and Irish studies, there has been an emphasis on "deep mapping" as both concept and artifact, with a particular attention being paid to the provisional and processual nature of deep mapping practices in general.[10] The legacy of visual artist and scholar Clifford McLucas and his engagement with the Welsh theater group Brith Gof in the 1980s provided a starting point for many people working in this area in Ireland and Britain today. Theater practitioner Mike Pearson and archaeologist Michael Shanks have written extensively about their collaborative deep mapping practices, as has artist-scholar Iain Biggs and cultural geographer Karen E. Till, who, although based in Ireland, works in a transnational context of memory work, trauma, and community-based deep mappings in Ireland, Germany, North America, and South Africa. More recently, I have come to agree with Eamonn Wall's assessment of Tim Robinson's work (mapping, writing, and walking the West of Ireland) as an exemplary form of deep mapping practice that has taken place over a forty-year period.

This (largely unconsciously formulated) deep mapping practice of the x-po Mapping Group took place over a long period of time, engaged with extensive historical archives and records, and employed visual, textual, and digital media to illuminate how the frequencies of place can be picked up and transmitted to a wider audience. It was conceived as being open-ended, and by incorporating various fragments of place into the work, it was big—the exhibition maps took up a whole gallery space. What was most important in many ways seemed to be one other key feature of "deep maps" that Clifford McLucas (1945–2002) originally outlined in the now famous short manifesto "Deep Mapping" in that the x-po mapping project brought together the amateur and the professional, the official and the unofficial, the national and the local.[11] The negotiation between these realms was instrumental in bringing the project to a wider audience through a public exhibition while also demonstrating that the story of Kilnaboy was a story replicated in many ways throughout the rest of rural Ireland. There were lessons for all to be learned from the project, whether in terms of local heritage conservation, public geographies, or how one can create different kinds of public spaces that foster and encourage alternative visions of national policy and planning with regard to the future needs of rural communities in Ireland today.[12] What was extraordinary about these men was that they were adamant that while they wanted a physical map that could be exhibited publically for all to see and use, they recognized from the outset that it would remain by definition unfinished and to some degree incomplete, as it was a map as much about people's relationship to place as the physical places they lived in.

The X-PO exhibition *The Full Story? Tracing Kilnaboy Townlands* took place at the Courthouse Gallery, Ennistymon, in County Clare, and showed the entirety of the group's research up to 2012—an exhibition that offered a picture of the homes and householders of the fifty-one townlands in Kilnaboy Parish over the past 150 years. We jointly decided that the exhibition space should incorporate several different elements of their mapping work and that it should not just be about presenting maps on a wall for people to passively view. Curated by O'Mahony, the exhibition incorporated the maps created by the group as anchor points in the exhibition space, with photographs, notes, memorabilia, and other items attached by pin and thread to the relevant site, field, house. Photographs associated with a particular house, family, or place were pinned by threads onto the edges of the map on the wall and so literally bound people to their home-places, capturing and evoking very personal maps and personal stories. As one journeyed through the exhibition, imaginatively walking across the townlands of Kilnaboy, one had a sense of encountering these people in some real yet also intangible way. There was also a short film of interviews with local people about what Kilnaboy meant to them on view in a small room off the main gallery space and a booklet listing all townland information of the parish that worked in tandem with the maps on display. I suggested that we incorporate an enlarged piece of a map on the gallery floor and invite visitors to walk, write, and "graffiti" the map, to inscribe it with their own place-names, family names, memories, and observations for use by future mapmakers.[13] On the evening of the exhibition opening, a public lecture on the importance of place in Ireland was delivered, and we also devised a "walking tour" of the gallery space, so as one walked through the space of the exhibition, one was also invited to walk through a carefully choreographed geography of Kilnaboy. Community mapping as a form of socially engaged arts practice can facilitate the honoring of place and the creation and sharing of an archive associated with such landscapes. The mapping group members and exhibition audience were exposed to a variety of creative spatial practices that they could consider using in their own communities in order to capture the landscape and lifeworlds of their own local place, and indeed many of the comments heard that evening were that people from other communities nearby wanted to start their own community mapping project as well after seeing the work of Brendan, Francis, Seán, and John.

"YOU'RE ALL THE TIME ADDING!"

While community mapping has been employed as an academic practice or tool for social scientists, the form and use of community mapping with the X-PO group display how community mapping not only represents a given world at a given time and space but can also *create* worlds of possibilities. This ability for community mappers to map and create alternative possible futures for their communities (often challenging the projected plans of local councils and national spatial strategies) was an issue that was much debated and discussed during a subsequent public mapping workshop that we ran with colleagues in the Galway City Museum as I realized that the work with the X-PO had a wider resonance for other communities across the West of Ireland. During this workshop Tom Varley, from the Slogadh Eachtaí group, stressed that one needs also to explore the possibility of failure with any community-based project and that there is "no right way" of doing community mapping.[14] While we were discussing what community mapping was, he argued that it's about "minute personal engagement with place" and that it's not about "closing things down, but [about] keeping them open."[15] Robert Macfarlane recollects a similar conversation he had in Scotland with Anne Campbell, who had worked with several others on collating "Some Lewis Moorland Terms: A Peat Glossary," a glossary that ran to over 120 terms, with the *some* in its title indicating its necessary incompleteness. "There's so much more to add to it," Campbell tells Macfarlane. "It represents only three villages' worth of words."[16] Francis Whelan from the x-po Mapping Group also argued that one needs to be reminded that such mappings are always open-ended: "You're all the time adding," he told our workshop participants, with an acknowledgment to all there not to expect to finish their maps anytime soon!

With a sophisticated understanding of the mapmaking process, such citizen-cartographers often appear to be more comfortable working within an ethos of possibility than the more professionally closed realms of probability belonging to their academic counterparts. Community mapping projects also show how socially engaged creative practices can function to make visible, activate, and critique the social geometries of power on a broader scale (where the local is most certainly ecologically connected to the global) while also developing a reflexive cultural praxis, one that is embedded within, and relevant to, the local community from which it emanated (and has responsibility toward) in the first instance. Through community mapping practices it can be seen that place is as much about attachment (through local affiliation to place), detachment (particularly through the imprint of the migrant experience in contemporary Ireland), and mobility, more than any conceptually preconceived ideas of ethnonationalism, chauvinism, or narrow iterations of place/identity politics—we live and move between places as the place ballets of our lives are constantly in motion. Additionally, projects that employ socially engaged creative practices (whether through songs, music, stories, dance, visual art, or performance) can capture the intangible lifeworld of a community while also addressing real-life concerns of that particular community, whether it be privatization of public spaces, gentrification of inner cities, or the impact of climate change on local environments. Such mappings provide a place and a platform, then, for archives and stores of different kinds of ground truthings to be created, particularly for tacit and traditional knowledges. Indeed, the lessons from such community mapping projects indicate that such ground truths are home truths: we don't need to travel very far to find the answers, and we are all the time adding . . .

NOTES

I would like to thank Deirdre O'Mahony and the x-po Mapping Group for their kind invitation to get involved with their extraordinary project and for patiently sharing their knowledge and expertise with me in recent years. I would also like to thank Paul Carter, Mícheál Ó Cúaig, and Tim Robinson for their insights into the many ways in which we make places, whether in Canberra, Connemara, or Carna.

1. *Sean-nós* (old style) singing is an ornate, unaccompanied style of singing associated with Irish-speaking (Gaeltacht) areas in Ireland.
2. This event took place as part of the "Unfolding Ideas: The Roundstone Colloquium," Roundstone, Connemara, April 25, 2008. On the life of George O'Malley, see Robinson, *Connemara*.
3. Robinson, "Seanchaí and the Database."
4. The concept of the "home-place" is fundamental to any understanding of the traditional relationship to place, locality, sense of belonging, in rural Ireland. The home-place usually references the ancestral family home, which more often than not denotes the family farm or dwelling in an Irish rural context.
5. See Heise, *Sense of Place and Sense of Planet*.
6. Carter, *Ground Truthing*, 9.
7. On the origins of this project, see *Publicart.ie* website, http://www.public art.ie/main/directory/directory/view/x-po/15ddcb42990656f8a991b79e 9f3cd847/; and Deirdre O'Mahony's public art blog http://www.deirdre -omahony.ie/public-art-projects/x-po.html, both accessed May 20, 2016.
8. Wood, "Mapping Deeply," 305.
9. Maher, *Deep Map Country*, 10–11.
10. See the work of visual artist and academic Sylvia Loeffler and her arts project that explores the emotional responses of a community to its locality in the Dublin harbor area, "Glas Journal: A Deep Mapping of Dún Laoghaire Harbour," 2014–16, accessed May 20, 2016, http:// www.research.ie/intro_slide/glas-journal-deep-mapping-d%C3%BAn -laoghaire-harbour-silvia-loeffler-irish-research-council-g.

11. See McLucas, "Deep Mapping."
12. An example of this in the context of community-led heritage policy and management is the *Village Design Statement Toolkit*, coordinated and devised by the Heritage Council of Ireland, accessed May 20, 2016, http://www.heritagecouncil.ie/planning/our-initiatives/village-design -statement-programme/vds-toolkit/.
13. This was inspired by a similar project by Tim Robinson in which an enlarged version of his map of the Aran Islands was displayed as a public art project as part of the Cork European Capital of Culture series of events in 2006. See Cronin, "Landscape Cultures."
14. The Slógadh Eachtaí group provides a focus for information and discussion about the Slieve Aughty uplands in Counties Clare and Galway in the West of Ireland. See http://www.aughty.org/, accessed February 21, 2016.
15. Tom Varley, discussant at "Know Your Place! Community Mapping Workshop," Galway City Museum, Galway, Ireland, March 29, 2014.
16. Macfarlane, *Landmarks*, 17.

BIBLIOGRAPHY

Biggs, Iain. "The Spaces of "Deep Mapping: A Partial Account." *Journal of Arts and Communities* 2, no. 1 (2011): 5–25.
Carter, Paul. *Ground Truthing: Explorations in a Creative Region*. Crawley: University of Western Australia Press, 2010.
Cronin, Nessa. "'The Fineness of Things': The Deep Mapping Projects of Tim Robinson's Art and Writings, 1969–72." In *Unfolding Irish Landscapes: Tim Robinson, Culture and Environment*, edited by Christine Cusick and Derek Gladwin, 53–72. Manchester: Manchester University Press, 2016.
———. "Landscape Cultures: Writing the Irish Natural World and the 'Geophanic' Projects of Tim Robinson." *Canadian Journal of Irish Studies*. Special issue on Irish Environmental Writing, edited by Maureen O'Connor and Derek Gladwin (forthcoming).
Heise, Ursula K. *Sense of Place and Sense of Planet: The Environmental Imagination of the Global*. Oxford: Oxford University Press, 2008.
Macfarlane, Robert. *Landmarks*. London: Hamish Hamilton, 2015.
Maher, Susan Naramore. *Deep Map Country: Literary Cartography of the Great Plains*. Lincoln: University of Nebraska Press, 2014.
McLucas, Clifford. "Deep Mapping." Accessed February 23, 2016. http:// cliffordmclucas.info/deep-mapping.html.
Pearson, Mike, and Michael Shanks. *Theatre/Archaeology: Disciplinary Dialogues*. London: Routledge, 2001.

Robinson, Tim. *Connemara: Last Pool of Darkness.* London: Penguin, 2010.

———. "The Seanchaí and the Database." *Irish Pages* 2, no. 1 (2003): 43–53.

Till, Karen E., ed. *Mapping Spectral Traces.* Blacksburg: Virginia Tech College of Architecture and Urban Affairs, 2010.

Wall, Eamonn. *Writing the Irish West: Ecologies and Traditions.* Notre Dame IN: University of Notre Dame Press, 2011.

Wood, Denis. "Mapping Deeply." *Humanities* 4, no. 3 (2015): 304–18.

Where Narratives Met

*Microplace and Macrospace in Early Fascist
Primary School Textbooks and the Case of
Eugenio Cirese's* Gente buona *(1925)*

FABIANA DIMPFLMEIER

The Italian nation-building process has been characterized by a
never-dormant clash between national hegemonic and subaltern
cultures. In the early twentieth century, despite strong nationalis-
tic views that denied local particularism, a new regional idea took
hold in the Italian peninsula. In part uneven economic develop-
ment, corruption in Rome, and the policies of Giovanni Giolitti
encouraged the regions to raise awareness of local strengths and
identities in areas of Italy. This cultural neoregionalism followed an
increased attention to the many Italian dialects and to the histor-
ical and prehistorical peculiarities of the peninsula since the mid-
nineteenth century, on the long trail of the federalist claims that
spread in Italy since 1796.

In the first decade of the twentieth century a widespread dissat-
isfaction with the incomplete historical and moral formation of
national unity gave way to countless debates in newborn local maga-
zines, most notably Giuseppe Prezzolini's *La Voce* (The Voice). What
the young generation of intellectuals perceived to be missing was
the spirit of the nation—its soul—that could only rise through a
revolution of ideas and eventually lead to the full formation of the
moral conscience of the Italians. This renewal of culture and of its
function in society became a national education process originat-
ing from below, or as it was called by Benito Mussolini, "the intro-
duction of Italy to Italians."

La Voce modeled a conception of localism that aimed at a deep re-
foundation of the state. Local, regional, and municipal identity—a
true "Italian-ness"—was being born, strengthening the national

identity, rooting it into a historical consciousness far beyond any previous mythical vision of the nation. Everything thought of as "local"—history, landscape, men and women—was envisioned as part of a bigger project, a contribution of individual areas to the national life. Particularly emphasized were the regional inhabitants' "primitive" characteristics, their contribution to the Renaissance and the First World War, a general rejection of politics, several anti-urban and antimodern stances, the relationship between humans and environment, and the values of popular culture, such as spontaneity and creativity as opposed to artistic and literary academicism.

Beginning in 1904, Giovanni Crocioni—teacher, local intellectual, and a man deeply in love with his region of the Marche—began reformulating regionalism as distinct. His thinking did not discount the federalist Carlo Cattaneo and was concordant in some respects with Antonio Gramsci. Trained at the Roman school of Ernesto Monaci, creator of the Italian Romance philology, Crocioni inherited from his master the dedication and care for the study of Italian dialects conceived in a practical and educational way. Monaci considered dialects as the distinct voices of the Italian populations that in their similarities recalled the common homeland, and he felt their study was the best way to strengthen the voice of the whole nation. Crocioni perceived Italian dialects as a means to connect literary language to popular language, region to nation, starting from a scholastic reform that contemplated the official entrance of the regional culture into classrooms. What was needed to return the lifeblood to the national culture, he argued, was the adoption of the dialect in the teaching practice and the introduction of "small encyclopedias of the region . . . that [touched] each aspect of civil living, revealed what was glorious in the past, useful and visible in the present, and promising for the future."[1]

Eventually, in 1923 the new regionalist views were adopted in the elementary school curriculum approved by the school reform of Giovanni Gentile (the "Riforma Gentile"). By that time Giovanni Lombardo-Radice—the new general director of primary and secondary school education—had been working for quite some time on a profound renewal of the school system that found its base in the bilingualism of the children, in the specific traditions of their villages and regions, and in their real and vivid experiences. Lombardo-Radice proposed to teach the Italian language through a continuous comparison between local and national narratives on the basis of "a pedagogy of discovery and knowledge, rooted in the life and historical memory of the community, which has a fundamental trust in the ability of the child and in the folk world to which he belongs and of which the child must become aware . . . ; a journey that will lead him also to acquire the awareness of the dignity of the popular world."[2]

Following the Riforma Gentile from 1924 until 1928 a considerable number of regional primary school textbooks for the third, fourth, and fifth grade flourished and were promoted by Lombardo-Radice as having a "near to the student" educational base and being students' first link to the *Heimatkunde* (local history).

MICRONARRATIVES AT WORK: *GENTE BUONA*

Important to the movement was a primary school textbook dedicated to the Molise region, a stretch of land laying on the Adriatic coast of Italy—at the time the fifth province of the Abruzzi and Molise region. Written in 1925 by Eugenio Cirese and published by Carabba, *Gente buona* (*Good People*) valorized regionalism and local uses, practices, and traditions as well as dialect. As a local intellectual, Cirese represented the social base supporting the promotion of the regionalist movement, in line with a long tradition of studies focusing on the problems of the South of Italy. Moreover, he was a primary school teacher, which placed him at the heart of the early-twentieth-century practice of cultural mediation between national culture, local intellectuals, and common people in the process of unifying and modernizing the nation. Finally, he was a dialect poet. *Gente buona*, although written in didactic poetic prose, stands as the first nucleus of the "poetry of everyday life" that would characterize Cirese as a mature poet and that finds a raison d'être in his attempt to anchor the dignity of the popular world in the consciences of the Molise people.

The textbook is structured on the cycles of the seasons, divided into months starting from October, the beginning of the school year. Every month shows a small page dedicated to the "national calendar" listing the most important events related to Italian history. Notions of geography and history follow, alternating contemporary events and older historical memories that date back to Roman times. A section contains the description of the historical, artistic, and natural wonders of the region and its "great men" enriched by numerous photographs and maps. Further, *Gente buona* contains technical paragraphs on key activities related to land cultivation, weights and measures, local businesses, and hygiene and first aid. Finally—the book is most of all an anthology of literary texts—the author includes folk songs, nursery rhymes, and proverbs in dialect and in Italian.

Anthropologist Pietro Clemente has noted that *Gente buona* appears as halfway between an almanac, a popular newspaper, and a tour guide, enhancing popular elements, educating through notions meant to encourage students' embrace of the nation, and introducing its readers to the process of socialization of the masses that was rapidly taking foot in the country.[3]

Particularly significant is the poem in dialect written by Cirese that opens the book:

Chest'è la terra de la bona genta	This is the land of the good people
Che penza e parla senza furbaria;	who think and speak without guile;
veste all'antica, tira a la fatia,	dress the old way, live through fatigue,
vò bene a la fameglia e iè cuntenta.[4]	love their family, and are happy.

Composed to illustrate the title of the work and condense the characteristics of the inhabitants of the region, the poem clarifies immediately that the author feels like an "insider" and shares the perspective, values, and language of his readers. At the same time, it clearly presents the synthesis of the Molise identity as the final goal of the textbook. In other words, the poem represents a yet-to-be built identity of the Molise region.

The words of the philologist Francesco D'Ovidio quoted in the introduction clearly point in this direction. Addressing the Molise people, he invites them to start feeling respect for and being supportive of their region. "You cannot prescribe a small squad of politicians to create the ardor that others do not feel," he says, "and the others are naive if they believe they can exert patriotism by delegation or proxy!"[5] He argues in short that a gap existed between Molise as considered by academics and politicians and Molise as perceived by its inhabitants.

A need to connect the feelings and experiences of the common people, who daily live in their region and benefit from its specificities, breathes life into the regional construction. The main role of the textbook and of the teacher, perceived as "intellectual-participant," is exactly to create a bridge between these two extremes and harmonize them: to move from the map to the territory, from the abstract boundaries, the lines showing roads and rivers, to the living reality of the region, its memories and its soul. From this point of view *Gente buona* appears from the very first moment not only as the tool of the hegemonic spread of a regionalism built by the local intellectuals but also as the creative forge of a regionalism that moves from below and is actually rooted in the life of the inhabitants of the region.

SENSE OF PLACE: AT THE HEART OF THE REGION

Gente buona highlights the relationship between people and their environment. This connection plays an essential part in the creation of the identity of the Molise region and its anchoring to the national context, intertwining with the process of modernization of the Italian peninsula and the contemporary spread of mass tourism. Cirese employs four strategies to fulfill these aims: to valorize the everyday life of the inhabitants of the region; to attribute new significances to the territory they inhabit; to symbolically condense their region in specific loci of identity; and to focus on the importance of agriculture for the future well-being of Italy.

I will start from the process of enhancement of the rural world that is central to the textbook and is rooted in what Clifford Geertz calls the "primordial loyalties": the set of interactions between language, environment, and personal relationships that Cirese uses as a kind of centerpiece and then positions them as significant and characteristic elements of the Molise identity. In particular, considering that place "provides a profound center of human existence to which people have deep emotional and psychological ties [so much so it can be described as a multidimensional construct representing beliefs, emotions and behavioral commitments] and is part of complex processes through which individuals and groups define themselves,"[6] one can state that Cirese uses the local sense of place to build the imagined soul of the region.

A paragraph at the opening of the month of October reads: "The sun appears as a rosy disk behind the thick veil of mist that rises from the valley and surrounds the benumbed nature. . . . It seems that the earth tells man: 'I'm tired: hurry to pick the last fruits and give me the new seeds that I will warm in my bosom during the winter.' And the man hears the silent prayer: he collects olives; picks apples, pears, and chestnuts; plucks yellow and black grapes from the vines; chooses in the granary the seed he will sow in November."[7] The school year, like the sun slowly rising in the sky, opens on a scenario familiar to the pupils. It is harvest time, and nature, like a benevolent mother, is preparing to safeguard again the efforts of the men. The work in the fields, divided into activities in which the parents of the schoolchildren are engaged, outlines the answer to a call, almost as a whispered confidence. From the beginning an exclusive relationship between humanity and nature proceeds in the book through deep understanding and visceral attachment.

The worlds of people and nature often mirror each other. The month of April, for example, proclaims: "If every day of the year and all the years of life had the sun, the songs and the scents of an April morning, men would be better. . . . Tear yourselves away, children, from the gentle caress of sleep and run into the fields; the sweet and mysterious voices of nature; the songs of the women who uproot the weeds in the cornfields; that of the men who, in a long row, hoe and fallow; the trill of the lark that rises towards the sun will make you feel an infinite sweetness."[8] Spring affects not only the mood of the men but their own characters as well. With the awakening of the season, the children likewise waken, and the mysterious voices of nature blend with those of happy women and men committed to working in the fields. Almost as if a secret life-giving whisper spreads through the air, all living creatures rejoice in a refreshing communion.

An intimacy can also be discerned in the darkest and saddest moments of the year, such as November:

> The Matese has put on its white hood again. The last leaves, stripped by force by the wind, shiver in the gray sky and go to find a nook close to their dead sisters. On the yellow carpet fall the cold tears of the trees and the sky, and the sun has not the strength to dry them anymore.
>
> On the hills the sower, alone with his hopes, is intent on the great fatigue: moves slowly and scatters the seed with a sweeping and regular gesture. . . .
>
> From the nearby oak grove the thud of the hatchets that strike on the trunks arrives; it seems like the sad voice of the winter, and it resounds melancholically in everyone's breast, fearful in the soul of those—so many still!—that do not have any more wood to light in the empty hearth, that have no longer hopes to light in the desert life.[9]

It is nature this time that assumes human form and voice: the Matese mountain—overlooking the entire region of Molise, towering over it like a benevolent god of nature—is covered with a hood of snow, a seeming cap to protect it from the cold. The leaves shiver, and tears of sadness drop from the sky and the trees. Winter is coming, and its voice fills the dry mountain air through the work of men cutting wood. The labor marks the passing of the days of the inhabitants of the Molise region, while the very hope of survival is linked to the resources that the territory cannot always provide to all.

Cirese uses these monthly interludes, sometimes similar to small visual ethnographies and repeatedly focused on the simplicity of the daily gestures, to strengthen the living reality made of the peasants' fatigue and labor, configuring it as an intense and exclusive dialogue, almost perceptible in its voices, between the humans and nature. This relationship of mutual exchange comes to define the very essence of the Molise identity in its simplicity, austerity, dedication, and kindness. The caring for the land, then, in the succession of days, moons, and seasons, assumes in the textbook symbolic power and potent educational worth, capable of giving dignity and value to the lives of the students and, more generally, to the inhabitants of the region.

INTRODUCE MOLISE TO MOLISANS

Two other strategies Cirese uses in the construction of the regional identity of the Molise region are "the re-signification" and "symbolic condensation" of its environment. This time it is not about enhancing an already existing feeling. Rather, Cirese seeks to empower and partly replace it by acquainting children with their region and its problems and guiding them to the appreciation of regional beauties, understood as symbolic places of identification. In this regard I would like to analyze some school trips described in Cirese's book that, together with many geography lessons, maps, and photographs, also give *Gente buona* the quality of a small tour guide.

The first "instructive walk" starts from the village of Castropignano and continues along the river Biferno. Through an imagined dialogue between teacher and students, the children learn to orient themselves and identify wellsprings and rivers as well as to invest the territory with new data and meaning. Cirese writes: "Many times the children had been to that place, and the river and the villages clinging to the hills had not awakened in them any curiosity. Why? Because almost always the cattle track was the way, often very long, to arrive at the grove full of nests or to the tree full of cherries or to the hidden Muscat grapevine. . . . The day before, instead, the teachers said: Tomorrow morning we will do an instructive walk. . . . And now all the minds were willing to understand and enjoy the beauty."[10] In fact, the outing teaches children not only to recognize the geography of the area but also to identify and give new value to the elements that are part of it. In particular, Cirese connects natural resources to more modern and practical uses, showing the importance of a correct system of field irrigation and the production of hydropower, so much so that canals, dikes, and hydroelectric plants become symbolic loci of importance in the future of the region.

Moreover, the trip is a means to render the students responsible for environment-related issues, such as the salubrity of the waters. Firmly connecting land, regional identity, progress, and political commitment, Cirese writes:

> Children, our people, good, disciplined, strong, and hard-working, are entitled to better hygienic conditions so that they can attend with greater confidence to the work in the fields. When you grow up, perhaps the water problem will be among the issues of life that are still waiting to be resolved. Well, you will have to solve it, by participating, directly or indirectly, in the administration of your country. And you do not have to ask for everything and expect everything from the government. Strong people do not ask: with common work one opens the way to improvement and progress and knows how to find the voice for the triumph of their rights. . . . I hope my words will enter you, endure in time, and become the voices of your souls, moving the will power and, becoming indistinguishable from the murmur of water in our squares, one day fostering the triumphant anthem of a new civilization.[11]

These few lines show the ultimate goal of *Gente buona*: to ensure not only that the students identify themselves with the region but also that they take care of its development, feeling it as their own, and not delegate to others this responsibility. The Molisans, then, who derive their identity from the strong bond they have with the territory that helps characterize their essence, can succeed in protecting and improving their living conditions by strengthening, in a kind of virtuous circle, the same bond that connects them to the earth.

In another point in the text Cirese describes a second instructive walk, this time focusing on the importance of building rural roads linking the fields to the villages in order to facilitate agricultural work. Cirese calls for the formation of a proper agrarian consciousness. In such a case, indeed, he thinks that "the work will be less difficult, more fruitful, and the farmer will be convinced that America, free and beautiful, is in his field, with his family."[12] Replacing the dream of a faraway land of opportunities, the destination of many Italian emigrants of the time, with the love of a nearby reality, the teacher hopes that this awareness, translated into a "new civilization" built by his students, will become the new vivifying soul of the territory, entering the very essence of the region so that it is indistinguishable from "the murmur of water in our squares."

Finally, the school trip made to the provincial capital of Campobasso explicates the process of symbolic condensation undergone by the territory of Molise. Unlike the previous trip, the capital tour is made by bus (a rarity at the time) and comes across as a hybrid between an educational outing and tourist travel. After seeing the town hall, the prefecture, and the national monuments of Giuseppe Garibaldi and Gabriele Pepe, Italian heroes of the unification of the Italian peninsula, the teacher takes his students to the Museum of the Sanniti (the first inhabitants of the Molise), where they discover the glorious past of their region. After supper they continue their journey through history, attending a lesson on the castles of Molise, accompanied by a lantern show. The next morning the pupils visit the House of the Orphans of War, where they learn about the harsh realities of the battlefields and the importance of defending the homeland. Eventually, the tour ends at the Trombetta Photographic Studio, where they have the opportunity to observe magnificent photographs of folk costumes, landscapes, and monuments: pictures that they will bring back home to hang on the walls of their classrooms.

The choice of symbolic sites made by Cirese clearly operates as a short program of mirroring and rooting of the identity of the young students in the region and in the nation. He traverses a range from national history, represented by the statues of the heroes of the Risorgimento but also alive in the sacrifice of the fathers of the many orphans gathered in the House of Orphans of War, to local history, anchored in the mythical past of the Sanniti displayed in the museum: a proud and independent people who long opposed the Roman conquest and have now been adopted as founding ancestors of the local homeland.

From monuments and museums, simulacra of significance that make a bond with established traditions, the author moves to more subtle, modern, and mobile forms of symbolic condensation such as lantern shows and photographs. These reproductions enable students "to love their birthplace more, for its past of strength and its present of labor."[13] Thanks to the magic of a technical medium still almost unknown at that time, Cirese proceeds to anchor more firmly in the eyes and hearts of the children the historical, artistic, natural, and folkloric beauty of their region. The Molisan children, in addition to bringing home memories of their trip to Campobasso, will take with them small capsules of "Molise-ness."

CONNECTING MICRO- AND MACROSPACES

In conclusion I would like to focus on how Cirese employs the relationship with the environment to anchor Molise to the Italian nation and to open it up to modernity. Already at the beginning of the volume, in addition to the poetry presented here, the schoolteacher cites two other quotations. The first is the wish of the Latin poet Virgil: "that the year will be abundant with fruits and prolific with cattle; that the harvest will fill the furrows and stock the granaries,"[14] which indicates the core of the "everyday life poetic" already described. The second text, by the contemporary poet Giosuè Carducci, explicitly points to the importance of agriculture for the Italian nation. "Oh Italians," writes Carducci, "raise and free agriculture! Pacify the countryside! Drive out hunger from the furrows, pellagra from the bodies, and the grim ignorance from the souls! Pacify the countryside and the workers! And the Roman eagle will dress her feathers once again and will cry out our rights on the mountains and the seas."[15]

Both quotations give value to and place agriculture at the center of the narrative; moreover, they also indicate its permanence as a focus of identity over time. The land and its cultivation have been typical features of the region since ancient times; at the same time, they are the focus of the present and the future of a region that is part of a nation that, to return to its ancient glories, has to learn to invest in the landscape, modernizing and healing it. Under the heading "From the Journal of the Countryman," Cirese quotes others to make his point:

> When I have completed the unification of Italy, all my thoughts should be directed to the improvement of agriculture, the only source from which one can expect real wealth and prosperity. (C. Cavour)

> True wealth is only that which comes from the earth. Whoever improves their own harvest, tills the lands, dries up the marshes, is the one who makes the greatest achievements. (Federico II)

> The agricultural conditions of a country express the level of its civilization and well-being. (G. B. Say) [16]

Underscoring the prominence of agriculture not only for the region but also for the entire nation, Cirese intertwines microplace and macrospace, regional and national destinies, making them inextricably one. At the same time he outlines the specificity, the role, and the importance of Molise for the sustenance and flourishing of the Italian nation in present and future times. From the local scene a larger national narrative is born.

Gente buona contains several paragraphs explaining the importance of a monthly accounting, highlighting the most suitable crops and innovations to enhance the agricultural productivity and livelihood of the rural Molise—how to grow wheat, corn, potatoes, barley, oats, and rye; how to operate the agricultural rotation, to reap and prepare a granary; how to breed pigs; and how to manage fruit farming. Once invested in the regional agriculture, Cirese explains, "Italy could satiate with her bread all her children." [17]

The specificity of the regional culture, although not blending with the national, would then bring to Italy a priceless contribution that finds its lifeblood in the very essence of the region: its relationship with the land. As explained so well by Cirese, the Molise region "is for the most part a rural region; the economic well-being of our families, which will also be the wealth of the motherland, has to be expected only from the fields, which require thoughtful and assiduous care. Whoever neglects the fields neglects himself and does not love Italy because only one who works can be truly called Italian."[18] With these words Cirese binds regional and national identity, amplifying one of its core values: the labor derived from the inhabitants' daily fatigue.

TRA COSMO E CAMPANILE

In this brief essay I have described some of the mechanisms of the construction and rooting of the regional Molise identity, focusing on the relationship between humanity and nature at work in teacher and poet Eugenio Cirese's 1925 primary school textbook *Gente buona.*[19] His volume is a touchstone into a larger intellectual movement, focused on the enhancement of the *piccole patrie* (small local homelands) in Italy. Furthermore, it promotes a sensitivity deeply rooted in territorial knowledge, love for landscape, and unity of purpose and feeling derived from a relationship with nature tinged with early ecological and environmental insights.

By the end of the 1920s the Fascist interest in dialects and regional culture was overshadowed by a top-down process of language nationalization increasingly structured according to a rigid propaganda. However, the work of Cirese, perpetuating and enriching a long tradition of studies focusing on the problems of the South of Italy, highlighted instances inside and beyond Fascism that resulted in the construction of an independent Molise (1963) and a specific identity in a dialogue of complex continuity.

In 2007 *Gente buona* was reedited by the province of Campobasso. The publication can be read as a tribute to the dialect poet, as a mirror of the current cultural re-functionalization of his work, and as an operation of renewed and explicit identity recognition—but also, from a "glocal" (global-local) perspective, as the sign of the encounter between the *piccole patrie* sharing a vision of nature and the contemporary Westerner developing a sensibility toward a new way of being human and living an intimate relationship with the environment. Thus, *Gente buona* lies again at the intersection of microplace and macrospace.

NOTES

1. Anceschi, *Giovanni Crocioni*, 69.
2. Martelli, "I sussidiari per le culture regionali," 291.
3. Clemente, "Scolari e contadini nel Molise degli anni Venti," xxx–xxxi.
4. Cirese, *Gente buona*, 1. All translations from the work are mine.
5. Cirese, *Gente buona*, 3.
6. Convery et al., "Introduction," 1.
7. Cirese, *Gente buona*, 5.
8. Cirese, *Gente buona*, 113.
9. Cirese, *Gente buona*, 22.
10. Cirese, *Gente buona*, 12.
11. Cirese, *Gente buona*, 17–18.
12. Cirese, *Gente buona*, 32.
13. Cirese, *Gente buona*, 170.
14. Cirese, *Gente buona*, 1.
15. Cirese, *Gente buona*, 1.
16. Cirese, *Gente buona*, 18, 110, 198.
17. Cirese, *Gente buona*, 9.
18. Cirese, *Gente buona*, 32.
19. The phrase in the subheading, which translates to "Between cosmos and bell tower," refers to the title of the book *Tra cosmo e campanile. Regioni etiche e identità sociale* by the anthropologist Alberto Mario Cirese, son of Eugenio, and to his reflections on the relationships between local and global identities.

BIBLIOGRAPHY

Ambrosoli, Luigi, Giuseppe Anceschi, Carlo Dionisetti, and Enzo Santarelli. *Il regionalismo di Giovanni Crocioni*. Florence: Olschki, 1972.

Anceschi, Giovanni. *Giovanni Crocioni. Un regionalista marchigiano nella cultura italiana tra positivismo e idealismo*. Urbino: Argalia, 1977.

Ascenzi, Anna, and Roberto Sani, eds. *Il libro per le scuole nel Ventennio fascista. La normativa sui libri di testo dalla Riforma Gentile alla fine della seconda guerra mondiale (1923–1945)*. Macerata: Alfabetica edizioni, 2009.

Cavazza, Stefano. *Piccole patrie. Feste popolari tra regione e nazione durante il fascismo*. Bologna: il Mulino, 2003.

Cirese, Alberto Mario. "Il Molise e la sua identità." *Basilicata. Rassegna di politica e cronache meridionali* 29, nos, 5–6 (1987): 12–15.

———. *Tra cosmo e campanile. Regioni etiche e identità sociale.* Firenze: Protagon, 2003.

Cirese, Eugenio. *Gente buona. Libro sussidiario per le scuole del Molise.* Lanciano: Giuseppe Carabba Editore, 1925.

Clemente, Pietro. "Scolari e contadini nel Molise degli anni Venti. Storie di un altro mondo." In *Gente buona* by Eugenio Cirese, xvii–xliv. Campobasso: Provincia di Campobasso, 2007.

Clemente, Pietro, and Antonio Fanelli. "'Intenso nel sentire ma sobrio nell'esprimersi.' Il Molise dei due Cirese." *Glocale. Rivista molisana di storia e scienze sociali* 6–7 (2013): 51–79.

Convery, Ian, Gerard Corsane, and Peter Davis. "Introduction: Making Sense of Place." In *Making Sense of Place: Multidisciplinary Perspectives,* edited by Ian Convery, Gerard Corsane, and Peter Davis, 1–8. Woodbridge: Boydell Press, 2012.

Crocioni, Giovanni. *Le regioni e la cultura nazionale.* Catania: F. Battiato Editore, 1914.

Dimpflmeier, Fabiana. "Vivere la regione per vivere la nazione. La valorizzazione del patrimonio locale nei sussidiari per le culture regionali degli anni Venti." In *Costruire una nazione. Politiche, discorsi e rappresentazioni che hanno fatto l'Italia,* edited by Silvia Aru and Valeria Deplano, 92–106. Verona: Ombre Corte, 2013.

Geertz, Clifford. "Primordial Loyalties and Standing Entities: Anthropological Reflections on the Politics of Identities." Lecture delivered at Institute for Advanced Study, Budapest, 1993, http://www.colbud.hu/main_old /PubArchive/PL/PL07-Geertz.pdf.

Gentile, Emilio. *La Voce e l'età giolittiana.* Milano: Pan, 1972.

Martelli, Sebastiano. "I sussidiari per le culture regionali." In *La Casa Editrice Carabba e la cultura italiana ed europea tra Otto e Novecento,* edited by Gianni Oliva, 289–305. Roma: Bulzoni, 1999.

Imagining the Memory of the Earth

Geo-Site and the Aesthetic of the Anthropocene

ANDREA BENASSI

This essay starts from ethnographic fieldwork done in an Italian nat-ural park: the Romagna's Gypsum Mountain Park.[1] This is a place where geology and rocks have a special identity and heritage sta-tus. This project investigates the nature of this new *geo-heritage* park, which links micro- and macrospace and how this heritage develops in the new idea and network of global geoparks.[2] Nature parks have an important role in the creation of a new heritage. The establish-ment of new regulatory and discursive regimes can deeply change the relationship between communities, territories, and economic strategies.[3] From this point of view, under the narrative of environ-mental protection, natural parks become an anthropological place where new essentialisms take shape and reinforce the old dichot-omy between nature and culture.[4] Moreover, these public spaces also become political spaces that can generate conflicts about the idea of "nature."[5] The essay aims to show the relationship between micro- and macro-narratives about geo-heritage and its practices and how this may have ties with the emergence of a new vision of nature: a nature's *reseau* full of human and nonhuman actors.[6]

GYPSUM MOUNTAIN AND GEOHISTORY

In 2013 a UNESCO delegation visited Mount Tondo in Gypsum Moun-tain Park in order to evaluate the request for it to be recognized as part of a global geopark network (GGN):"Mount Tondo is a sym-bolic site, not only for the Gypsum Mountain but also for the entire Romagna region. It is an absolute concentration of natural and cul-tural values."[7] The park, based on its geological features, is part of the ERAGP project that aims to create a wide geopark connecting and defining the identity of the Apennines in the area of Bologna and Ravenna provinces in Italy.[8] Geoparks, structured at the institutional level, are formed as part of a large European and global network sponsored and defined by UNESCO:[9] "Is a geopark only about geology? No! While a geopark must demonstrate the geological heritage of international significance, the purpose of a geopark is to explore, develop and celebrate the links between that geological heritage and all other aspects of the area's natural, cultural and intangible heritages. It is about reconnecting human society at all levels to the planet we all call home and to celebrate how our planet and its 4.600 million year long history has shaped every aspect of our lives and our societies."[10]

Defined as a new instrument for a holistic view of the territories and of their development, geological parks build a new kind of vision in which geological interpretation becomes a central axis of reality. Whether it's old protected areas or the new territories, connecting with the GGN network allows such parks to identify themselves under a new label, one able to transform local space in a geohistorical planetary heritage under the auspices of the geosciences. With the creation of Gypsum Park, the gypsum as a rock becomes a valuable geological landscape in itself: a perception and vision that coexist with a large quarry of the same mineral in the same mountain; it is a presence able to generate a landscape antithetical to mining and a landscape with important local economic and social aspects.[11] From this perspective there is a dialectical conflict between different actors. Farmers, politicians, environmentalists, cavers, tour operators, and government officials are competitors in imagining the true nature of gypsum and drawing up a moral code. From one side the gypsum is characterized by the idea of biological and geological uniqueness. Another perspective highlights the idea of the power and mystery of nature; another focuses on those who interpret the rock and its presence as part of a local social and economic narrative. Political arrangements allow the mining excavation (gypsum as material resource) but also sponsor actions and narratives about a new vision (a raw rock bearing absolute values that redefine the whole territory as subspecies gypsum).

In terms of educational and recreational activities, the story of the Gypsum Park territory is told through the great geological cycles. A deep history identifies the timescale, historical and transcendent, of these phenomena.[12] From this perspective the human relationship with landscape only enables us to interpret, protect, or destroy: "Why starting from Geology? In our opinion, when you know the rocky structure of a territory and its geological history, you can better understand both the landscape shape, the distribution of plants and animals and also—even if less obvious—the story and economy of human settlements. Notice that the Park itself is named by its geological and mineralogical essence—gypsum—that identifies a specific area."[13]

This territory embracing a geopark's paradigm as a tool for development and standardization becomes a place transformed, *subspecies geo-logos*, where biological and sociohistorical elements are subordinated to geology. Local transient epiphenomena interpret the narrative as a new global transcendent history that creates a new essentialist approach between identity and territory: "Cultural aspects within a Geopark, significant for regional identity, are living tangible and intangible components, and are an integral part of a Geopark. They are closely related to the landscape people live in."[14]

Geo-heritage, something of a hybrid compared to traditional cultural or natural heritage, forces us to question the nature of cultural heritage and those cultural coordinates underlying natural heritage.[15] It must be identified and protected globally because of its ability to narrate the story and power of the earth through a new category of microspaces: the geo-sites.[16] Geology—the depths and time of the earth—becomes in this way the path for a new institutional and emotional sense of place, a sort of descent into hell, led and defined by disciplinary knowledge: experts capable of showing a correct exegesis of a new techno-nature, where geodiversity becomes the new interpretative paradigm.[17] The geo-sites are presented in a new spatiotemporal frame: local points capable of acting as nodes in a living system of heritage and global memory, one capable of conceiving the planet as an organic whole, marked and defined by nonhuman crises. Through a multiplicity of practices Gypsum Park defines itself through the transformation of a large quantity of places in geo-sites.[18] In other words, a new geo-aesthetic manifests under the frame of gypsum.

In this new vision not only the quarry but also agricultural activities are perceived as negative and dangerous, capable of changing the shape of valleys, outcrops, or other geological landscape elements exposed in a sort of meta-museum. From this perspective the agricultural use of the land, as contemporary human agency, contrasts with the land as testimony of a deep global time. When we talk with Marco, a local farmer, about some sites visible in his farmland, he is amazed by their existence. Surveyed in terms of their conservation status, private places become public narrative spaces. In the management plan each site is described, mapped, and photographed to define it scientifically in time and verify it as both temporal yet timeless. The farm activity that moves stones, pieces of limestone, or gypsum, is stigmatized as negative. Through the information panels along the trails and organized events, individual sites become visible manifestations of discoveries, skills, and actions, undertaken by the community of scientific experts.

Geologists and cavers share the same epistemic coordinates and actions in the park. Such actions affect a transfiguration of the places themselves as signs of a new sacred nature focused not so much on the idea of wilderness as on that of a planet resembling *Gaia* and its power: something reflecting a coherent and objective original global memory of the planet before its corruption by humans.[19] The scientific community of Gypsum Park then rewrites time and history, a process that gives voice to layers, faults, discrepancies, fossil levels, sediments. Along the way the *anthropos* is placed completely on the edge of these great phenomena. The park territory is defined by a new narrative from the geological theory of the Messinian Salinity Crisis that arises in explanation for the existence of the gypsum. This narrative operates as a foundation myth: "A story that begins 6 million years ago, when the Mediterranean Sea underwent the so called 'Messinian salinity crisis' when the water dried out and salt and gypsum concentrated in large deposits. One of these, probably the most important for continuity and purity, is the Gypsum's Mountain of Romagna."[20]

The gypsum as rock, through the public geological narrative, becomes the incipit for a new vision of the entire Mediterranean basin as a geohistorical and biological macrospace.

GYPSUM IN THE ANTHROPOCENE

In 2011 the Geological Society of America titled a lecture "From Archean to Anthropocene: The Past Is the Key to the Future." Year after year out of geology emerges the idea that the planet and humanity, from the peaceful stability of the Holocene, are entering a new geological epoch edged by uncertain behavior: the Anthropocene. A working group on the Anthropocene, as part of Geological Sciences International, currently works to ratify the Anthropocene as a unit of the globally recognized geological time scales.[21] Since the Nobel Prize winner Paul Crutzen proposed the word *Anthropocene* to define the entry of humanity into a new geologic time,[22] the concept has spread globally as a container capable of synthesizing the current ecological crisis as well as designing new relationships and modes of governance between humanity and nature.[23] For some it remains a controversial concept.[24] To think ourselves into the Anthropocene allows us to define and witness the transition to a new era in Earth's history, in which humanity, the *Anthropos*, is considered as a geological force.[25]

The adoption of the geosphere as a last frontier reached by human agency puts an end to the planet's image as a projection of nature.[26] From a place of powerful forces able to overwhelm human beings, Earth becomes a space of memory, a record of nature's past creative power. This space claims a nostalgia for the Holocene epoch, the mother and cradle of humanity. The planet seems, from this perspective, a place to try and preserve the traces of the past creative power of nature as nonhuman agent. But if the Anthropocene is a powerful theoretical category capable of determining the global, it must be localized and experimented within the *friction* of local space in order to exist. This new way of thinking of the geological heritage as a public space seems to conform to the Anthropocene's vision of nature. Academic theory that links gypsum to the evaporation of the entire Mediterranean Sea transforms a local element into something like global geo-heritage, as witnessed by the prehuman history of the planet. The territory in these temporal coordinates experiences a particular aesthetic perception as a result of a particular frame of knowledge and power, a sensorial mutation able to activate a new aesthetic vision.[27]

Throughout a multiplicity of possible times, the park chooses an unimaginable time, a glacial time based on geological cycles.[28] This perspective creates sanctuary places full of time that cast a nostalgic shadow on the entire territory as a space in which a different ontology of time can be experienced. In the park you can identify a site with these characteristics in the Monticino quarry, a former mining area. This is shown by a new aesthetic of the quarry as a place redeemed, transformed from the space of mining into the beginning of a new morality. The space of the formerly productive mining landscape, linked to a local human history, becomes a vision of the gypsum bank and its stratigraphy, itself a huge fresco of planetary history. In this vision geological layers become pages of a new and absolute stone book:

> In 1985 a very important scientific discovery occurred in Monticino Gypsum quarry near Brisighella: an impressive deposit of fossils of the final Messinian Age (about 5–5½ million years ago) with continental fauna species already disappeared a long time ago from our environment: antelopes, rhinos, horses, anteaters, monkeys, hyenas, as well as a large number of small rodents and insectivores, whose disarticulated bones were trapped. The primitive Gypsum Vein was like a "piece of Africa" hot and dry, until it was again submerged by the sea following the opening of the Strait of Gibraltar.[29]

The site is presented as a kind of entertainment event, a sanctuary where dramatic events in world history can be seen: the crisis of salinity, the waters that come from distant oceans, an entire sea that opens and closes sixteen times, exotic animals struggling for life, footprints of past life. It functions as a museum where these tracks became witness of their presence. Educational practices that involve the site want to convey the signs of aging that are inscribed in it—for example, mountains that rise and fall. Everything looks amazing and yet real in front of the visitor. Stratigraphy discloses a cosmogony and at the same time shows visitors a future in which crisis and apocalypse now seem linked to human activity. Starting from this *sanctuary*, through the creation of specific trails, the mountains become a kind of scientific museum en plein air, a *reseau* where geological theory and history take shape in well-defined times and spaces. For the park geologist the territory is incorrectly administered, given the emphasis upon the geological sciences for a wide audience. After all, the geologist imagines the territory alive in its nonhuman evolutionary processes. Therefore, the paradigm of geo-conservation will protect a geodiversity that is the basis of biodiversity. This paradigm embodies both educational and tourism practices.[30] Gypsum in the park must therefore be protected because it is able to embody the essence of life.

TIBERIUS'S CAVE AND THE NATURE OF THE VACUUM

When we arrive close to Sasso church, Anna, a caver for Forli, stops and watches the big quarry, the huge white spot before us, on the other side of the valley. In particular its whiteness permeates the landscape and fascinates us, conveying a negative power, emptiness, absence—an entity that can eat the mountain. Anna, though a caver, does not know the inside of the quarry, yet despite her partial view, her judgment is clear. She defines a homogeneous group: the miners and owners along with the local population that has not struggled against the mine. The local mining history is simplified and essentialized. She describes this work as "unlawful." Mount Tondo and the nearby Tiberius's Cave have always been emblems of environmental struggle. The cave, already an ancient sacred archaeological site, is interpreted as a symbol of a sacred and protected nature rather than a nature exploited and subjugated. Its fragile survival against the surrounding quarry makes it a bastion and witness of primitive nature and the central value of study and contemplation, a perspective that clashes with those who see the gypsum as a source of labor.

Paul is the director of the plant close to the quarry that produces gypsum board. In his mind the quarry resembles a great work. The value of organized human labor shines in his description. But when he tells me about the "amphitheater," the bottom of the excavation, he reveals his personal aesthetics of the mine. He takes a sheet of paper and draws the galleries, the square, trying to transmit to me the wonder of the unexpected. His aesthetic perception of the place becomes a matter of sensation, light and dust. Everything represents material to create and show his relations with the mining landscape. Here in the active quarry, the heart of the conflict between natural and artificial, the image of a new mountain takes shape: an image created out of a vacuum but able to trigger a process of imagining nature.[31] The space of the mine is partly underground—an artificial vacuum intercepting and crossing the natural caves. The mountain from this perspective becomes a place where two antithetical networks intertwine and contrast with one another: the galleries of the quarry and the galleries of the underground karst systems—two sets of straight and curved lines, designed and explored, drawn on the conservation map and embodying a real and symbolic juxtaposition between a natural vacuum and the artificial one.

In this way the explorations of the cavers build the image and story of a new natural heart of the mountain and its hollowness. These derive from an aesthetics made of water and air and grow through descriptions and personal experiences. The passing of water creates, through experiments and explorations, a new huge underground entity that exceeds the single caves and individual fragments intercepted by the quarry. This entity, of course, relates to the original air and water circulation, an auratic atmosphere or geochemical vascular system that the quarry had injured.[32] Tiberius's Cave grows and extends itself, branching across the mountain as part of the same prehuman vacuum system. From an archaeological site the cave becomes a powerful entity, able to cross and bind the whole mountain through its lines and networks, something to be protected as a whole. Carlo, an old miner, told me how the encounter with the natural vacuum, during the excavation of tunnels, was unexpected. Today the proximity of these two types of emptiness is perceived as wrong and unnatural. The possibility of contact of these two modes, the risk of finding human traces during the exploration of caves (quarry expansion), creates a narrative oxymoron. Holocene and Anthropocene face off in galleries and the hollow mountain by materializing lines between the two eras—between human power and the power of nature. The simple contact between these vacuums generates the idea of a contamination, erasing the deep time that the cave represents by the human time of the quarry. Such contamination can falsify the truth that exists in the stone book of nature.[33]

FORMS OF AIR, ROCK, AND LIFE

The human incursion into the depths of the earth is seen as an intolerable incursion into the history of time, both a crisis and a heritage. The opening of the quarry in 1954 becomes a social and geological marker, embodying the arrival of the Anthropocene into the mountain: something able to twist the times and block its geological life. If the circulation of water is seen as a reticulum of geo-life in sync with the external environment, the evolution of the cave's galleries is related to the evolution of the valley of the nearby Senio River. In protectionist narratives the cave becomes an instrument and memory about the whole territory, a coherent archive of the time.[34] The karst process becomes a live and active indicator of environmental changes. Mutations are inscribed in the rocks like scars to read and interpret, transforming each individual morphological variation into a kind of archive of geological history but also of the external environmental life tout court. In an attempt to give an age and a biography to the cave, the karst is transformed into something almost living, and Tiberius's Cave is the oldest "living" cave in Emilia Romagna.[35] In a mode of re-enchantment the cave is then interpreted as something sentient, like negentropy, which witnesses the whole external history and preserves traces inside it.[36]

Following this reading, 1954 becomes a pivotal year in which this dialogue between inside and outside is interrupted because of humanity. This vision links the local time of the quarry with the global time of the "Great Acceleration." Simultaneously, the human traces in the rock layers become witness to human beings turned into a geological force. This denunciation is interwoven into narratives about disfigurement of the mountain skyline that are also charged with the responsibility of modifying the vital flows of air. The mine becomes something that produces not only aesthetic but ontological damage to human and nonhuman habitat, turning it into a less healthy space, allowing the spread of fog and unhealthy air from the lowlands. The scarred mountain, evident by its whiteness, becomes the cause and the explanation of the appearance of an evanescent white mass that erases the boundaries, confuses identities and traits. Traces of the artificial nitrogen cycle, triggered by the Green Revolution, use the Haber-Bosch process from gypsum to create fertilizers.[37] This mass symbolizes a cry of urgency in which the danger as rhetorical object moves in the narrative space between local and global contexts.[38] The risk of destruction slips and moves from a gallery—the single karst system—to the entire gypsum outcrop and beyond, up to climate change and life itself, a hazard of compromised nature but not yet a matter of fact.

I'm in a pub, near the mine. Outside there is fog, even a bit of snow. Maybe it will turn to the good, but the fog that you see across the street is enough to talk about the quarry and the weather: "They say that the fog has come since they lowered the mountain. Before, it stopped on the mountain and did not arrive in the village." Antonio says this, laughing a little, as he tries to understand what I believe. His report, an example of expert local knowledge, is something valuable and makes a good impression, a rumor, or only a fairy tale.

NOTES

1. See Benassi, "Simulacri di natura." The park covers six thousand hectares in the territories of six villages within the provinces of Bologna and Ravenna, in the Apennine Mountains, where there is a sort of small mountain range entirely made of gypsum.
2. The Global Geoparks Network is a UNESCO program launched in 1998

under the Earth Sciences Division. Its mission is to preserve and promote the geological heritage of the planet from a geotourism perspective. UNESCO currently recognizes 111 geoparks.

3. See Benassi, "Walking."
4. See Descola and Lloyd, *Beyond Nature and Culture*.
5. See Brosius, "Analyses and Interventions."
6. See Latour, *Politiche*; and Kirksey and Helmreich, "Emergence."
7. See Rondinini, "L'UNESCO."
8. See Gentilini and Panizza, *Emilia Romagna*.
9. European Geopark Network (EGN). *Geoparks Programme Feasibility Study Report* and *Global Geoparks Network* sponsored and defined by UNESCO. See Komoo and Patzak, "Global Geoparks Network," 13.
10. See Global Geoparks Network.
11. Currently the mining site of Mount Tondo, owned by Saint Gobein Corporation, is the largest European gypsum quarry.
12. See Irvine, "Deep Time."
13. Sami, "Geologia e geomorfologia," 13.
14. See Global Geoparks Network.
15. Olwig, "Introduction: The Nature of Cultural Heritage," 3.
16. Casto, *I beni culturali*, 17.
17. See Dei, *La discesa*; and Simonetti, "Between the Vertical and the Horizontal."
18. See Lucci and Rossi, *Speleologia e geositi*.
19. See Latour, "Facing Gaia."
20. Fusignani and Costa, "Presentazione," 7.
21. See Boes and Marshall, "Writing the Anthropocene."
22. Crutzen, "Geology of Mankind,"23.
23. See Lynas, *God Species*.
24. Autin and Holbrook, "Is the Anthropocene an Issue," 60; also see Malm and Hornborg, "Geology of Mankind"; and Baskin, "Paradigm Dressed as Epoch."
25. See Chakrabarty, "Climate of History."
26. Szerszynski, "End of the End of Nature," 65–84; also see Sloterdijk, "Atmospheric Politics."
27. Bender, "Time and Landscape,"104; also see Mirzoeff, "Visualizing the Anthropocene."
28. See Macnaghten and Urry, *Contested Natures*.
29. Bentini, "Per un parco," 13.
30. See Torabi Farsani, *Geoparks*.
31. See Roepstorff, Bubandt, and Kull, *Imagining Nature*.
32. See Menely, "Anthropocene Air."

33. Szerszynski, "End of the End of Nature," 74.
34. See Taylor, "Auras and Ice Cores."
35. Ercolani et al., "I gessi," 98.
36. *Negentropy* is the reverse of *entropy*. It refers to things becoming more orderly. Time in science is defined as the direction of entropy. Life is considered to be negentropic because it takes things that are less orderly and turns them into things that are more orderly, putting more information inside of them.
37. The Haber Bosch process fixes atmospheric nitrogen to synthesize ammonia, one of the ingredients for chemical fertilizer. In the past the quarry worked together with the ENI's ANIC petrochemical plant in the town of Ravenna, which specialized in the manufacture of chemical fertilizer.
38. See Beck, "Critical Theory of World Risk Society."

BIBLIOGRAPHY

Autin, Whitney J., and John M. Holbrook. "Is the Anthropocene an Issue of Stratigraphy or Pop Culture?" *GSA Today* (2012): 60–61. doi:10.1130/gl53gw.1.

Baskin, Jeremy. "Paradigm Dressed as Epoch: The Ideology of the Anthropocene." *Environmental Values* 24, no. 1 (2015): 9–29. doi:10.3197/096327115x14183182353746.

Beck, Ulrich. "Critical Theory of World Risk Society: A Cosmopolitan Vision." *Constellations* 16, no. 1 (2009): 3–22. doi:10.1111/j.1467–8675.2009.00534.x.

Benassi, Andrea. "Simulacri di natura. Politiche del patrimonio, retorica dell'identità e conflitto nel parco della Vena del Gesso." PhD diss., La Sapienza, Univerita di Roma, 2014.

———. "Walking in 'The Forest of Taboos': ecoturismo e patrimonio nel Manusela National Park." *VOCI* 10, no. 1 (2013): 285–331.

Bender, Barbara. "Time and Landscape." *Current Anthropology* 43, no. S4, special issue on "Repertoires of Timekeeping in Anthropology" (2002): 103–12.

Bentini, Luciano. "Per un parco della Vena del Gesso." *Museo in Forma. Rivista Quadrimestrale della Prov. di Ravenna.* 1999.

Boes, T., and K. Marshall. "Writing the Anthropocene: An Introduction." *Minnesota Review* 83 (2014): 60–72. doi:10.1215/00265667–2782243.

Brosius, J. Peter. "Analyses and Interventions: Anthropological Engagements with Environmentalism." *Current Anthropology* 40, no. 3 (1999): 277–309. doi:10.2307/2991397.

Casto, Lucrezia. *I beni culturali a carattere geologico del Lazio.* [Rome]: Regione Lazio. 2005.

Chakrabarty, Dipesh. "The Climate of History: Four Theses." *Critical Inquiry* 35, no. 2 (2009): 197–222. doi:10.1086/596640.

Crutzen, Paul J. "Geology of Mankind." *Nature* 415, no. 23 (2002): 23–23. doi:10.1038/415023a.

Dei, Fabio. *La discesa agli inferi.* Lecce: Argo, 1998.

Descola, Philippe, and Janet Lloyd. *Beyond Nature and Culture.* Chicago: University of Chicago Press, 2013.

Ercolani, Massimo, Piero Lucci, Stefano Piastra, and Baldo Sansavini. "I gessi e la cava di Monte Tondo." *Memorie dell'Istituto Italiano di Speleologia.* Bologna, 2013.

Fusignani, Eugenio, and Massimiliano Costa. "Presentazione." In *La casa rurale nella Vena del Gesso romagnola. Quaderni del parco,* 1st ed., 7. Faenza: Carta Bianca, 2011.

Gentilini, Sara, and Mario Panizza. *Emilia Romagna Apennine Geopark Project: Application Dossier.* Bologna: GAL Appennino Bolognese, 2012.

Global Geoparks Network. "What Is a UNESCO Global Geopark?" Accessed July 1, 2016. http://www.globalgeopark. org/aboutGGN/6398.htm.

Irvine, Richard. "Deep Time: An Anthropological Problem." *Social Anthropology* 22, no. 2 (2014): 157–72. doi:10.1111/1469-8676.12067.

Kirksey, S. Eben, and Stefan Helmreich. "The Emergence of Multispecies Ethnography." *Cultural Anthropology* 25, no. 4 (2010): 545–76. doi:10.1111 /j.1548-1360.2010.01069.x.

Komoo, Ibrahim, and Margarete Patzak. "Global Geoparks Network: An Integrated Approach for Heritage Conservation and Sustainable Use." In *Geoheritage of East and Southeast Asia,* edited by Mohd Shafeea Leman, Anthony Reedman, and Chen Shick Pei, 1–13. Kuala Lumpur: Ampang Press, 2008.

Latour, Bruno. "Facing Gaia. A New Inquiry into Natural Religion. Six Lectures on the Political Theology of Nature." Lecture Series, University of Edinburgh, February 18–28, 2013.

——. *Politiche della natura.* Milano: Cortina, 2000.

Latour, Bruno, and Peter Weibel. *Making Things Public: Atmospheres of Democracy.* Cambridge: MIT Press, 2005.

Lucci, Piero, and Antonio Rossi. *Speleologia e geositi carsici in Emilia-Romagna.* Bologna: Pendragon, 2011.

Lynas, Mark. *The God Species.* London: Fourth Estate, 2011.

Macnaghten, Phil, and John Urry. *Contested Natures.* London: SAGE Publications, 1998.

Malm, A., and A. Hornborg. "The Geology of Mankind? A Critique of the Anthropocene Narrative." *Anthropocene Review* 1, no. 1 (2014): 62–69. doi:10.1177/2053019613516291.

Menely, T. "Anthropocene Air." *Minnesota Review* 83 (2014): 93–101. doi:10 .1215/00265667-2782279.

Mirzoeff, N. "Visualizing the Anthropocene." *Public Culture* 26, no. 2 (2014): 213–32. doi:10.1215/ 08992363-2392039.

Olwig, Kenneth R. "Introduction: The Nature of Cultural Heritage, and the Culture of Natural Heritage—Northern Perspective on a Contested Patrimony." *International Journal of Heritage Studies* 11, no. 1 (2005): 3–7. http://www.tandfonline.com/doi/abs/10.1080/13527250500036742 ?journalCode=rjhs20.

Roepstorff, Andreas, Nils Bubandt, and Kalevi Kull. *Imagining Nature.* Aarhus, Denmark: Aarhus University Press, 2003

Rondinini, Margherita. "L'UNESCO nel Parco dei Gessi." *Il Resto del Carlino,* 2013.

Sami, Marco. "Geologia e geomorfologia." In *Parco regionale della Vena del Gesso Romagnola,* 13–40. Parma: Diabasis, 2010.

Simonetti, C. "Between the Vertical and the Horizontal: Time and Space in Archaeology." *History of the Human Sciences* 26, no. 1 (2013): 90–110. doi:10 .1177/0952695112473618.

Sloterdijk, Peter. "Atmospheric Politics." In *Making Things Public: Atmospheres of Democracy, Zentrum fur Kunst und Medentechnologie,* edited by Bruno Latour and P. Weibel, 944–51. Cambridge: MIT Press, 2005.

Szerszynski, Bronislaw. "The End of the End of Nature: The Anthropocene and the Fate of the Human." *Oxford Literary Review* 34, no. 2 (2012): 165–84.

Taylor, J. O. "Auras and Ice Cores: Atmospheric Archives and the Anthropocene." *Minnesota Review* 83 (2014): 73–82. doi:10.1215/00265667–2782255.

Torabi Farsani, Neda. *Geoparks and Geotourism.* Boca Raton: BrownWalker Press, 2012.

UNESCO. *Geoparks Programme Feasibility Study Report.* Paris: Division of Ecological and Earth Science UNESCO's Executive Board at the 161th Session, 2001.

———. *Global Geoparks Network.* Paris: UNESCO Division of Ecological and Earth Science, 2006.

Cacophonous Silence
(The Sound of Falling Wildly)

A Transnational Experiment in
Ecological Performance Poiesis

JESS ALLEN AND BRONWYN PREECE

If a tree falls in the forest and no one is there
to hear, does it still make a sound?

11. A fallen sycamore in Coed Penglais, Aberystwyth, Wales: the site chosen by coauthor Jess Allen for her half of this falling performance intervention. Copyright © Jess Allen and Bronwyn Preece.

Authors' note. The pages that follow are a collaboratively constructed, reflexive-poetic reading of the multi-month, transnational performance *The Sound of Falling Wildly*. Each author's voice is made "visible" with a different font: Jess's text appears in Neutraface, interspersed with Bronwyn's poetic writing, insertions, and provocations, which appear in Chaparral. Cowritten text is displayed in New Baskerville. This writing is intended to offer multiple points of entry to engaging with this work, as one might when witnessing live performance. It is not necessarily linear: it opens with two poems, the role and significance of which only become clear as the rest of the writing unfolds. In constructing the work in this way, we invite readers to fall, as we did: embracing uncertainty. The split-screen film—part dance film, part visual video poem—that represents the culmination of this process can be viewed on Vimeo at https://vimeo.com/116579557.

this is the sound of (my) Falling Wildly . . .

cacophonous silence. quiet volume. discordant rhythm. a pulse thrummed melodic. movement texturing a palpable and pastiched presence. unfurling rupture. raucous rapture. activist fuel for fossilization.

life. living. cycles. continuous. always.
hopefully . . . always.

if a tree falls in the forest and no one is there to hear, does it still make a sound?
YES.
earth's voice rising up—reminding me, reminding us, that "it" and everything is not about "one," it's not about "no one"—
"solo" is an impossibility . . . sound is present—a constant, lingering vibration: the music of interconnection . . . my inextricable embeddedness with being.

when I fall wildly, I rise up.

a tree, every tree—always falling, always rising—lubricates the
xylem that spreads the oxygen I breathe—
the zephyrs of my carbon dioxide exhalations sounding a
photosynthetic relay between birth and decay, action and hope.
simultaneous time chroniclers. documenting this time, that time.
*"oh pardon me thou bleeding piece of earth, that i am meek and gentle
with these butchers."*
i fall wildly to the striking sound of being both implicated butcher
and axed—limb to branch, trunk to torso, bark to bone.
inhale. exhale.
fall. rise.
stein. clayoquot. walbran. carmanah.
quote the past, query the present.
great bear rainforest. amazon. phone books and big macs.
this is our embodiment.
together we shape our current koans.
we are the sounds of one hand clapping the forest for the trees . . .
the trees for the forest.

standing, i and we meet the ground.

This is the sound of (my) falling wildly:
the silence of a long (with)held scream
freefalling through layers of disbelief
accumulated like leaf mold
the teenage activist's naïveté
grown a healthy bark of cynicism
                              reduced
at wild_(er)ness restricted
                              rerouted
to the space between
understanding and action

{held}
at the wild edges of our (dis)comfort
complacent dwelling

and yet
"the mountain is humming"
we hear its calling
in the itch of our skin
only soothed by our falling
air rushing over outstretched wing

untamed
disquieted
the scratch of our nails in the earth
clawing our way back to
[civilized?] wildness
shrugging off this fur coat, this fleece
of propriety
with a heavy thump

then listen
to the cumulative
noisy quiet
of insects
the biomass of busyness
without our loudness
ripping through it
like a road
like a storm
with a song in it
wrestling trees to the ground
laying them down with a whisper:
the crown's falling sigh
is an exhalation

and

this last breath
is our first

The whole wood was listening with me, the trees and the bushes, the little animals hiding in the undergrowth and the birds roosting in the branches. All were listening. Even the silence was listening. Silence was listening to silence.

—ROALD DAHL, *Danny, the Champion of the World*

Joseph Conrad . . . describes forests [as]–"the wilderness without a sound."

—JAY GRIFFITHS, *Wild: An Elemental Journey*

FALLING WILDLY (PRE-AMBULATION)

On February 13, 2014–later named "Wild Wednesday" by the tabloid press–I walked to the woods with my dog. I did not know that the MET office had issued a rare red weather warning for the west coast of Wales.

Extreme weather is expected. Follow the advice of the emergency services.

[warning: nature / nature: warning]

As I walked under the flailing groan of the Scots pines that line the edge of the university campus, I noticed there was an evacuation in progress. I saw a policeman attempting to direct the traffic around a fallen conifer. Silhouetted against the sea-sky line, he was blown about like a marionette on the storm's strings.

Take action to keep yourself and others safe.

At the entrance to Penglais Woods, I was stopped by two young men, who tried to dissuade me from proceeding. Meanwhile, my delighted dog chased leaves round the adjacent car park.

Avoid dangerous areas.

Then in front of our astonished eyes, as if waiting for this small audience, an old oak fell heavily across the path, with a sound of rending wood.

Risk to life is likely.

[we are self-immolating ourselves as earth]

After some moments' deafening wind-silence, I said: "That would have been an ironic way to go for an ecological performance artist." And with polite incredulity one of them—an ecologist, as it happens—responded: "Ecological *performance*? . . . What can performance do for ecology?"

And this is a question I have been taking back to the woods ever since . . .

[questions-shared-questions]

Conceived many months after this storm, *The Sound of Falling Wildly* was a transnational performance project that forms part of our ongoing and extensive series of remote collaborations. It was constructed around the oft-cited conundrum—not dissimilar to a Zen koan—*If a tree falls in the forest and no one is there to hear, does it still make a sound?* We were curious to see if this somewhat platitudinous paradox might be reclaimed and performatively (re) enacted to unsettle, or contribute usefully to, current debates around contemporary perceptions of "the wild." We were also curious about how, exactly, an ecological performance practice could provide a frame/work through which to do this, at the same time as drawing out the reciprocal possibilities it might awaken for a "re-wilding" of performance.

[there would be no zafus, no zabutons to cushion our falls. ~~this was wild zen.~~ an implosion of comforts and knowns; appropriations and philosophies; ground and gravity]

12. A fallen lodgepole pine on Lasqueti Island, British Columbia: the site chosen by coauthor Bronwyn Preece for her half of this falling performance intervention. Copyright © Jess Allen and Bronwyn Preece.

We are both ecofeminist performers, artists, activists, scholars, both living off grid in rural (if not "wild") locations in the United Kingdom and Canada, respectively. As women in our thirties, our own current conceptions of wildness derive from many things—not least a childhood spent recreationally climbing trees in ancient woodland (me), a young adulthood campaigning to save them (Bronwyn), later adulthood spent dancing and performing in them (both). And so perhaps it was also a subliminal desire to revisit and unsettle our own notions of the wild that prompted us to construct a performance score around falling in the woods.

Falling Wildly takes its form from the ritual process we have begun to establish through our other collaborative works. These typically begin with (i) the selection of an outdoor performance site usually in "nature"; (ii) the collection of physical objects from that site; and (iii) the writing of a piece of text and a loose score (series of rules or instructions) for movement—all of which we exchange though the mail as a precursor to (iv) a filmed movement-based response on site.

instructions to get unruled by: a series

–fall away from a lexicon of nouns.
        i am a verb. "wild," "nature" &
        "environment" are moving, are
movement.
–fall deeply into s/Self as environmental
evocation: wildly natural, inextricably   connected
–fall away from illusions of distance, into a
"silence" of engaged co-dependent   arising . . .
–fall the constant flux that we are. . . .

        push record. . . .

Independently, we both struggled with the choice of an appropriate site for this work: in rural mid-Wales and on Lasqueti Island, British Columbia, both of us have access to what might be regarded—even in stringent, ecological terms—as true wild land: "old-growth" trees or "ancient woodland." Yet both of us were repeatedly drawn toward particular (fallen) trees in far more recent, more managed, more public, even more "domestic" sites. Bronwyn's was a lodgepole pine on a bluff above her home. Mine was not even a native species: a sycamore that had fallen in those same dog-walking woods on the edge of town, in those same storms. Taking with it the entire bank of winter-quiescent bluebells that had lain in the earth over its root system, they went on still to flower gloriously in spring [i can attest].

Committing, then, to these instinctively chosen sites and the layered, personal metaphors they offered us, we agreed on a day on which to collect plant matter from our respective forest/woodland floors. We also purchased the same day's national and local newspapers. In them we sought out those articles that touched on themes we considered to be remotely "ecological": wild(er)ness, activism, climate change. Subsequently mulching wild plants and newsprint together, we "wild-crafted" the pulp into bioregional, eco-political paper "tablets." Onto these we would then scribe, with willow charcoal, a long piece of text about our own relationships to, conceptions of, hopes for, wildness: drawing variously from our embodied reading of the news articles, childhood memories, experiences of ecological activism, direct action, our lives off the grid.

[our hands were covered in dye for days . . . inked imprints of the toxicity of our news . . .]

Exchanged in the mail, these writings were then taken out to their counterpart woodland sites, where they bore witness to our execution of a simple movement score for camera, with a single directive: to explore falling. This video footage was then edited together with wild(audio)track and intercalated fragments of the written text. The result is a form of visual poem, or a three-way dance dialogue that forms a mediated, virtual arboreal arc across the northern hemisphere.

A koan is by definition paradoxical: an anecdote or riddle without solution, used in Zen Buddhism to demonstrate the inadequacy of logical reasoning and provoke enlightenment. As such, this essay takes the form of both the koan-like provocation with which we began and the gesture of falling at its core: documenting our startled descent into uncertainty without ready resolution.

Who hears?

Does a person who practices with great devotion still fall into cause and effect?

We are the sounds of a fall rising up to meet the
Anthropocene—the effect/cause of wilding a here from the over
there of wilderness—
one hand clapping   ⟶   the remaining forest for the
trees. . . . the clearcuts for the forest

listening with devotion

13. Film still of Jess "listening" to the sounds of the woods in Wales through an aperture in the paper tablet handcrafted by Bronwyn from the detritus on the forest floor in Canada. Copyright © Jess Allen and Bronwyn Preece.

The act of falling is currently enjoying great prominence in performance scholarship; falling might yet prove to be the new walking, such are the claims made for its dramatic potential.[1] Perhaps this is because falling is such a perfect metaphor for contemporary precarity and has long been a universal one for human (female) culpability. Women fall, but so do children, apples, rain, autumn leaves. Trees fall, but so, too, do civilizations, with an inevitability that "The Dark Mountain Manifesto" reminds us "is as much a law of history as gravity is a law of physics" so we'd do well to remember that, in a changing climate. "What remains after the fall," they continue, "is a wild mixture of cultural debris."[2]

[i stand: socialized flotsam and jetsam

empathetically: i fall]

Deconstructing the debris—the wild fallout—of our own performance has proven challenging. For a start, if falling itself is such a powerful metaphor for uncertainty (say, about the future of wild[er]ness), then why go to the woods to do it? Especially when (eco-activist) women falling off (and apparently hugging) fallen trees could be construed as reinforcing several tired clichés. Yet for us both—trained in site-based environmental movement—it was an obvious choice for a different reason: it is widely accepted that the practices of embodiment practiced outdoors give more ready access to a sense of interconnection with the more-than-human world.[3] Falling onto, softening into, jumping off, moving on and with, surfaces and objects is to recognize their autonomy at the same time as foregrounding the equality of "vital" materiality we share with them.[4] In other words, the conscious practice of outdoor movement is radically decentering, countering the "heresy of aloofness" that Robert Macfarlane posits might be at the heart of our troubled relationship with the natural world, precisely because "we have begun turning away from a felt relationship" with it.[5] We hoped the film might convey something of this imperative to its viewers.

Trees, too, have a particular symbolic potency: a "longevity" and "self-generating energy" we (humans) have long admired.[6] We feel an affinity with them not least because of their form, which "like the upright human body . . . [appears] majestically defenceless. . . . Road protesters, hugging their adopted tree trunks for dear life, appear naturally entwined, trunk to trunk, arms, legs and branches, in a passionate embrace of living bodies."[7] This notion of shared vulnerability with trees is more potent in the film, when I watch it, for knowing that Bronwyn and I were both diagnosed with (potentially physically) disabling medical conditions in our twenties. In this sense our falling is not wild at all: after our very first falls, in which we both hurt and shocked ourselves, we play it safe. (As Amy Sharrocks warns, "Falling and failing get mythologized, romanticized as sites of potential, when they can hurt drastically.")[8] This is a different kind of letting go here—at least for me—of the wild physicality of a formerly fearless dancer, replaced with an acceptance of the body's frailty. This is my literal fall from grace.

[void of religion, dogma, ideology . . . *full of radical hope*. . . .
subversive, critical, creative]

Our trees, in contrast, had indeed fallen wildly—as a result of natural processes, not human endeavor—and so perhaps their presence on film is all the more "potent" when set against the field (audio) recording that contains audible-but-invisible presence of human "interference": a building site on the edge of the (Welsh) woods where human-operated machines are taming and reclaiming natural greenspace. Intentionally, the film footage and text were edited together in silence, based purely on how the choreography of falling—our improvised responses to the contingencies of our (different) sites and bodies—could work with (animated) written word. The audio score, edited independently to the desired length, was then overlaid directly on top of this, with almost no editorial tweaking. Consequently, the subtle synchronicities between words and movement, movement and sound, are all the more striking: at one point Bronwyn, in Canada, drops to her knees, coincidentally at the same time as the clanking of a digger bucket, in Wales, as if her own joints were mechanical, metallic; at another the text *discordant rhythm* appears on screen, as if subtitling the syncopated shriek of seagulls that we can hear.

[i am the/your hole in the bucket . . .
my/our bucket list: earthed]

Throughout, then, the viewer can weave his or her own story about wildness—from this juxtaposition of sounds, words, and images— that may variously be about hubris, vulnerability, the quixotic nature of human endeavor, but one that is also thoroughly enmeshed within wider—wilder—processes. Perhaps this multiple, layered "narrativizing" is inevitable because, as Hayden Lorimer and John Wylie observe: "Sounds lend grace, or violence, to scenery . . . Sounds can seem the more untrustworthy for being beyond sight or reach, lacking a source point evident to the eye. The conditioning of human being is such that you don't engage innocently with sound."[9]

We had originally intended to overlay the images with recorded speech, as in our previous film work, but immediately it was apparent that the human voice was most unwelcome here.[10] Intuitively as we watch someone in the unintuitive act of preparing to make a planned fall, we have an empathic sense of what must be an internal monologue. As Sharrocks writes of watching the late Dutch performance artist Bas Jan Ader's famous filmed falls: "The tense moments of waiting, knowing what is coming, watching while the artist approaches the moment of letting go . . . You have time to consider what he is waiting for . . . He seems to be gearing up for the moment of most feeling, to wrest every ounce of emotion [from] this act . . . and is present in it wholeheartedly."[11]

And so, superimposing our falls with an external commentary seemed incongruous and disingenuous. It got in the way of the potential for the viewer's kinesthetic empathy with our simple commitment to fall together, transnationally—"two bodies committing to two trajectories"—in doing so, demonstrating a shared vulnerability that might, just might, rescue us from cliché.[12] The act of deliberate falling also offers an almost palpable sense of will. For if true wild land is "self-willed," then we were embodying the metaphor, albeit in a self-destructive way for aesthetic ends that true "nature" would not countenance (though activism—and performance art—frequently exploits).

]to fall from/
with the tree
"of" a friend

touched/touch-
ing first
through *home-*
made paper (posted,
overseas, received)–
bits of bark and
branch roughing
up the contours of
charcoal—
penned words
through black,
petrified trees: compress-
ing cries, screams
(withheld)—this is
contact, this is context . . .
sycamore syntax
then split through
screen—2D
foliage whispering
wind through
leaves moved and
moving:
pushing the film edges
(filmedges) of "my" half
as i *pine*-d the (shared)
telematic exhale . . .
this, my
second contact—"fixed
projection" . . . second
context
sycamore screen(ed)

dreaming away distance. . . .

14. On a visit to Aberystwyth from Canada the authors make a ceremonial visit to the woods, and Bronwyn re-creates Jess's fall from the sycamore in Coed Penglais. Copyright © Jess Allen and Bronwyn Preece.

i landed in a bluebell forest,
Penglais Woods
an early spring greeting
distorting the paradoxical
justifications of a jet-
fueled journey—
transnational collaboration
landing on/in a runway,
a fallway, a
way-we-fall
together . . .
red dreads replaced
with brown hair,
and an embrace of
spring muddied earth
this the third—
imbricated—

contact, context
"local"-"nonnative"
sycamore streaks
on a "foreign" Canadian w/
dual citizenships (UK):
a poeisis of the
ethics of
exchange . . . [

The act of falling is of course also a perfect metaphor for wildness, as both have a rebellious, elusive quality that evades fixity, perhaps because they only truly exist in motion, in being, in becoming. This is akin to the "arc between two deaths" (the stases of vertical balance and horizontal repose) that Doris Humphrey so famously regarded as the essence of all movement, what gave modern dance life.[13] Or perhaps made it more like the fallibility of real life than the escapism of ballet—trying so hard to maintain uprightness and make it look effortless. In his plenary address at a recent symposium for ecological performance makers, Simon Bayly issued the provocation that in an era of ecological crisis and uncertainty, we ought indeed to pursue practices that help us to "lose our uprightness."[14] Falling might indeed then live up to its promise as a performative device for eco-activist performance. And postmodern dance practices such as contact improvisation teach us how to fall, which is a ready metaphor—and model—for wild resilience.[15] As Rilke writes:

This is what things can teach us:
to fall,
patiently to trust our heaviness.
Even a bird has to do that
before he can fly.[16]

Ultimately, for all our trying, the sound of falling wildly was not to be heard, or rather, it was cacophonously silent. Wildness, after all, was not to be "found," too elusive to be penned, too exuberant to be contained in a piece of handmade paper. Wildness was shy of the camera, too big to be constrained by the frame. Skeptical of contemporary performance, it would not enter into a dance with us. Holding on to our original provocations was anyway impossible: the letting go of falling was a totality. Like walking into a room and forgetting what you came there for: standing, falling, lying in the woods, there was suddenly no longer really a question for us to answer. The brief moment of falling focuses the mind, but the sudden shock of landing disperses the purpose into a different kind of learning. In this way the fall is the koan-like riddle itself—its own answer and its own question, eternally enfolded in the wild tumult of being.

if
a tree falls in the forest
and there is no one there
to hear
does it still
make a sound?

this
is the sound
of falling wildly
cacophonous silence
quiet volume
discordant rhythm
a pulse thrummed
the silence
of a long withheld scream
freefalling
through layers of disbelief
accumulated
like leaf mold
unfurling rupture
raucous rapture
a constant, lingering
vibration

i fall wildly to the striking sound of being
implicated;
butcher
and axed
held
at the wild edges of our discomfort
complacent dwelling
shrugging off
this fur coat, this fleece
of propriety
the scratch of our nails in the earth
clawing our way back to
civilized? wildness
this
is our embodiment
always falling
always rising
a photosynthetic relay between
birth and decay
action and hope
listen
to the
noisy quiet
like a storm with a song in it
together
we shape
our current koans
the tree's falling sigh
is an exhalation
and
standing
i and we
meet the ground

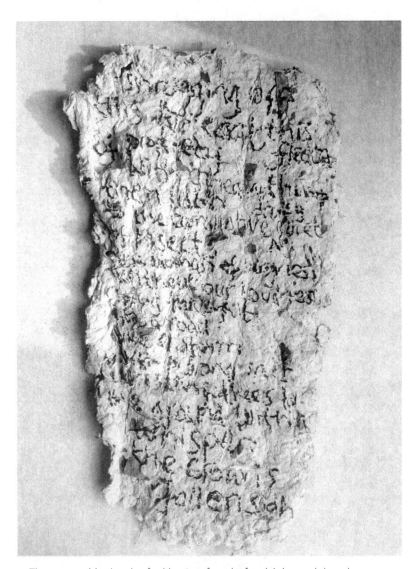

15. The paper tablet handcrafted by Jess from leaf mulch beneath her chosen syca-more in Wales, scribed with the words of her poem in willow charcoal, shortly before posting to Bronwyn in Canada, an exchange that marked the start of the collaboration. Copyright © Jess Allen and Bronwyn Preece.

NOTES

1. See Albright, "Falling"; Claid, "Can I Let You Fall"; and Sharrocks, "Anatomy of Falling."
2. Kingsnorth and Hine, "Uncivilisation," n.p.
3. See Olsen, *Body and Earth*; Poynor; Stewart, "Dancing"; Orr and Sweeney, "Surface Tension."
4. See Kramer, "Bodies, Rivers, Rocks and Trees"; and Bennett, *Vibrant Matter*.
5. Macfarlane, *Wild Places*, 203.
6. Macnaghten and Urry, "Bodies in the Woods," 27.
7. Macnaghten and Urry, "Bodies in the Woods," 27.
8. Sharrocks, "Anatomy of Falling," 48.
9. Lorimer and Wylie, "LOOP," 7–8.
10. *Dropped in the Ocean*, https://vimeo.com/87669240; *Triangulating Caplor*, https://vimeo.com/104126385 or https://vimeo.com/104118100.
11. Sharrocks, "Anatomy of Falling," 48.
12. Lorimer and Wylie, "LOOP," 7.
13. See Humphrey, *Art of Making Dances*.
14. See Bayly, "Plenary."
15. See Albright, "Falling."
16. Rilke, "Wenn etwas mir vom Fenster fällt," 117.

BIBLIOGRAPHY

Albright, Anne Cooper. "Falling." *Performance Research* 18, no. 4 (2013): 36–41.

Bayly, Simon. "Plenary." Performance and Environment: New Perspectives on Ecological Performance Making Symposium. Royal Central School of Speech and Drama, London, November 1, 2013.

Bennett, Jane. *Vibrant Matter: A Political Ecology of Things*. Durham NC: Duke University Press, 2010.

Claid, Emilyn. "Can I Let You Fall?" *Performance Research* 18, no. 4 (2013): 73–82.

Dahl, Roald. *Danny, the Champion of the World*. London: Jonathan Cape, 1975.

Griffiths, Jay. *Wild: An Elemental Journey*. London: Penguin, 2006.

Humphrey, Doris. *The Art of Making Dances*. Alton: Dance Books, 1959.

Kingsnorth, Paul, and Dougald Hine. "Uncivilisation: The Dark Mountain Manifesto." *The Dark Mountain Project*, 2009. Accessed June 22, 2014. http://dark-mountain.net/about/manifesto/.

Kramer, Paula. "Bodies, Rivers, Rocks and Trees: Meeting Agentic Materiality in Contemporary Outdoor Dance Practices." *Performance Research* 17, no. 4 (2012): 83–91.

Lorimer, Hayden, and John Wylie. "LOOP: A Geography." *Performance Research* 15, no. 4 (2010): 6–13.

Macfarlane, Robert. *The Wild Places*. London: Granta, 2007.

Macnaghten, Phil, and John Urry. "Bodies in the Woods." In *Bodies in Nature*, edited by Paul Macnaghten and John Urry, 166–83. London: SAGE Publications, 2001.

Olsen, Andrea. *Body and Earth: An Experiential Guide*. Lebanon NH: University Press of New England, 2009.

Orr, Marnie, and Rachel Sweeney. "Surface Tension: Land and Body Relations through Live Research Enquiry: ROCKface." *Double Dialogues* 14 (2011). Accessed January 19, 2012. http://www.doubledialogues.com/article/surface-tensions-land-and-body-relations-through-live-research-inquiry-rockface/.

Rilke, Rainer Maria. "Wenn etwas mir vom Fenster fällt." *Rilke's Book of Hours: Love Poems to God*, 116–17. Translated and edited by Anita Barrows and Joanna Macy. New York: Riverhead Books, 2005.

Sharrocks, Amy. "The Anatomy of Falling." *Performance Research* 18, no. 4 (2013): 48–55.

Stewart, Nigel. "Dancing the Face of Place: Environmental Dance and Eco-Phenomenology." *Performance Research* 15, no. 4 (2011): 32–39.

POETRY 1 | *Ground Truths*

Meadows and Fireflies

ALIKI BARNSTONE

Sometimes I'm an anachronism remembering the meadows
    of my childhood in the Green Mountains,
        the fireflies mirroring the Milky Way
on a moonless night, the dark almost true black,
    for miles around, the absence of light interrupted
        only meekly by the two houses on our dirt road.
Acres of meadows illumined by bugs, homely things in the day
    we discovered in morning, having wandered
        with our Mason jars into unmowed grasses
and wildflowers, waist high to a child, shoulder high
    to the youngest—to emerge from the pollen-heavy
        dusky field with a lantern
of orbiting and blinking insects and to place them
    on the nightstand beside our heads, watching
        until sleep and to dreamwalk tiny
onto the fireflies' backs, gliding beyond the glass prison
    to float beneath a cascade of Goldenrod blooms,
        or alight on a downy bedspread of Queen Anne's Lace.
In the tall, sheltering, necessary darkness, fireflies' bioluminescence
    attracts mates, and females lay fertilized eggs
        among the seeds on the ground's surface, or just below,
and the universe in miniature sleeps in winter, to bloom and fly
    in the next year, and the next, and in all the years to come,
        could the meadows survive the future.

Sonoran Desert

Winter Afternoon Singing Itself

ALBERTO RÍOS

Five birds fly in a line,
A black part in the white hair of the cloudy sky.

They waver for moments, each bird,
As if someone were playing them as the black keys on a piano,

Making a faint, distant music of wing and hurry and purpose,
A chance measure performed on the immense, grand
    instrument.

Too Easy

GREG DELANTY

A robin bashes his blood-breasted body
      against a neighbor's windowpane.
Maybe he beholds bird-heaven within; his family
      past, present and future: chirpy friends,
mates singing merrily over a feast
      of divine cutworms, angelic larvae. Or, he eyes
the Helen, Marilyn Monroe, Sheba, Aphrodite
      of robinesses. But the bird-book explains
how the male American robin works himself
      into such a territorial frenzy that he's often seen
attacking his own reflection, convinced his own image
      is the enemy. Too easy to turn into allegory.

Communion

TWYLA M. HANSEN

I worshipped amid the regulars—
families of Cedar, Cottonwood and Pine—
child on a carpet of rotted leaves
wandering the long pews
of the planted windbreak,

while the wind sighed its hymn
through limb and needle,
the hollow root filled with rainwater
a baptismal font, a pet cemetery
marked by mishmash of stone and wood,

where I first believed—the miracle
of seed and soil, the magic of sun
and rain, the might of machine
and harvest and yield—sheltered
there in my private sanctuary.

Could any place be more sacred?
Once-treeless plain where the first
people sipped from that cool spring
down in the field, where the graves
of Native children dotted those hills.

I was alone, but never lonely,
surrounded, kneeling to the season
at a shrine of piled sticks and rocks,
chorus of birdsong from the balcony,
litany of bee and mosquito and wasp.

Those fields now a factory of corn
and soybean, no trace of livestock
or silo, no milk barn or nearby farms,
windbreaks and contours obliterated
to accommodate center pivots.

Oh Christ! your body broken, eaten,
your blood shed over this land.
Forgive us for not remembering.
Before it is too late, teach us how
to love our one and only Earth.

Strata Songs

Galway and Arizona

SUSAN MILLAR DUMARS

I

Barna Woods are sleeping.

Every side of every war
buried the inconvenient
here. I tread on bones,
hidden histories,
on the slush of secrets
and sodden leaves.

The trees—wet brushstrokes
on white sky—taper, drip dark.
Green moss, sudden and sweet
as a lover's tongue.
Beech limbs reach
for light. Birds joke
in their own language.

II

The Grand Canyon is awake.

On the South Rim
snow falls fast
and the ruts in the path
hammocked by ice make me clutch
at the offered arms
of oaks. No guardrail
between me and consequence.

Nothing hidden—
I'm face to face
with time's
hard carving.

Now the naked canyon
slips from cloud-shadow
bedclothes—
reveals
her iron blush.

Sutra, in Umber

KIMBERLY BLAESER

November 2009. In gracious remnants of fall sun, my hair warms
to its roots. Now, silent as heat, deer materialize amid columns
of Fort Snelling oak, recede again into weathered wood. We walk
with uncertain ghosts.

Here is old Dakota Territory. A confluence of rivers, a mythic
place of origin. Makoce Cokaya Kin. Where the Minnesota meets
the Mississippi. Center of the Earth. Here, too, 1,600 Dakota
women, children, and heartbroken old men became prisoners.
Interred on these grounds.

I pass like breath into the hollow, slowly move among the deer.
In the stillness of intrusion time falls away. On the ground
of trampled leaves, in a light of indistinguishable origin, I
remember the story. Imagine the way history sinks into sepia.

Winter 1862. Starvation and disease here beneath the trees.
The Dakota camp already overcrowded—occupied by the dark
specter of murder. Memories of thirty-eight warrior bodies swing
like pendulums on the colonial metronome. Mass execution.
Each day until May more Dakota spirits slip away, step into dusky
rumors about vanished heathens. 300 prisoners never leave
these grounds.

Spring enters amid vacant-eyed strangers. Steamboats churn
sacred waters. And survivors again leave their homelands, their
relatives, their dead. Passing into exile. Before me now longing
fills the forest like dew. Each burr, each blade of copper grass,
remembers. And soon every black bark knot becomes eyes.

I tell myself only the deer live here now. Glimpse their branch antlers curved, leaf ears erect. But in this wavering between one being and another, in the vital shimmer of unknowing, I see the tree bark faces of the many sentient. Earth—the simple ink-trace of ancients. As if story and landscape converge. Forever inseparable.

After Taiwan

KIMBERLY BLAESER

I watch the umbrella tip walk slowly up the Erzihping Trail and the deep scarlet fleece at the woman's waist swing slightly side to side, unfurling like a conquering flag. One step ahead, a navy backpack bounces just below her husband's abundant gray hair. Now the tall grasses of Mount Datun rise on each side of the figures, closing around them as they diminish into smaller and smaller memory.

They wanted a photo. Their ancient everyday. My foreign face. In the digital window where we stand together in the Tamsui morning, my wide smile reflects the joy I feel in their presence. Eighty. Still hiking. In tandem. I imagine the island years, the long sequence of suns. Like this January orb that warms my shoulders. Or later plays so generously across the tiles at Tian Yuan. Showing to perfect effect the temple's scores of brilliant dragons, the wall of hungry tigers.

What we found in the mountain morning: No serow, wild boar, Formosan sambar. No clouded leopard or any of the other twenty-eight mammal species. Many are rare, endangered. Some have not been sighted for years, may already have gone with the older suns.

Not so the stone lions who welcome visitors and guard the temple grounds. Not so the extravagant tropical flowers in fiery palettes, the sweet-scented incense sticks, the overflowing bowls of ripe fruit presented at altars. Not so the simple solemnity of bowing before good.

After Taiwan, I wondered at the artist's way. With a wealth of words or watercolors, what to place in the foreground, what receding at the edge of vision?

Birth of a Nation

COLM TÓIBÍN

In a doorway in a grimy street, a crowd
Of like-minded old patriots has grouped
To add a new color to the glistening dawn,

Which rises from the side of the flattened earth,
And longs, in grim boredom, for variation.
They mix the dawn-paint in grainy silence;

They will do anything to help, now that
The blaring car sirens and cops on wheels
Have ruined the delicate country they fought

For, burned down great houses to achieve.
Danton is dead and De Valera blind.
The men have been left only sticks and pots

And the fierce urge, impelling and intense,
To make something permanent, like God
Makes, or the constitution that they wrote

So happily, having consulted all
Parties who had influence at the time.
No need to talk, one says, but simply paint,

Throw colors over the abyss, that they
Might land on the holy place where the dawn
Is parked, duly waiting for its great chance.

No, the argument went on, we must
Wait till the appointed hour when light,
All tentative and raw, comes in the sky,

And then spread out, inch toward the edge, and pounce;
With bright splashes, gold-yellow, cream and red
Startle the grayness of the empty dawn.

Hey, one man went on, remember dawns you saw!
Small rays of yellow against the cold and dark,
And then the lift of day, banal and bright.

We must paint it by surprise, one said,
Find new colors, streaks of violent azure,
And lift the morning from its lifelong gloom.

Down in the depths, the night grew still, holding
In its arms the half-made throbbing dawn,
Dreading the catastrophe of time, clockwork

Spreading its evil havoc through the world.
The night and its colleagues longed for this
To cease, but it was all hopeless in those years.

At the doorway in a grimy street, six men
Blew warmth into their freezing fists, appealed
For reason to prevail in times of need.

In the meantime, rays of stealthy light,
The strange stark grayness in the eastern sky,
Touched them, made them wince and call out loud

That nothing could compare to what they'd planned.
In time, they shouted, the world will learn to
Replace chaos with artful immanence and warmth.

They walked then, armed and determined, their voices
Hoarse with ideals, while below them
The night lay ignorant that time relents,

That even the spiteful earth yields up its source,
Until slowly, in graceful measured beats,
The light slides down, dark order is restored.

Encounter

TESS GALLAGHER

Over the rain-rutted avenue
I've walked in to horses at Kingsborough,
neglected estate, now plundered
by gatekeepers, the twisted arms of wild
rhododendrons hacked for firewood; the locals'
mild compensatory salute: "it's grand
to finally be able to see the lake!"

I hold my palm to the muzzle of a mare,
her deep eye that sinks me in,
its richly fringed eyelid closing over
my reflection, then lifting me
like an emissary of unknown offerings
down corridors burnished with inklings
of hounds and masters, of drops of port

spilled from a flask accidently onto
its neck, or of Cromwellian plunder of silver
dug into the pasture while they, unbridled,
looked on. She snuffles my empty
hand then tosses me and history into her
farthest cavern. She'll keep me for the contraband
I am, a lonely walker who doesn't know

what she wants in a borrowed land
far from home. A small entitlement of steps
led me to mystery, seeking to be
left out. How else let difference tell you
what you are?

Matters of Geneva

DAWN DUPLER

In the heart of Geneva, a town surrounds a tomb
of an Allobrogian chieftain, whom we know by debris
brushed from his bones,
by his grit under our nails.
We laid him down to complete his death.

Not far from St. Pierre's funerary crypt,
miles below the sloping Swiss fields, men dug tunnels
in the dirt like animals desperate for escape,
a back channel to channel back to their beginnings,
to God's quick breath after the Big Bang.

Here, in the depths of the Large Hadron Collider,
immured scientists crash protons together
head on like children playing Chicken,
where no one flinches, like James Dean
driving into himself, and photons fly

and fall. Gluons and bosons, muons and more detritus,
all flash that never flew above ground,
are now a slice of new terrain
where a pair of lonely photons explain how matter
came to be, not from clay, but from the fray of an energy field.

Had some peoples' predictions come true,
that finding the God Particle
would turn each air molecule into a fireball,
we would have become the Emperor's Terra-Cotta Soldiers,
standing upright in underground graves.

But the world's matter did not burn. Still, particles
are portions, never complete. They scamper in tunnels,
unseen, untouched, daring us over the edge.
Excavate and cast away all but bones
beneath St. Pierre's Cathedral, and let us do what we do best

beneath the earth, our most innocent deed:
remain dead.

The Course of the Peculiar

MICHAEL HEFFERNAN

I made my mind up to combine my arts
as the neighborhood Monet or young Rimbaud,
or old Rimbaud and young Monet, to see
who had the strongest stroke of pen or brush
to gain the angle of the mind's or the tree's light,
so I went out and sat down in the shade
of our umbrella on the backyard's edge
before you come to the jungle at the back,
which goes into a great beyond beyond
the farthest cul-de-sac that no one knows
or ever has seen anyone drive out of
in whole or in part since the twelfth century,
when the last Proto-Caddoans were here
at the high point of their fourth lost kingdom
before their last, mad king had sold them all,
including his own crazed self, to the Archeo-Jibways,
who were zestful cannibals, and ate the king
at a huge dinner party where he danced and sang
and did a sort of stand-up act and smeared
the last of his own possum butter on his head
before they chopped it off and carved him up
in tidbits to stack on skewers and pass around.
I had in mind to talk about my art.
Enough of all that jabber about the Jibways
and the king they ate who ended up a joke.
My neighbors can't imagine what I do
around the backyard moving back and forth
from light to shadow staking out the perfect
angle from which to throw a spoon of paint
onto a virgin canvas freshly stretched

on old tomato stakes I gave up planting
when I thought a gardener was what I was
before I knew the magic of Scarlet Lake
from Daler-Rowney, Bracknell, Berkshire, England,
which happens to be the very most elegant
naphthol red pigment that you can get
to throw around with only the dog to watch.
And what this dog enjoys about my work
is not the color (being color-blind)
but the graceful turns I make around the lawn
before I sashay up to an arm's length
and make a sidewise fling of Scarlet Lake
within a hefty splatter from her nose
while she is halfway blinking through a drowse
and not yet in a frame of mind to wonder
who is this figure flinging himself around
who looks familiar and whose scent is one
she recognizes as someone's who gave her food
and now is throwing paint that reaches someplace
far from where a dog would dream to be
in this or any place a dog belonged
before she came to know what she was doing.
Wily as she can be from time to time,
she seems to have no scheme for what to do.
From where she watches this, the rest is sadness.

Tsé Bit'a'í

CHRISTINE CASSON

—"Rock with Wings" in Navajo, the name given to a volcanic
monadnock in northwestern New Mexico that was once,
according to legend, a great bird that transported the Navajo
people fleeing from a warlike tribe, and from the cold
northlands, to safety in the Four Corners Region.

Her wings shudder, splintering their sheath
of ice, her eyes' translucent membranes
swept aside, the long-entrenched fervor
of glacial winds slackening grip;

upheaved bone and muscle, leg's tendons
unflexed and the headlong rush, cliff's edge
beneath, massive wings pressuring air
downward, the load so fierce she's lifted up,

thrust and drag in equilibrium—
and their insistent prayers breaching
her ears' auriculars—a language
she's never known, its modulated

pitches, affricates and fricatives,
scouring her ears, entreating her help,
so unlike her own mellifluous
trill. She sounds the continent, heads south—

the only course out of winter's grip,
more than five thousand kilometers
soaring on thermals as she surveys
the terrain like a cartographer:

the boreal and hardwood forests,
mountain ranges, woodlands, and rivers
coiled like ouroboroi: to basalt
mesa, a caprock to match her breadth.

Exhausted, she slows, tilts toward heaven
for a moment, pinions raised, digits
outstretched; femur, fibula angled
for descent. She lands and earth shivers,

winds whisper at her back, dust plumes rise
and settle. She waits and they climb down,
disfiguring feathers in their haste
and relief, the sun's light quickening.

Konza Prairie

O. ALAN WELTZIEN

At tallgrass prairie south
of Kansas River, no endless
quilt of pastures:

Grass hills roll, hardwood copses wind
along wet seams, perennials
bunch and gleam in late spring's wet heat.
Horizontal beads of chert
line slopes, just below rounding tops:
off-white jewels, rough cut,
stretched necklace trace
green swells in and out,
stony high tide wrack
mark of old Flint Hills
ebb and flow, geology's dance
extrude at uniform height.

Raised pattern on giant archaic amphora,
rock ribbon atop brows
of earth's own swollen tumuli.

Glaciers, Mountains, Falls

DAVID BRANNAN

I keep looking at the maps posted
not because I'm afraid of getting lost

(I'm all too familiar with loss)
but because I need to be reminded

among the bears feasting on huckleberries
among the elk grazing on the meadows

in the creeping haze
in the waltz of light and shadow

in the pirouettes of hissing milky water
and the promise of the iris:

You Are Here

PART 2 | *Watershed Ways*

Braided Channels of
Watershed Consciousness

Loren Eiseley's "The Flow of the River"
and the Platte Basin Timelapse Project

TOM LYNCH

Heavy rain batters my window, waking me from sleep. I roll over, grab my cell phone, open the weather app to check conditions. On the radar large state-sized swaths of green, punctuated with areas of yellow and red, glide northward. Nothing looks too threatening, no tornado warnings at least. As I put the radar in motion, I can virtually witness the warm moisture lifted out of the Gulf of Mexico flowing due north across the center of the continent, drifting over my house in Nebraska nearly a thousand miles away. I listen to the rain roar on the roof, the rattle of water on metal as it circles the downspout, flowing out into the driveway. Through my second-story window I see sheets of water on the road, shimmering in the glow of the streetlight, all rushing away—fortunately away—from my house here on what passes for a ridgeline in eastern Nebraska.

≈

Theoretical conversations regarding place and space studies often revolve around the competing claims of lococentrism versus a global perspective. I would suggest that this formulation is a false and unproductive dichotomy, and I offer the bioregional concept of what Gary Snyder refers to as "watershed consciousness" as a useful and rigorously materialist venue in which to demonstrate a more holistic perspective. In "Coming into the Watershed" Snyder explains that "a watershed is a marvelous thing to consider: this process of rain falling, streams flowing, and oceans evaporating causes every molecule of water on earth to make the complete trip once every two million years. The surface is carved into watersheds—a kind

137

of familial branching, a chart of relationships, and a definition of place. The watershed is the first and last nation whose boundaries, though subtly shifting, are unarguable."[1] Lawrence Buell has noted that "'watershed' [has] become the most popular defining gestalt in contemporary bioregionalism, at least in the United States." He explains there is good reason for this: "The logic is not simply aesthetic, not simply that waterways are eye-catching, picturesque landscape definers. Equally if not more fundamental and long-standing have been the economic function of rivers as supply lines (and later also as power sources) and the social settlement patterns following from that."[2] That is, watershed consciousness works to integrate the social and cultural with the natural and ecological in ways that other forms of place identity have difficulty doing.

I would like to examine two efforts to develop this sort of watershed consciousness within the drainage basin of the watershed in which I reside, the Platte River in the interior of the North American continent. One is Loren Eiseley's essay "The Flow of the River," published in 1957 as the second chapter of *The Immense Journey*. In this essay Eiseley combines personal experience narratives and geological and evolutionary knowledge along with a powerfully imagined extension of his senses in order to generate a watershed consciousness that encompasses and indeed exceeds the Platte River. I will then braid Eiseley's essay with a newly emerging and quite different effort, the Platte Basin Timelapse (PBT) Project, which uses the latest in digital media to generate a comparable sort of consciousness. Meandering throughout the discussion will be personal experience narratives and theoretical reflections. As Buell has proposed, "The imagination is key to making watershed consciousness a potent force."[3] I hope to show in this essay, and in the two projects considered, how imagination can serve the expansion and deepening of our watershed consciousness.

≈

On the morning news I hear reports of flooding in town. More than seven inches of rain fell overnight, on ground already saturated from weeks of rainfall: a one hundred–year event, they say. As I ride my bike to a meeting on campus, I descend the casual drainage toward town. The bike trail first follows a neighborhood creek, normally just a trickle and too small to have a name. In her essay "Meanderings" local writer Lisa Knopp discusses this drainage, notes that this creek is indeed nameless, and so, on the assumption that it had been diverted to its present location when the nearby neighborhood was constructed in the 1920s, christens it "Diversion Creek."[4] As far as I can tell, however, that name has not been officially adopted, and the lack of a formal name for a fairly prominent feature of the local landscape suggests a certain impoverishment in the watershed consciousness of the local officials and residents.

≈

Places and their distinctive features exist at a complexly graduated range of scales, revealing nested and interconnected characteristics from the smallest to the largest level. Few planetary landforms illustrate this more cogently than watersheds and the larger hydrological cycle of which they are a part. Being fractals, watersheds can be envisioned at a seemingly infinite range of self-similar, recursive, and mutually constitutive scales:

- at the molecular level soil moisture is absorbed into plant tissue via the root and xylem to eventually transpire into the atmosphere;
- at the bodily level water flows from aquifer to tap and courses through our bodies in dendritic patterns of blood flow that (also being fractals) uncannily resemble watercourses in drainage basins, which in a sense they are;
- at the neighborhood level the rainwater shed from rooftops passes through gardens, yards, and streets;
- at the community level water discharges accumulate in storm drains and local streams, posing sometimes vexing problems for flood control;
- at the bioregional level larger streams and rivers gather community runoff and create often bountiful riparian ecosystems;

- at the continental level major river systems discharge into the ocean the accumulated water (as well as soil, trash, and toxins) of continental interiors;
- at the planetary level the hydrologic cycle powered by solar energy lifts water out of the oceans into the atmosphere and eventually deposits it as rain or snow onto distant terrains;
- and indeed even at the cosmic level we are now exploring comets as potential sources for the water we find on Earth.

In short the movement of a water molecule through bodies, watersheds, oceans, continents, and even interplanetary space gives the lie to the local versus global polarity. Buell concludes that thinking in terms of watersheds "challenges parochialism not only of jurisdictional borders of whatever sort but also of 'natural' borders that fail to take larger interdependencies into account, interdependencies that finally reach out to include the whole planet."[5]

≈

Tree branches and gravel from adjacent side streets have been washed across the bike trail, and I slow to wend my way through the debris. At one low spot near the zoo, the trail is covered in a pool of shallow standing water, perhaps twenty yards in length. A cyclist in front of me turns back. "I'm not going through that," he remarks over his shoulder. I fail to heed his caution, creep slowly but inexorably into the water. As I advance, water splays from my rolling tires. With each downstroke of the pedal, my foot goes closer to the water, closer, closer, then into, deeper, deeper. I'm getting nervous, but it's too late. I can't turn around, and if I get off the bike, I'll only get wetter. Soon the water is halfway up my calf, pouring over the tops of my boots and drenching my socks. Nothing to do now but pedal carefully through the last stretch and ride up the other side.

Chagrined as drenched socks slosh with every pedal stroke, I soldier on. Where the bike trail joins Antelope Creek—the major drainage in this neighborhood—the creek and the trail both go under a road, South Twenty-Seventh Street, but that underpass looks flooded, and chastened by my recent experience, I'm not going to risk it. I cross the street above ground at the pedestrian crosswalk and rejoin the trail on the other side. As I advance, I note storm sewers dumping increasing amounts of runoff, and the usually shallow creek below the trail is a swollen and surging brown. A bit farther on I note where the water has backed up behind a large impoundment, the recently constructed labyrinth weir, part of a new multimillion dollar flood control project now being put to its first test. What is typically a mudflat is now a broad brown lake. Below the weir the trail descends into the Union Plaza section, a city park through which the normally small placid stream flows between decorative channels, plantings, and sculpture. That area is now beneath eight or ten feet of water, with my bike trail at the bottom. I turn around, head up to the city streets to continue to campus.

Were I to have pursued my course along Antelope Creek, perhaps in a kayak, I would have soon arrived at Salt Creek, which was breeching the top of its levee and flooding low-lying neighborhoods. My journey would have continued down Salt Creek to its eventual confluence with the Platte River, near Ashland, then shortly afterward into the Missouri for a long slow trip to St. Louis and the Mississippi River, and then downward with increasingly meandering leisure to New Orleans and the Gulf of Mexico . . . where all the water came from in the first place.

≈

As portrayed in "The Flow of the River," Loren Eiseley had been searching for fossils among the debris along a channel of the Platte, probably the North Platte near Bridgeport, Nebraska. The book in which his essay appears as a chapter, *The Immense Journey*, is concerned with evolution, that immense journey upon which we and all other living things find ourselves (and a phenomenon whose structure, being fractal as well, can also be illustrated in a way that resembles the dendritic patterns of watersheds). As his book as a whole makes clear, life seems to have originated in the warm seas of an early Earth, and much of the process of evolution has involved figuring out how life can move into increasingly drier regions and still maintain the original watery bath that is its origin and upon which it still depends for survival. The main evolutionary problem, in a way, is how to extend the reach of the watershed, and life itself is the medium of extension.

Eiseley's essay opens, a bit surprisingly, with an urban scene, a view from his office window as our narrator looks down upon the rooftop of an adjacent building, where a pool of rainwater, rippled by the wind, "may be translating itself into life." "I have a constant feeling," he relates, "that some time I may witness that momentous miracle on a city roof, see life veritably and suddenly boiling out of a heap of rusted pipes and old television aerials."[6] All it takes, it seems, to generate life out of inanimate matter is a bit of water and a stray breeze.

Buell observes that compared to other forms of traditional place identity, "the watershed as a defining image of community has the . . . advantages of being a quick and easy way of calling attention to the arbitrariness of official borders (country, state, county, town, private property lines), an equally obvious reminder of common dependence on shared natural resources, and an appeal to an imagined community defined by 'natural' rather than governmental fiat that promises to feel larger than most people's habitats or locales, yet still manageable in size."[7]

Each of these traits can be seen in the work of the Platte Basin Timelapse Project, established in 2011 by Nebraska photographers Mike Forsberg and Michael Farrell. The PBT has installed more than forty cameras placed strategically throughout the 90,000 square-mile Platte watershed, from Colorado's Lake Agnes, at 11,000 feet elevation, down to Plattsmouth, Nebraska, at 900 feet, where the Platte débouchés into the Missouri River. Each of these cameras takes a photograph every thirty seconds, photos that are then combined into stunning visual displays of the changing characteristics of the river that are made publicly available via the internet and public television. Forsberg and Farrell liken each camera to a chapter in a book in which each camera "tells one part of the story of [a] proverbial drop of water as it makes a journey of roughly 900 river miles through the heart of North America."[8] Their time-lapse imagery allows us to view multiyear changes in the river and its basin in only a few minutes. The goal of the project is to enable people to see an entire watershed in motion, to appreciate their place within its wider context, to understand the functional interconnectedness of land and water, and to generate advocacy for river restoration and protection.

≈

It is difficult for the human imagination to move nimbly between the sorts of changes of scale, involving both time and space, that are necessary to generate a comprehensive watershed consciousness. In celebrating watersheds, Snyder illustrates their reach through time and space: "For the watershed, cities and dams are ephemeral and of no more account than a boulder that falls in the river or a landslide that temporarily alters the channel. The water will always be there, and it will always find its way down. . . . But we who live in terms of centuries rather than millions of years must hold the watershed and its communities together, so our children might enjoy the clear water and fresh life of this landscape we have chosen. From the tiniest rivulet at the crest of a ridge to the main trunk of a river approaching the lowlands, the river is all one place and all one land."[9] One of the major tasks for environmental writers and artists is to find ways to evoke and personalize the long spans of time and the long reaches of space that, as Snyder's discussion illustrates, are necessary both to comprehend watersheds in their full richness and complex dimensions and to motivate us to proper ethical action for their protection and enhancement.

≈

Eiseley's "The Flow of the River" shifts registers from the personally intimate to the geologically comprehensive, from the narrator's immediate present to the early Pleistocene, with gestures toward much deeper time. Eiseley struggled with this sense of scale in his writing. We can see his efforts in a passage such as the following, which seeks to collapse unimaginable lengths of time into the experience of a single afternoon: "Once in a lifetime, perhaps, one escapes the actual confines of the flesh. Once in a lifetime, if one is lucky, one so merges with sunlight and air and running water that whole eons, the eons that mountains and deserts know, might pass in a single afternoon without discomfort."[10] In this passage Eiseley evokes what has often been considered his mystical side, the now oft-maligned nature writer's gesture toward a sense of at-one-ment with the natural world. But I would argue, there's nothing especially mystical about the experience; it is indeed relentlessly materialist. For it is indubitably the case that our flesh is composed of, among other things, sunlight, air, and running water. We can merge with such elements and forces, become, as it were, *one with them*, not because of some supernatural mystical agency but because we are ourselves composed of such elements and forces. We are indeed always and already one with them, we *are* them, and to refer to such an insight as mystical is not just to miss the point but to invert it, to dematerialize and mystify that which is intensely and marvelously material.

≈

Serenella Iovino, writing about Italy's Po River valley, has proposed that

place imagination entails ethical and aesthetic values; it entails memory and identity. Being parts of this imagination, the stories of a place belong to this place's ecology of mind; and as such they are part of the "survival unity" that includes ourselves and the world in which we live. What I call "narrative reinhabitation" is a cultural-educational practice that consists of restoring the ecological imagination of place by working with place-based stories. Visualizing the ecological connection of people and place through place-based stories is a way to remember a dismembered unity, to enliven our cultural and ecological potentialities—to reanimate the world.[11]

The Platte Basin Timelapse Project is an effort to do what Iovino describes, to share the imagination and stories of place, and so to re-member what has been dis-membered in a particular place and to reanimate the world of that place as part of a process of narrative reinhabitation.

Although cameras are set up throughout the watershed, much of the PBT work focuses on the Central Platte in Nebraska, where the river exhibits an extensive system of braided channels. The Central Platte is most notable today as the staging ground of the largest migration event in North America (and one of the largest in the world), the spring arrival of the sandhill cranes, who descend upon the river in February and March in numbers up to 500,000. Mixed among the sandhill cranes one can also find, if one is very lucky, a few endangered whooping cranes.

One section of the PBT website is organized around the themes of Settlement (1800s–1930), Awareness (1930s–1980s), and Recovery (1980s–today). Essentially, the tale that is told involves accumulating narratives regarding the character of the Platte River and our human relationship to it and to its wildlife. It begins with some information about the human populations that had originally settled the region, primarily the Pawnee, whose homeland this was before they were forcibly relocated to Oklahoma. This is followed by a consideration of stories of the era of European settlement. Because the Oregon Trail followed its channel, the Platte served as a major corridor for European settler colonial westward expansion. Today this section of the river is followed by Interstate 80, one of the major east-west corridors in the United States. European settlers brought new forms of agriculture, which caused massive disruptions, a sort of dis-membering of the river, as it were. As the tales told on the website sediment and stratify, the evidence of environmental problems begins to accumulate, particularly in the 1930s, and culminates with the listing of the whooping crane as an endangered species in 1967. The most significant tipping point, the website explains, involved a proposed dam:

> When [in the 1960s] a group of public power companies proposed a new dam and reservoir on the Laramie River, a tributary of the North Platte in Wyoming, environmental groups mobilized behind the brand-new endangered species legislation to fight it. The National Wildlife Federation and state of Nebraska opposed the project, arguing the dam would further compromise wildlife habitat and irrigation needs downstream.

After a series of lawsuits and negotiations, parties finally reached agreement in 1978. Construction of Grayrocks Dam and Reservoir was allowed to proceed as long as the power companies limited their annual water use and created a trust fund dedicated to protecting and enhancing whooping crane habitat.[12]

The PBT website includes numerous short sections involving history, wildlife, agriculture, prairie restoration efforts, climate, hydrology, groundwater, irrigation technology, and urban and rural communities. Embedded within many of the stories are short video clips or a sequence of time-lapse images covering several years of changes. Ariana Brocious's story "Whooper Recovery," for example, describes efforts to protect the whooping cranes during their migratory passage through the watershed. It includes an audio file of a public radio program she produced as well as several videos of whooping cranes and their protectors in action. Kat Shiffler's "Inside Wet Meadows" describes a seasonal wetland and includes interviews with biologists and conservationists about the value of such wetlands, a type of landscape whose protection is often challenged. It presents a three-year-long time-lapse sequence of changes at one wetland meadow, Mormon Island, during which one sees muddy, marshy conditions convert to grassy fields: grasses wave in the wind, cows appear, dart around, then vanish, storm clouds replace blue skies, grasses turn brown and snow blankets the scene, the snow melts, pools of water rise, then sandhill cranes briefly populate the landscape, the wetlands disappear, and green grasses emerge again. Underlying and animating these transformations is the pulsing rise and fall of the water level. What most people would consider to be an extremely dull, flat scene with little to draw interest comes to life and is revealed as a dynamic, ever-changing, dramatic system.

≈

Eiseley explains the circumstances that prompted his experience on the river, referring to a time in his early twenties when as a college student he worked during the summer on university- and state museum–sponsored paleontological digs in western Nebraska: "Many years ago, in the course of some scientific investigations in a remote western county, I experienced, by chance, precisely the sort of curious absorption by water—the extension of shape by osmosis—at which I have been hinting."[13] Eiseley describes this experience in a way that is very much a matter of an embodied watershed consciousness: "You have probably never experienced in yourself the meandering roots of a whole watershed or felt your outstretched fingers touching, by some kind of clairvoyant extension, the brooks of snow-line glaciers at the same time that you were flowing toward the Gulf over the eroded debris of worndown mountains."[14]

The word *extension* appears twice in these passages, and later in the paragraph Eiseley refers to an "extension of the senses," something that is "not unique" but is nevertheless "hard to come by."[15] In a way extending the senses is his task and is in fact the task of any author attempting to create a watershed consciousness, or the consciousness of anything too large, or too vast in time, to be immediately perceptible to the common senses—"hyperobjects," as they have recently been termed. (Climate change comes to mind as an obvious example.)

Eiseley then describes the Platte, which "normally . . . is a rambling, dispersed series of streamlets flowing erratically over great sand and gravel fans that are, in part, the remnants of a mightier Ice Age stream bed." He explains that while fossil hunting in the scorching summer heat of the high plains, he decided to try his luck along the riverbank: "I know the kinds of bones that come gurgling up through the gravel pumps and the arrowheads of shining chalcedony that occasionally spill out of water-loosened sand."[16] In the heat, though, he became "parched with miles of walking" and so decided to hop into the river for a cool splash in the shallows. At this point, he recalls, "a great desire to stretch out and go with this gently insistent water began to pluck at me." Carrying out this impulse, however, does not come easily to him. Indeed, he is filled with a vague disquiet. As he explains, he is a tad prudish, and so stripping naked to go skinny dipping does not come naturally: "Now to this bronzed, bold, modern generation, the struggle I waged with timidity while standing there in knee-deep water can only seem farcical; yet actually for me it was not so." To exacerbate his anxiety, he mentions a "near-drowning accident in childhood" and reminds us that he is a nonswimmer. He further explains that although the Platte is typically shallow enough to wade across, especially in this middle stretch, there is still considerable danger because "'this inch-deep river' was treacherous with holes and quicksands. Death was not precisely infrequent along its wandering and illusory channels." Because of the remoteness, "a man in trouble would cry out in vain."[17]

On the one hand, this sort of information serves the dramatic purpose of increasing tension: our author might die. But it also serves, I think, a more pertinent purpose to the theme of extending the senses; it positions Eiseley in a liminal and very vulnerable state. His senses are heightened both by his nakedness and by his fear, and such a state makes him receptive to both a literal and subsequently an imaginative extension of his senses:

> Then I lay back in the floating position that left my face to the sky, and shoved off. The sky wheeled over me. For an instant, as I bobbed into the main channel, I had the sensation of gliding down the vast tilted face of the continent. It was then that I felt the cold needles of the alpine springs at my fingertips, and the warmth of the Gulf pulling me southward. Moving with me, leaving its taste upon my mouth and spouting under me in dancing springs of sand, was the immense body of the continent itself, flowing like the river was flowing, grain by grain, mountain by mountain, down to the sea. I was streaming over ancient sea beds thrust aloft where giant reptiles had once sported; I was wearing down the face of time and trundling cloud-wreathed ranges into oblivion. I touched my margins with the delicacy of a crayfish's antennae, and felt great fishes glide about their work.[18]

In this passage we can witness Eiseley's imaginative effort to extend his senses, both in space, from mountain summit in Colorado to the waters of the Gulf of Mexico, and in time, from the Laramide orogeny that began to raise the Rocky Mountains eighty million years ago to the immediate present, when fish drifted beneath him as he floated. The experience culminates in his sensation that "I was water and the unspeakable alchemies that gestate and take shape in water."[19] This revelation leads him to ponder that aquatic animals consist of the very substance they inhabit, noting that "turtle and fish and the pinpoint chirpings of individual frogs are all watery projections, concentrations—as man himself is a concentration—of that indescribable and liquid brew which is compounded in varying proportions of salt and sun and time."[20] Following up on his parenthetical leap to the human dimension, he continues: "As for men, those myriad little detached ponds with their own swarming corpuscular life, what were they but a way that water has of going about beyond the reach of rivers? I, too, was a microcosm of pouring rivulets and floating driftwood gnawed by the mysterious animalcules of my own creation. I was three fourths water, rising and subsiding according to the hollow knocking in my veins: a minute pulse like the eternal pulse that lifts Himalayas and which, in the following systole, will carry them away."[21] Here Eiseley blends an evolutionary consciousness with a watershed consciousness, suggesting that they are in a very real way just different expressions of the same deep process by which time and change manifest in the material world.

≈

Eiseley experienced his watershed epiphany in his naked body unaided by any technology, by a stripping away of the cultural apparatus. His extension of the senses was an imaginative act, not a technological one. But he also notes that it was a rare experience, perhaps a "once in a lifetime" epiphany. The Platte Basin Timelapse Project, on the other hand, employs the latest in digital technology in order to create a large-scale representation of the ever-changing Platte River watershed over the course of years, employing, we might say, a digital extension of the senses in a way that does not depend upon chance encounters and epiphanies but that can be experienced more casually and frequently, if, no doubt, less intensely.

≈

About four in the afternoon, a few weeks after the floods, I arrive at a parking area near the junction of the Platte and Missouri Rivers outside the suitably named town of Plattsmouth, Nebraska. It's a warm, humid day, with storms threatening later in the evening. Next to the parking area a large sign announces that Lewis and Clark had camped near here on July 14, 1804. Their passage above the Platte was a major milestone on their journey, as the Missouri River upstream from here had been little explored by American citizens, and so they were about to enter into what was for them largely unknown territory. As the sign notes, Captain Clark recorded, with his typical arbitrary spelling and capitalization, that "the Current of This river Comes with great Velocity roleing its Sands into the Missouri, filling up its Bend. . . . We found great dificuelty in passing around the Sand at the mouth."

To be frank, this is a rather unscenic location, part of the Schilling Wildlife Management area, which has been established for fishing and waterfowl hunting and not on account of its visual virtues. Eight or ten cars are parked here, which I at first attribute to the Lewis and Clark significance but later realize is due to the excellent fishing access. I notice a tall pole near the Lewis and Clark sign, glance up, and see a white box at the top with PBT stenciled on the back. It's the housing for the final Platte Basin Timelapse camera, something I had not anticipated seeing, though I should have known one would be nearby. I've watched the photo sequences from this camera on the website.

From the point of junction where the Platte becomes the Missouri, a long breakwater of white rocks and piled-up logs divides the two rivers for one hundred yards. Today the waters of the Platte are distinctly browner than the waters of the Missouri, and the two rivers seem to flow side by side in the same channel for as far as I can see around the bend.

To my surprise I note first one then two kayakers on the far side of the Platte with fishing poles poking out of the stern of their vessels. A man and a woman slowly drift and paddle toward my shore, more placidly than I would have guessed possible given the turgid flow of the river. There's something treacherous to my eye about the water here, flowing steady and muddy, with lots of drifting branches swirling in foamy whirlpools. Somehow a raging whitewater would seem less intimidating. The kayakers come to shore fifty yards down-stream, cast their lines listlessly for a while, then shove off into the current and float out of sight around the bend onto the Missouri. Shadows of clouds pass rapidly across the roiled water.

NOTES

1. Snyder, "Coming into the Watershed," 229.
2. Buell, "Watershed Aesthetics," 246.
3. Buell, "Watershed Aesthetics," 249.
4. Knopp, "Meanderings," 210.
5. Buell, "Watershed Aesthetics," 264.
6. Eiseley, "Flow of the River," 15.
7. Buell, "Watershed Aesthetics," 246.
8. Forsberg and Farrell, "About."
9. Snyder, "Coming into the Watershed," 229–30.
10. Eiseley, "Flow of the River," 16.
11. Iovino, "Restoring the Imagination," 105–6.
12. Forsberg and Farrell, "Awareness."
13. Eiseley, "Flow of the River," 16.
14. Eiseley, "Flow of the River," 16.
15. Eiseley, "Flow of the River," 17.
16. Eiseley, "Flow of the River," 18.
17. Eiseley, "Flow of the River," 18.
18. Eiseley, "Flow of the River," 19.
19. Eiseley, "Flow of the River," 19.
20. Eiseley, "Flow of the River," 20.
21. Eiseley, "Flow of the River," 20.

BIBLIOGRAPHY

Brocious, Ariana. "Whooper Recovery." In *Platte Basin Timelapse: Seeing a Watershed in Motion* by Mike Forsberg and Michael Farrell. Platte Basin Timelapse Project. Accessed October 22, 2015. http://plattebasintimelapse.com/2015/03/whooper-recovery/.

Buell, Lawrence. "Watershed Aesthetics." *Writing for an Endangered World: Literature, Culture, and Environment in the U.S. and Beyond*, 243–65. Cambridge: Harvard University Press, 2001.

Eiseley, Loren. "The Flow of the River." *The Immense Journey*, 15–28. New York: Random House, 1957.

Forsberg, Mike, and Michael Farrell. "About." *Platte Basin Timelapse: Seeing a Watershed in Motion*. Platte Basin Timelapse Project. Accessed October 22, 2015. http://plattebasintimelapse.com/about/.

———. "Awareness." *Platte Basin Timelapse: Seeing a Watershed in Motion.*
Platte Basin Timelapse Project. Accessed October 22, 2015. http://
projects.plattebasintimelapse.com/into-the-current/awareness/.

Iovino, Serenella. "Restoring the Imagination of Place: Narrative Reinhab-
itation and the Po Valley." In *The Bioregional Imagination: Literature, Ecol-
ogy, Place,* edited by Tom Lynch, Cheryll Glotfelty, and Karla Armbruster,
100–117. Athens: University of Georgia Press, 2012.

Knopp, Lisa. "Meanderings." In *What the River Carries: Encounters with the Mis-
sissippi, Missouri, and Platte.* Columbia: University of Missouri Press, 2012.

Shiffler, Kat. "Inside Wet Meadows." In *Platte Basin Timelapse: See-
ing a Watershed in Motion* by Mike Forsberg and Michael Farrell.
Platte Basin Timelapse Project. Accessed October 22, 2015. http://
plattebasintimelapse.com/2015/03/inside-wet-meadows/.

Snyder, Gary. "Coming into the Watershed." *A Place in Space: Ethics, Aesthetics,
and Watersheds: New and Selected Prose.* 219–35. Berkeley: Counterpoint, 1995.

Plovers, Great Blues, Horned Owl

A Poet's Ecotone

BRENDAN GALVIN

More than a hundred years ago, my maternal grandfather, Ned McLaughlin, went sailing on a friend's schooner out of Boston, delivering lumber at several of the harbors along Cape Cod Bay. He was taken by the beauty of the dunes as the boat sailed past because they reminded him of those on the Inishowen Peninsula in Donegal, Ireland, where he was born. They attracted my grandfather enough that he wanted to see what the cape looked like from the landward side, and he soon began bringing his wife and daughters to Pond Village, North Truro, for the summer. So my mother and my aunts did some of their growing up only a couple of miles from the dunes at Corn Hill and the surrounding area, where I live now. When I reflect on it, I see that he has given me much more than his pattern baldness.

These days I go out walking on a road that edges a vast salt marsh. A stream meanders through the marsh, and where it parallels the road, I walk beside it, out to a bay beach, then down the strand a half-mile or so to a stone jetty, one of two that keeps the tide- and wind-mauled sands from closing the entrance to the harbor. At the jetty I am midway between two high dunes, each about a half-mile away. One, Corn Hill, marks the northern extent of the Pamet River's fluctuations over time, while the other dune, beyond Fishers Beach, is the southern extremity. Over generations the river has moved back and forth on the land between these two hills like a whip cracked in very slow motion.

At the jetty I turn back but by an inside route that takes me between a dune we call Egg Island and a vast tract of eelgrass on the north side of the harbor. These days, before I leave the beach for the parking lot, I still check to see if anything of a gray streak of ashes with brighter particles embedded in it is left on the sand. The particles are bone chips, the remains of my fourteen-year-old border collie, Finn, who all his life loved to run this beach with a ball in his mouth. The ashes hung on for several weeks after I spread them, as though they were reluctant to part with this place. Finally the extreme high tides of the winter solstice gathered them in.

A few days later one of those events occurred that only the natural world can stage. Walking these sands, I heard a rush above my head that made me think the air was being ripped open. In the distance, after it passed, I could see it was a flock, probably of least sandpipers, though the birds were too fast for me to be sure. But they were white on their sharp turns, hundreds of them, and flattened over the river before coming together again, this time in a ball, and heading back out toward the bay. It was late in the year for a migration, especially of such small birds, and I wondered if they were a sign it was going to be an exceptionally mild winter or if they had left the north quite late and were building their strength and resolve here before moving out across the next Atlantic reach. Maybe they were a sign to a grieving man about his dog too. I stood there watching them fly down the beach, lost in the midst of my total ignorance about matter and its changes, shifts of being, the journeys of the soul. I remembered an Irish saying that for me has a double edge: When death comes, it does not go away empty.

Because we live in a pine grove above a marsh, I've become an amateur birder by default, merely from looking out the windows or splitting wood or working in my vegetable garden. We're on the Atlantic flyway, and during spring and fall especially, all kinds of birds appear. I've been keeping track in a bird guide for more than forty years now and can sometimes predict what's going to show up and when.

Egg Island is so called because it is the nesting area for common terns and usually a few pairs of sorely endangered piping plovers. The plovers arrive sometime in late March from their winter grounds in Florida and Georgia, right after the equinox. There's a day every year when I walk the beach and notice for the first time one or two moving along the tideline or in the softer sandy and stony berm above it. They look like they've arisen from the sand, gravel, and miscellaneous beach detritus around them, so fine is their protective coloring. More than once I have seen one take cover in a footprint I just made in passing.

I think of plovers as wind-ups, almost mechanical in their movements, as though a kid had turned a key in their sides. They will run a few feet, stop, then change direction and head off on a tangent. But should I get too close, they will fly out over the water and come back to land farther down the beach. They scratch a minimal foxhole in the ground above the tideline and lay their clutch of buff-colored, dark brown–spotted eggs, usually four. The eggs are only a trifle over an inch long.

The human threat is as great to piping plovers as the threat from natural predators. When swimmers and off-road vehicles are prohibited from their nesting grounds, in some places the little *Charadrius melodus* becomes an enemy of humans, who can't get around the idea that we are supposed to have dominion over everything, that it all exists for the recreation and commercial purposes of our species alone. Thus, the occasional newspaper story about the beachgoer who's arrested for disturbing the nests because it's his right as a taxpayer to be anywhere on the beach he wishes, and the occasional bumper sticker on beach-going vehicles: PLOVERS TASTE LIKE CHICKEN. In 1986 the total East Coast population of piping plovers was only eight hundred pairs. Since then, by posting the nesting areas and fencing off nests, that figure has increased to about fourteen hundred pairs, but it is till touch and go. One bad storm can wipe the slate of plover chicks for that nesting season. A clever coyote digging beneath an electrified fence can create local havoc as well.

The road I walk is called Corn Hill Road, the river is the north branch of the Pamet, these days called the Little Pamet, and the bayside beach is Corn Hill Beach. There are practical and aesthetic reasons for my route. For one there's no commute. When I step out my back door and head down the hill—early in the morning during the warmer months, after noon in the brisker ones—I'm on my way into perhaps the finest hour of the day. Over the years I've discovered that this one place, occupying maybe a square mile, is endless: I will never come close to unraveling or even understanding it. On any given day something new may be happening, so it will never bore me. Like William Faulkner's home-place, his "own little postage stamp of native soil," or those glacier-created kettle ponds back in the pine woods where we swam as kids and told ourselves stories about them, it appears bottomless.

One reason for my route was the hill at the beginning and end of my three-mile run. It provided a challenge on the return home, recalling a college football coach who had his team take just such a steep grade at full speed in full gear every day to get to the showers after practice. Forty-five years later, on Corn Hill Road there are two houses rather than one, and I am walking, not running or even jogging, because the two major bones in my left hip have apparently joined. Though I've never actually seen the X-rays, I've been assured that my hip joins me statistically with 2 percent of the population. I see the world at three miles an hour now at best and observe it closer and better because of my alleged infirmity.

The road, stream, and marshes are bracketed by two long hills— Tom's and Cathedral—the kind locally called hogbacks. Covered with pitch pines, they were created with the river and marshland. The pines are a more recent development. If you look at photos from the beginning of the last century, Truro is bare of trees, denuded of its hardwoods to heat houses and build ships for the whaling and fishing fleets. My godson's grandfather, passed away some thirty years now, told me that as a boy he had herded cows on the bare hillside where I live surrounded by a grove of seventy-foot pines.

Isolated blocks of ice, left behind as the glaciers withdrew under a quickly warming climate about twelve thousand years ago, began to melt and run off the land into the bay. To the matter-of-fact Algonquians who named the place, *pamet* meant "at the sea." But the technical meaning of a pamet to geologists is a channel caused by the flow of melting ice. I live on the edge of this definition, and while I walk on the bayside at sea level, the other end of the valley formed by this meandering river system is about sixty feet higher, making it in geological terms a *hanging valley*. It ends abruptly at the high dunes overlooking the Atlantic at Long Nook Beach. Ages ago, before the ocean ate so much of those backshore beaches, it would have been a lot higher than sixty feet and a lot farther away.

The New York, New Haven, and Hartford Railroad bed (completed in 1872) and the present Route 6 (once universally called "the state road") were built across the river's course too. Now the stream begins in that quarter-acre spring-fed pond back of the dike and flows toward Corn Hill Beach. Most ponds its size that I know of have a name, but this one doesn't. If asked, I'd probably call it Heron Pond, for the great blue that often wades in it alone like a true *isolato*, beak poised for whatever moves and is therefore edible. Or stands by the reeds for hours in every season like a contemplative deep in meditation and in winter hunches against the purgatorial cold.

Trains stopped at the bottom of Corn Hill, and a little village existed there that included the station house. There were a number of small buildings where trap fishermen who worked the weirs staked in the bay waters just offshore kept their gear. An old icehouse from that time a century ago still does duty as a summer cottage, and another at the bend where Corn Hill Road enters the beach parking lot appears to have evolved from one of the fishing shacks.

Walking my route over the years, I've discovered all kinds of vestigial remains of the folks who lived in the valley. There's a place at roadside where wild asparagus comes up every spring, drifted from a long-gone farm garden, no doubt, but healthy looking and thick as my thumb. Given the poison ivy they grow among and their proximity to the road and automobile by-products, I've never been tempted to taste one. There's the odd cedar fencepost too, sometimes with a rusty loop of barbed wire like a snapped fiddle string still held on by a staple. Until it rotted out and collapsed, wrens used to nest in one of these posts each year, stuffing the hole with fresh straw and giving their warning buzz to anyone who got too close. A sound that one morning had an out-of-town acquaintance of ours looking around his feet for the nonexistent rattlesnake.

Wild apple trees are in evidence too. On a day each September, as I turn left onto Castle Road from Corn Hill Road, just beyond that junction I'm struck with the aroma of apples off a tree—a tang that surprises me every year. In the last decade the scent from that particular tree—whose ancient trunk looks composed of wooden pelvic bones and vertebrae, sinking among the goldenrod and chokecherry into the marsh's ferment, yet flush with fruit—has ambushed me in a new way. It's a reminder now and may be for as long as I have memory. I was walking right about there when a young man on a bicycle went breezing past in one of those orange-and-red spandex superhero outfits they wear these days. He returned in a minute, pedaling slowly, sagging on the handlebars and speaking loudly, though there was no one there but me. *Both towers? Both?* He was screaming, another vacationer losing his mind at his leisure, I thought, not an uncommon event, until I noticed the little speakerphone clamped to his biking helmet. When I got home and turned on the TV, what I saw made me realize that someone had just telephoned him about the World Trade Center towers.

So this place is not a world apart from the one that begins about sixty miles away on the farther side of the Cape Cod Canal. It is not the es-Cape, as we sometimes called it in our hip, ironic twenties. All the problems of the twenty-first century extend their tentacles in here too. Take Corn Hill, which is now a development of McMansions owned mostly by psychiatrists willing to pay dearly for an August view of the bay and Provincetown. Occasionally it's referred to in realtor-speak as "The Corn Hill Collection." It has had a starring role in local history. It was here that the Pilgrims, on their way to Plymouth, found caches of maize the Pamet Indians had buried to see them through the winter. Depending on whom you read, the Pilgrims either repaid the owners for this First Felony, or they didn't. I'd bet on the latter version, given that believers of the former never provide any details on how, when, or where the restitution took place. The town seal of Truro memorializes this event with a Native standing by a cornstalk in what looks to me like a Great Plains warbonnet. He is looking down the bay at the approaching *Mayflower*. The wigwams in the background are a second wrong detail on the seal because the Pamets and other Wampanoags built their houses of woven mats stretched over a wooden frame.

A colony of steeply roofed two-story cottages, built by Lorenzo Dow Baker, a local boy from Wellfleet who grew up to be one of the principal figures in what became the United Fruit Company, still stands on Corn Hill. Built as the twentieth century began, the cottages are now individually owned. Recently one sold for $400,000, though they are unheated and uninsulated, habitable in comfort for fewer than six months of the year. Like a lot of Truro, they were borrowed by Edward Hopper for a rather ominous 1930 painting, whose perspective is from below the hill, right about where the Corn Hill Beach parking lot is now.

Three years before Hopper painted that picture, German glider pilots were using the hill much as hang gliders use it now. Bivouacked in a few of the cottages, the airmen used L. D. Baker's garage as a hangar. Forbidden after World War I by the Peace of Versailles to own motorized aircraft, the German government was training future *Luftwaffe* pilots on the high dunes of Truro, launching them into the air with a giant rubber slingshot-like device. Depending on whom you talk to or read, this scenario has taken on a dimension that may have been derived from *Hogan's Heroes* and other popular fare. In these versions the pilots wear monocles and use cigarette holders, click heels and salute a lot, and generally carry on like stiffs. Yet the same reporters claim that the Truro girls were smitten to a one by them.

Everyone ought to have a totemic bird. Mine is the great blue heron. I can still remember the first time I took notice of one. It was in May 1965, and as I came around a corner of North Pamet Road that brilliant late afternoon, there the bird was, standing in the middle of a small pond by an old cranberry bog, giving me its aloof profile. It never moved as I passed, and probably from that afternoon I began to think of the great blue as my personal representative from the other world.

When we moved into our present house a few years later, I began seeing great blues almost daily. They haunted the meanders of the Little Pamet, gaunt looking, eyeing the river for sustenance, or graded down the air on those broad wings, majestic as they dropped and let out their long-legged grapples for the river bottom. I have come upon one in winter, fifteen feet away from the road as I walked past, with an eel dangling from that functional bill. I have arrived at a place on the road only moments after one walked there, probably chasing a field mouse or other morsel, the rune tree–like marks of its feet pressed wetly on the asphalt. At times on the path by the far side of the marsh, I have walked beneath one without knowing it was up there sunning in a pine, until it panicked and took off with a loud *quork*, awkwardly clambering skyward above those eelgrass acres.

More than any other bird I can think of, there is something prehistoric about the great blue heron. Maybe its length and the size of its wings as it flies recall the pterodactyl, and its often slow and deliberate flight seems to demonstrate confidence in its ancient lineage. It is stately as it stands in the river and pond as well. The word *hieratic* is used to describe it sometimes and means "sacred" or "priestly." To me there are overtones of aristocracy and solitude bound up with both bird and word. Dylan Thomas spoke of "the heron-priested shore" and Theodore Roethke of "the heron's hieratic fishing," so it's a poet's bird, to be sure.

It may also be a "symbol of longevity" like the long-legged bird in W. B. Yeats's poem "Lapis Lazuli." The Egyptians certainly regarded the heron that way and as an emblem of justice, goodness, and diligence. When I visited my mother for the first time in her room at the elderly facility where she spent the last years of her life, I was surprised and gratified to see the silhouette of a great blue painted on the wall of the room, as if somehow it had become her totemic bird as well.

Last winter, a few days after a big blow, on Corn Hill Beach I noticed a large white bird flopping and rolling about in the dunes, but I had the dogs with me and couldn't risk taking a closer look. It seemed to be injured, and by the shape of its head I thought it might be a gannet. Northern gannets often appear in the winter months out here, but this bird was too large, and it lacked the yellow gannet clown face markings. The closest I could come to nailing it down in

The Sibley Guide to Birds were the illustrations of the Laysan albatross, but that was impossible because the albatross is a seabird and only comes ashore to nest. I wrote the sighting off as a bad guess, then, reading a local weekly a few days later, I saw that an albatross had been sighted on a bay beach in one of the cape towns about twenty miles below us. Okay, I thought. Maybe I did see that albatross, but I wished I'd had a closer look. Apparently it was possible because sightings of the huge seabirds have been made from the Canadian Maritimes to Texas—"accidental species," as the ornithologists say. Walking a few days later, I noticed on the inner side of the dune away from the surf, near where I'd initially spotted the bird, a large splash of white feathers. Usually that means a dead gull, except this one looked too big to be a gull. Sure enough, there was the tubenose bill—blue-gray, about four inches long, with the paired tubes atop it that carry air back to the bird's lungs—sticking out of the matted, frozen corpse. It was an albatross.

The beach in winter is often a graveyard and not just the site of birds' corpses but also those of seals, turtles. Headless dolphins possibly done in by ship propellers and pilot whales that strand for unknown reasons too. In theory it's because of inner ear problems caused by bacteria or a fallible leader who brings the pod too close to shore as the tide's falling, leaving them high and dry. It doesn't take long for the scavenging gulls, abetted sometimes by crows and four-legged feeders, to clean a corpse to its bones. Among the bird footprints around the wicket of bones, one sometimes sees the delicate prints of foxes and the more doglike ones of coyotes. Walking past a dead animal for a few days, it's distressing to notice how quickly it's being reduced to a skeleton. Still, one has to admire the way the natural world keeps house. Nothing is left lying around for long; everything that can be recycled is taken back. Out here on the ecotone where land and water collide, Mother Nature bats last.

In the deep cold of the January nights every year, when the light of the Wolf Moon falls like ringing iron through the trees, from Tom's Hill and Cathedral Hill on the opposite sides of the marsh and Little Pamet River come the calls of the great horned owls, those five-part queries and responses that translate into something like "Can you hear me?" and "I can hear you," "Are you near me?" "I am near you." Great horned owls, which mate for life, go through this chthonic courtship ritual every year, and lying deep under quilts, we can almost set the year's clock by them. In a few months, after their offspring have fledged and left the nest, some nights we'll hear one or the other owlet landing with a thump on the roof over our heads. Or one day I'll look up from turning the soil in the potato bed or feeding compost into a tomato patch because I just heard something say *Schrreeep!* and there'll be an owlet watching me with those black-pupiled eyes surrounded by bright yellow, the corpse candles of folklore.

But before that can happen, the male owl, the one with the higher voice of the two calling back and forth out there, has to bring his courtship gifts to the nest, presentation pieces he lays on the brim of a matted construction site the size of an automobile tire. Sometimes it's an old hawk's nest the two owls have appropriated, but at other times it's a nest they've returned to year after year. The gifts consist of rabbits, skunks, cats, mice, moles, voles, toads, frogs, and you name it. As the female sits her eggs, there's liable to be a heap of fur or rather furs hanging over the nest's edge, though not elegantly.

For years two owls used a nest in a pine about a 150 feet from our back door, and that meant there wouldn't be any frogs in the garden or that walking the dog I'd occasionally find a dead rabbit by the side of the road, intact but for a surgical-looking slit at the back of its head where the owl went for its brain. Owls apparently consider brains a delicacy, and when there's plenty of food around, they may leave the rest of the victim. Perhaps that's what the horned owl that zipped down just above my head intended one night at dusk, before it flew off and got lost among the trees. Surprised, maybe even embarrassed, to discover there was more to me than a sparse comb-over of white hair.

Because great horned owls swallow their smaller prey whole, they have to regurgitate "owl pellets" containing the parts that won't pass through their digestive systems without doing damage. These pellets are actually small white packages that fit in your palm, dropped wet from a tree branch where the owl was sitting onto the ground. Sometimes there's a streak of whitewash down the side of a tree or on some leaves, indicating where one has fallen. When they are dry, they can be opened, and at least some of what the resident owl has eaten recently can be deduced from the contents. Teeth are sometimes present and a variety of small bones that look like parts from an old typewriter. There might be a swatch of fur, even a set of bird feet, clutching the air as if still in pain.

It isn't unusual for us to get a whiff of skunk in broad daylight and begin looking for an owl in the trees because the mephitic skunk spray temporarily blinds the bird, who's out in the sun because it can't tell if it's dark or light. For years we observed the annual courtship ritual of the owls and the occupation of the nest and the owlets at the edge of the nest crying to their parents for food as the male and female decimated the area to stuff the throats of their offspring. Sibling rivalry begins early in the nest, we discovered, with the stronger of the offspring getting the highest proportion of the food. Usually two owlets could make out okay, but if there were three, the weakest one was usually doomed.

Fledging began when one of the little ones climbed up on the edge and fell out onto the ground. Or when the parents decided they'd had enough and nudged their offspring out. Then began a period of wandering around on the ground and learning to make short flights from branch to branch, under the eyes of one parent or another. One spring evening I looked out the kitchen window and saw an owlet trying to get back into the nest. It was shaggy looking and had huge feet, like one of those stuffed school mascots they sell in college bookstores. It would get about ten feet from the trunk of the pine the nest was in and take a run at the tree and continue running right up the trunk until gravity kicked in and it dropped back to the ground. It was still trying this ploy when it became too dark for me to see it anymore.

Superior

Reimagining the Interior of a Continent

SUSAN NARAMORE MAHER

Fourteen bald eagles wheel in the thermals hundreds of feet above my backyard. They represent a fraction of the larger migration, ancient in its origins, that brings raptors along the high ridges of Lake Superior each autumn. Since the last glaciers retreated from northern Minnesota around eleven thousand years ago, humans like me have stood transfixed by the sight of gathering birds. On warm, sunny days hawks fly in vortices, swirling and circling andante on the winds. I'm no expert, just a casual birder. Yet catching a glance of migrating birds in action stops me in my tracks, and I stand staring upward. I know that I am in the presence of something mysterious and urgent. These birds carry a history on their wings that reaches back eons. One recent afternoon a large immature eagle floated just above the treetops in my neighbor's yard. Something in its hovering seemed spectral, as if that bird's corpus shadowed all of eagledom, past and present. I turned to make sure my cat was inside, but I needn't have worried about a fell swoop. In that second the eagle disappeared.

Every fall the Audubon Society runs programming at Hawk Ridge Bird Observatory along the north shore of Lake Superior to assist serious birders and to educate the curious public on raptors and songbirds flying by the tens of thousands along the hill front. As science writers Chel Anderson and Adelheid Fischer declare, "Northern Minnesota is the place to be" for feathered creatures seeking "a complex of habitats that are intact enough to support diverse assemblages of birds in the long term."[1] Among the heights and dips, the bog lands and deep forests, birds of all kinds find just the right "vegetational niches."[2] In fall the birds begin their return south, some flying as far as South America, following an ancestral map directed by instinctual memory and guided by topography, by shoreline and ridge. At over eleven hundred feet above sea level—hundreds of feet above Lake Superior—Hawk Ridge provides a breathtaking view of this greatest of Great Lakes.

When a full moon rises, people, not birds, flock to the heights. Using my LightTracker app on my phone, I know exactly when each full moon peeks over the distant Wisconsin hills. Lots of people arrive early with picnics, cameras, and telescopes. Full moons are events around here. On clear nights the moonlight rides atop the lake, a silver band illuminating watery space. From the ridge you can scan the curve of the lake's southwestern reach. At times the heights feel dizzying, and the expanse of space brings something ecstatic to the soul. I can't experience the joy of riding above this landscape, but standing near a cliff, arms lifted high, I can still absorb some of the thrill of being airborne. As a young boy, writer William Least Heat-Moon traveled these shores with his father. What he felt, I feel: "the edge of something dangerously wild and intimidatingly mysterious."[3]

Movement, itinerancy, is a defining aspect of Superior's shores. The birds trace an ancient flyway, above the waters and hills of *gichi-gami*, the Anishinaabe name for the lake, making visible hidden wind roads that direct bird traffic north and south. Carving into the steep hills, rivers and creeks etch other old ways along the lake in the seasonal months when fish mark their own migration. At a certain point, when winter starts retreating, parked cars congregate at the mouths of the Lester and French Rivers on Duluth's slice of the North Shore. For millennia humans have exploited the movement of fish, eager for their release from the ice-out. Once the ice melts, trout seekers in hip waders cast their lines for Kamloops just offshore. These steelheads, nonnative fish bred in Minnesota fisheries, link back to Ice Age North America and the Columbia River watershed. Their attachment to Superior's waters is shallow, a mere forty-year experiment, but they are old-timers on the continent.[4] Large and meaty, loopers long for the journey upriver, and the spring run marks a turning cycle in the year for them and the people who fish for them. Up and down the lake, the river waters crash down steep slopes, a sure sign that arterial waters are pulsing back to life. Native and nonnative fish alike are an iconic part of the spring awakening, and their movement coincides with the return of migratory birds. Natal waters pull on these fish, compelling many species toward a return run, a circuitous passage. Upstream, life and death meld in watery alchemy.

These waters also served as passageways for the original people of North America. In the boreal and transitional forests of the North Woods, streams and rivers quickly connect disparate communities, often lacing through lakes that have made the Boundary Waters Canoe Area Wilderness north of Duluth so unique. Dugout and birch bark canoes navigated these waters long before European contact established fur trade routes. On high points along rivers archaeologists have found remains of human communities thousands of years old. The French, British, and American traders adopted the canoe and traveled far into the interior of North America in search of fortunes. Vestiges of their early camps and settlements dot Lake Superior and the interior rivers that discharge their rushing waters into the lake. The winds at times seem to carry the ghostly voices of rendezvous when "traders, voyageurs, Indians and tough men from the lonely interior renewed their friendships."[5] Standing at Hawk Ridge, I intuit this intricate cartography of movement, animal and human ways meeting and separating through the tributaries that empty out three ways in northern Minnesota: to Hudson Bay, to the Gulf of Mexico, and to the Atlantic Ocean.

Lake Superior is a place of transit and continental complexity. Thirty-one thousand square miles, 1,276 feet at its deepest, three quadrillion gallons of water, Lake Superior is enormous, the beating heart of the region. One tenth of the earth's freshwater resides in its basin. A complete circuit of the lake requires thirteen hundred miles of travel through three states and the province of Ontario. Few cities populate the Superior Basin, Duluth at 86,000 people being the largest American city on the lake, second only to Thunder Bay, Ontario, at nearly 122,000. "On the shores of Gitche Gumee, of the shining Big-Sea-Water," Duluth forges together routes of history, natural and human, buckling and joining continental stories that extend back billions of years. The angled slopes that define Duluth's western and northern borders channel the modern infrastructure that descends toward the harbor and passage out to the sea.

Modern engineering of locks and the St. Lawrence Seaway have made Duluth an Atlantic seaport, the westernmost in North America. The Twin Ports of Duluth and Superior, Wisconsin, organize a veining of rail lines, highways, and slipways to load and service the big freighters, salties, and lakers. Through this harbor wheat from the Great Plains, coal from the West, limestone from Midwest quarries, and taconite pellets from the Iron Range funnel through for transport to other Great Lakes ports or out to the oceanic seaways of global trade. During the coldest months of winter the harbor and lake are ice covered, and shipping traffic is stopped. The region slumbers, its heartbeat slows, often past the spring equinox. But at some point winter's spell breaks. "Aliveness" is how Sigurd F. Olson succinctly measures this changeover.[6]

When the first oceangoing vessel, or "saltie," arrives each year, the ship's crew is greeted with gifts and ceremony. The *Federal Hunter*, loading up with durum wheat, broke the record for earliest arrival in 2013, despite an ice covering that the chief officer from India called "beautiful . . . like heaven." The *Federal Hunter* is only 655 feet long. Seagoing ships tend to be smaller to pass through the Welland Canal farther east on the Great Lakes. When a laker's bow pushes under the Aerial Lift Bridge into Duluth harbor, people rush to the watery gauntlet, the slender passage that guides ships into the St. Louis River estuary. The *American Century*, which picks up coal and other cargo frequently in Duluth, is a thousand feet long and so wide you feel like you could touch its sides as it passes through the canal entrance to Duluth's bay.

Captains pilot these huge ships confidently into and out of harbor, and tourists and townspeople alike throng to wave at crew members and hear the loud, bone-shaking horns, one short, two long, of ship and bridge as they meet and part. When a laker slips its berth and heads out into the lake, I love to watch it grow smaller and smaller until all you see is a splotch of white, the ship's bridge, disappearing on the waters. Lakers fly American or Canadian flags, but when salties arrive, they bring colorful designs from around the world. Hundreds of years ago trade competition spurred continental wars, and it was here, in the interior of North America, that a young United States tested its ascendancy. Eventually the American industrial age built its foundation from Minnesota iron shipped eastward to steel foundry cities. The modern ships that sail Lake Superior churn through the routes of ancient people, trace the passages of contact, and extend the reach of the industrial age out into global currents.

After twenty-seven years living on the American grasslands, I uprooted my family for a new job in Duluth. Our migration was in spring, our movement tracing the northerly trajectory of birds and warmer weather. The challenge of new work, not the tug of family roots or primal landscape, untethered me. Interstate 35 threads its way north from Des Moines, Iowa, passing through hilly farm country and crossing the Mississippi River bluffs at the Twin Cities. Much of the way reflects the Nebraska landscape I had come to love, and I still find myself standing on Hawk Ridge or down at the shore to embrace the openness of water and sky that reminds me of the plains interior. Around Hinckley, Minnesota, the landscape changes. The woods-lined farmland switches over to northern coniferous forest, to the rugged Iron Range, and the boggy landscape left by retreating glaciers millennia ago. Glacial Lake Duluth, the proto lake of Superior, was higher then, and to the west and north stretched Glacial Lake Agassiz almost to Hudson Bay. You can see the old lake's terraces at Hawk Ridge. Ten thousand years is a nanosecond of time geologically, and when winter is long, the local woods with their pines and birches, ice-locked ponds, and craggy outcroppings bring this past into the present. I can imagine woolly megafauna back into existence, tramping across the frozen, open country or padding through the forest trails.

Interstate 35 intersects U.S. Highway 2 at Proctor, Minnesota, near the summit of Thompson Hill. Passing Spirit Mountain, a haven for snowboarders, zip line enthusiasts, and mountain bikers, I-35 breaks through the hardwood and conifer forest and begins one of the most spectacular descents on an American interstate. "You feel that you've entered another world," writes John Toren. "You have."[7] The deep waters of Superior stretch out below you. It's like reaching the apex of a roller coaster and suddenly plunging down, falling over the mountain to the harbor below. I-35 eventually reaches a tangle of interconnected roadways that locals call the "Can of Worms." Canadian National rail lines cross over and under the interstate, guiding cargo trains straight to the shipping yards and ore docks to unload taconite iron ore pellets. Modern transportation of all kinds mixes and merges where the St. Louis River estuary turns toward the great inland sea. When winds are westerly, jets follow the same route, skimming over the harbor and then taking the turn at the ridgeline to descend to the airport, another kind of bird, if less seasonal, that works migration.

Certain times of year fog obscures the descent. You feel the g-forces of each curve left and right down the slope, but the thrill of dropping hundreds of feet to lake level is missing in the thick, gray soup cloud. Among Duluth's nicknames is Fog City. Fog can sit for days, grounding migrating birds and air traffic, hiding the lake and the high hills. The perceived world shrinks. Sight is obscured. Fog blindness underscores the dangers in the landscape and seascape, from falling over rock faces to grounding vessels on reefs. Around Lake Superior historic lighthouses mark entrances to ports and treacherous coastline. Scores of undisturbed shipwrecks rest beneath the lake waters. Maritime maps use skeletal images of old masted sailing ships to mark their sites, some within a few hundred feet of Duluth's aerial lift bridge. The *Edmund Fitzgerald* left Duluth on its final voyage into those gales, not fogs, of November—the tenth exactly of 1975. Each November, in communities around the lake, mourners gather for remembrance ceremonies. At Split Rock Lighthouse, now a state park, rangers light the lamp, which beams out over twenty miles onto the black waters of Lake Superior. In between the sweeping pulses of light, evening's darkness heightens the palpable sadness in the crowd. To die in such deep, cold water, suddenly, in heavy seas and high winds, must have been terrifying. Hundreds of sailors and passengers, embarking on the mundane work of trade and travel, faced drowning in Superior's waters over the centuries and before them French voyageurs and Native people seeking swift passage in canoes: "The lake, it is said, never gives up her dead / When the skies of November turn gloomy."[8] Gordon Lightfoot's famous lyrics explain the finality of sinking on Superior, the reality of deep waters that keep vessels from surfacing after being wrecked. "Superior," author Jerry Dennis concludes, "is merciless."[9]

Spring can bring dramatic weather too. Fog, gale-force winds, and intense rains often follow ice-out, giving Midwest surfers the rare chance to follow ten-foot waves to shore at Stony Point and other popular surfing beaches. The hardcore don wet and dry suits to surf in freezing temperatures if squalls create big waves. More common are kayaks and sailboats once spring takes hold, flocking together like the returning cormorants and loons. But it will be months before the lake's waters are warm enough for swimming. Even late in summer the waters offshore remain dangerously cold. Lake Superior demands respect, and even experienced sailors leave port vigilant. Expert kayakers have tipped over in sudden rough seas within sight of the Lake Walk in Duluth, their wet suits unable to stave off the churning forty-degree water for long. In 2012 a kayaker nearly died while beer drinkers watched his rescue from a local watering hole.

Duluth is called the "San Francisco of the Midwest." Hills rise dramatically from Lake Superior, and a hundred miles northeast the Sawtooth Mountains dominate the landscape. John R. Tester tells us that "about 2.7 billion years ago and again at about 1.8 billion years ago, the area that was to become Minnesota had sizable mountain ranges."[10] Vestiges of volcanic activity that stopped around 1.1 billion years ago gave birth to much of the beauty of the North Shore. Duluth's topography determines street directions. For a flatlander who drove for decades on gridded sections, this cartography is challenging. I often have no idea what direction I am traveling, and after half a decade here I still get turned around frequently. My woodland neighborhood, many hundreds of feet higher than Lake Superior, is broken up by resistant rock formations that jut up, block construction, and force roads around them. These outcroppings are Precambrian, remnants of continental worlds that once were equatorial before tectonics shifted them north toward the Arctic. Across northeastern Minnesota the rocks reveal the deep past: Precambrian glaciation, ancient iron-rich seas, mountain orogenies, vestiges of a Paleozoic equatorial zone, more seas, uplift, tectonic shifting, and the icy Pleistocene. Outcroppings up the North Shore record the etchings from the last great Ice Age, quaternary cross-hatchings on ancient Precambrian rock. The granites, gabbros, and basalts record more ancient temporal passages, paleomagnetic archives of origin and change.[11]

Bedrock is cut by the many streams and rivers that cascade down from the heights. As the snowmelt intensifies each year, these falls thunder downslope. The river names leave one record of European contact: St. Louis River, French River, Knife River, Encampment River, Baptism River, Temperance River. Their waters flush snowmelt, scoured rock, and organic matter into Lake Superior and the St. Lawrence watershed. This thin slice of the Arrowhead drains Atlantic-wise. The continent divides three ways in northern Minnesota, with watersheds draining east to the Atlantic, north to Hudson Bay, and south to the Gulf of Mexico through the wetlands of Louisiana, quite the continental span. Three biomes roughly follow these drainages: northern coniferous forests, once filled with white and red pines before lumbering began, vestiges of tallgrass prairie, and deciduous forest. In the parlance of biology the meeting of biomes "forms a continental-scale ecotone."[12] Here eastern deciduous and northern boreal forests meet, a zone that connects the North Shore to Maine.[13]

The confluence of lakes and rivers, a landscape robust and fertile, has supported generations of Native people, Dakota and Ojibwe in modern centuries, going all the way back to paleo-Indian tribes. Well before European priests, coureurs de bois, and voyageurs entered this landscape (and maybe Vikings for all we know), Native communities traded and networked across North America. The bounty that nourished these people, in Mary Lethert Wingard's description, was multiple: "The forest, lakes, and rivers teemed with game, water fowl, and fish; herds of buffalo still roamed the prairie; lush vegetation provided a variety of foodstuffs that included wild rice, berries, nuts, and edible roots; and sugar maples yielded the sweetness of their sap."[14] Modern locavores continue to make use of these traditional foodstuffs, including venison, waterfowl, meat from restored bison herds, and freshwater fish from the lake. In 2013 spring's late snowfall produced a record sugaring on the North Shore as tons of sap were boiled down for syrup and candy.

Famous for Jeno's Pizza Rolls and Chun King canned foods, Duluth is seeking a different future through return to what the landscape provides. Wild rice, walleye, fiddleheads, bog cranberries, retain their integrity in North Woods cuisine and encourage a lake-anchored food palate. Forty years ago, when U.S. Steel left Duluth, few could have imagined the city's phoenixlike rise out of the industrial ash heap, borne on the wings of the genius loci. At the beginning of the twentieth century the area in and around Duluth produced most of the food for the population's consumption. In the twenty-first century citizens are seeking ways to reinhabit and reproduce these older ways of sustaining life. Researchers at the University of Minnesota–Duluth, for instance, have reestablished a large organic vegetable farm on a once abandoned land grant field station. It now feeds students with a plethora of fresh-grown vegetables. A century-old apple orchard, tended and pruned again, is reemerging from slumber. The North Woods of North America are not the continent's breadbasket, but the arable land that exists is surprisingly productive.

Before the captains of industry dug out the iron, logged the forests, and built harbors to transport raw materials for mass consumption, the French and British trading companies set up a nimble infrastructure for the fur trade. The seventeenth century, then, marked "the industrial-scale exploitation of the region."[15] Traders followed the long-established routes of Native people. Historian Claiborne Skinner explains:

This northern country was a region of dense forests, lakes, and rivers. To avoid the trackless woods and the clouds of biting insects which infested them, people used the water as highways: first with rafts and then dugout canoes. These worked well enough on the rivers south of the Great Lakes, but were too low-sided for open water and too heavy to be carried around the rapids and waterfalls characteristic of northern rivers. At some point, however, the Indians developed a new craft both lighter and more versatile than the dugout: the birch bark canoe. . . . The birch bark canoe allowed hunters to travel greater distances in search of game and fostered a long-distance trade in luxury commodities like copper, shells, mica, and tobacco.[16]

The French wanted pelts, *castor gras*, the "greasy beaver."[17] Rain repelling, beaver fur made great hats, and for fashion these mammals were trapped close to extinction. Spring was a busy season for fur traders such as Daniel Greysolon, Sieur du Luth, the namesake of my city. Once ice-out happened, the river highways opened. Greysolon and other fur traders could move expeditiously from Lake Superior to the Mississippi. Lithe, swift birch bark canoes allowed them to penetrate thousands of miles into the North American interior. As Skinner puts it, "[It] was a corrupt, chaotic time of fast money and few rules and in it the *coureurs de bois* attracted more than their share of rogues and scoundrels."[18] Eventually this industry collapsed, presaging the boom and bust of future extractive enterprises. Lake Superior, at the cusp of three important watersheds, provoked a collision of cultures.

All of this is ghost past now, a faded tracing beneath the current passing show. The violence of the fur trade era has receded, and the legends have been domesticated. Greysolon is a ballroom for rent and a city street; Radisson is a hotel chain and Cadillac a car. The spring melts that once led coureurs de bois downriver and up-country now provoke the invasion of the tourists on the North Shore hankering to witness crashing waters. The old warehouse, brothel, and saloon district, Canal Park, boasts hotels, art galleries, restaurants, and the durable goods of Duluth Pack. Once a depressed burial ground of lost industry, the tourist district now houses all forms of kitschy Gitche Gumee shops selling mementos of the place, T-shirts, mugs, whiskey shot glasses, lighthouse magnets, and the like. The shipping season itself has become a major draw. The fanatics call Boatwatcher Hotline: 218-722-6489. Not far from Canal Park, archaeological palimpsests of fur trade activity, barely known to the locals, faintly mark this history. The juxtaposition of fur trade and tourist trade, however, is at once jarring and true.

The return of ships is among northern Minnesota's delights each spring. Global trade in the twenty-first century repeats the ice-out cycle of the fur trade, with ships that winter over leaving first. The opening of the shipping season varies considerably. The snow load into the spring of 2014 was among the deepest: 130.2 inches of snow stopped just short of the record. When winter holds on tenaciously, cold, foggy days add up well into May. Delayed ice-outs are dramatic and swift when winter shifts to summer. Winters that freeze up the Great Lakes are less and less common as the Anthropocene era warms the planet, but 2014 was anomalous. Throughout May ice still packed into the southwestern corner of Lake Superior, and icebreakers plowed out of Duluth harbor. On thick foggy mornings the city disappeared, and the sun struggled to burn off the ground cloud. By afternoons glinting parts of the aerial lift bridge appeared briefly, but the ice floes on the lake kept generating fog. The world for days remained in silvery opaqueness. Wind-sculpted ice walls slowly retreated from the beaches, allowing the detritus of winter storms to emerge. A late ice-out keeps waters cold longer and prolongs the wet fogs that hang over the city and cool down the summer. Garden crops such as kale, lettuce, and broccoli love this coolness, but cold summers after long winters try the soul. As Jerry Dennis explains, "Winter's cold remains impounded, damping the wind. Often the lake is covered in fog—thick white rafts of it."[19] These are good days for beach fires and long lonely walks.

In 2014 icebreakers worked overtime to open up the harbor for business. Hundreds of ships were waiting for the locks of Sault Sainte Marie to unfreeze. When they did, ships in convoys closely followed the icebreakers to make their way to Thunder Bay, Ontario; Silver Bay, Minnesota; and the Twin Ports. Ship spotters were treated to unusual numbers of ships, lakers first and then the first saltie of the year, the *Diana* from Antigua, arriving to load 11,500 metric tons of grain. A year after the *Federal Hunter* set the early arrival record, *Diana* marked the latest arrival of a seagoing vessel to Duluth harbor. The back and forth of the shorter oceangoing vessels and longer lakers punctuates late spring days, while smaller yachts and sailing boats accrue in number, their colorful sails and names adding dashes of energy and sparkle. Invariably, slowly, the lake's waters warm near Duluth, and life renews itself. The old patterns, the enduring cycles, pulse under the thin skin of the modern city.

These dramatic changes, palpable and invigorating, spur my appreciation for and adaptation to the frequently unforgiving northern landscape that others find unimaginably harsh. The Norwegians say there is no bad weather, just bad clothes, and living here toughens the energies of body and mind. Summer unlocks all kinds of energies up and down the North Shore. Forest floors soften up, spring to life. The days lengthen, and by June the skies still feel light at 10:00 p.m. As the birds return, other changes occur on the landscape. By the time hummingbirds are hovering around the feeders, bears have emerged from winter dens. In Duluth, where wild and domestic spaces rub up intimately, people thrill at reports of sows and cubs afoot, eagerly share news of bear sightings. There's an edginess when bears are wandering the neighborhoods. I've heard wolves calling from our woods, though I have yet to see one. Closest of all are white-tailed deer, who treat my front yard like a twenty-four-hour grocery store. Wild encounters stay with you: the young cub that pops out of the woods onto the street; a fast-moving loon flying parallel to your car; a fox at night in the headlights, a quick rush of fur and movement. I long to see moose, though disruption to the ecosystem is driving them ever northward.

North Woods animals are part of the cultural iconography, their images plastered everywhere and on everything, from chainsaw art in doorways to loon-shaped flower baskets in cemeteries. Coffee mugs, T-shirts, postcards, hats, you name it, all proclaim alliance with wolves, bears, moose, and loons. North Woods fauna sell a lot of goods. At the same time, changes in the landscape make contact with these animals less likely. Loons face challenges at both ends of their migration, and parasites, warming waters, and wolf predation are thinning out moose populations. Wolves, despite their comeback, remain a tenuous species in northern Minnesota. Disappearances, collapse, and extinction happen over life spans. On the surface forest song, paw tracks, and brief sightings animate the magical months between May and October. The biome around Lake Superior may seem static, but it's not. Those longtimers and scientists who study the signs in the waters and on the land discern unsettling disturbances to flora and fauna. Dramatic changes on a global level threaten the integrity of every living thing along Superior's shores.

I have moved to the North Woods of Minnesota, but I am not of the North Woods. Not yet, and maybe not ever. Out of the city, on county highways, I resist the enclosure of forest, and I find bog country impenetrable, alien. There is much that I don't understand about the place I live in. I listen, I read, I practice my moves, expanding out incrementally through road trips or hiking. But I also return to trails I have walked, looking at them seasonally, learning to mark what changes, what stays the same. Much of my own adaptation is slowly earned. I try to remember the names of things, breeds of birds, species of trees, types of pebbles on the beach. Intimacy takes time.

Hawk Ridge has become one of my necessary places of return. The whole reach of Earth's critical zone from bedrock to atmosphere stands out here. Hawk Ridge is a touchstone into the deeper matrix of Lake Superior. In *Sustaining Earth's Critical Zone* the multiple authors, all scientists, explain that the Critical Zone "is a complex natural reactor where inputs of solar energy and atmospheric deposition and gases interact with the biota and rock mass of the continents to maintain soil, nourish ecosystems and yield clean water."[20] Moreover, the temporal and spatial dimensions expand and contract at the Critical Zone. "The wide range of physical, chemical and biological mechanisms," they project, "interact at different timescales ranging from seconds to 1000s of millennia, and at spatial scales of single molecules to the entire earth."[21]

Standing at Hawk Ridge, I intuit this grand exchange, this immense expanse of history. The flight of a bird across this landscape carries with it eons of knowing intimately the full reach of a landscape, a continent, even a hemisphere. Some of this knowledge is hardwired at birth. In comparison my tenure here is negligible.

I am as native as the Kamloops, which is to say not at all. But like them, I am settling in. From the ridgeline I perceive a reality that reaches across a continent and projects out into the oceans of the planet. I stand on rock over a billion years old, extant because it is the craton, the Canadian Shield, the foundational rock of continents. Though nothing as physically durable exists in me, not even my bones, I share with this world an ancient code of memory, DNA, history chronicled within helix strands. The information organized within this DNA predates my own humanity and presages the world beyond my species when North America will have rejoined some other continental mass and formed a new configuration of planet Earth. I cannot physically fly with the birds at Hawk Ridge, but my imagination wings across space and time, helping me peel away some of what covers the mystery, exposing some of the deep layering of this place I now call home.

NOTES

1. Anderson and Fischer, *North Shore*, 60.
2. Anderson and Fischer, *North Shore*, 63.
3. Heat-Moon, *Here, There, Elsewhere*, 274.
4. Greg Breining tells us that the Minnesota Department of Natural Resources introduced "a domesticated, easy-to-raise version of the lake-dwelling Kamloops, which they began stocking along the North Shore in the 1980s." *Fishing Minnesota*, 22.
5. Hart and Ziegler, *Landscapes of Minnesota*, 62.
6. Olson, *Reflections from the North Country*, 73.
7. Toren, *Seven States of Minnesota*, 245.
8. Lightfoot, "Wreck of the Edmund Fitzgerald."
9. Dennis, *Living Great Lakes*, 115.
10. Tester, *Minnesota's Natural Heritage*, 8.
11. Tester gives a vivid description of North Shore geology in *Minnesota's Natural Heritage*.
12. Anderson and Fischer, *North Shore*, 20.
13. Anderson and Fischer discuss the Laurentian Mixed Forest Province in their chapter "Headwaters" in *North Shore*.
14. Wingerd, *North Country*, 4.
15. Anderson and Fischer, *North Shore*, 28.
16. Skinner, *Upper Country*, 5–6.
17. Skinner, *Upper Country*, 6.

18. Skinner, *Upper Country*, 27–28.
19. Dennis, *Living Great Lakes*, 84.
20. Banwart et al., *Sustaining Earth's Critical Zone*, 5.
21. Banwart et al., *Sustaining Earth's Critical Zone*, 5.

BIBLIOGRAPHY

Anderson, Chel, and Adelheid Fischer. *North Shore: A Natural History of Minnesota's Superior Coast.* Minneapolis: University of Minnesota Press, 2015.

Banwart, S. A., J. Chorover, J. Gaillardet, D. Sparks, T. White, S. Anderson, A. Aufdenkampe, S. Bernasconi, S. Brantley, O. Chadwick, C. Duffy, M. Goldhaber, K. Lenhart, N. P. Nikolaidis, and K. V. Ragnarsdottir. *Sustaining Earth's Critical Zone: Basic Science and Interdisciplinary Solutions for Global Challenges.* Sheffield: University of Sheffield Press, 2013.

Breining, Greg. *Fishing Minnesota: Angling with the Experts in the Land of 10,000 Lakes.* Minneapolis: University of Minnesota Press, 2003.

Dennis, Jerry. *The Living Great Lakes: Searching for the Heart of the Inland Seas.* New York: St. Martin's, 2003.

Hart, John Fraser, and Susy Svatek Ziegler. *Landscapes of Minnesota: A Geography.* St. Paul: Minnesota Historical Society Press, 2006.

Heat-Moon, William Least. *Here, There, Elsewhere: Stories from the Road.* New York: Little, Brown, 2013.

Lightfoot, Gordon. "The Wreck of the Edmund Fitzgerald." Moose Music, Ltd., 1976. Accessed July 2, 2016. http://www.azlyrics.com/lyrics/gordonlightfoot/thewreckoftheedmundfitzgerald.html.

Olson, Sigurd. *Reflections from the North Country.* Minneapolis: University of Minnesota Press, 1976.

Skinner, Claiborne A. *The Upper Country: French Enterprise in the Colonial Great Lakes.* Baltimore: Johns Hopkins University Press, 2008.

Tester, John R. *Minnesota's Natural Heritage: An Ecological Perspective.* Minneapolis: University of Minnesota Press, 1995.

Toren, John. *The Seven States of Minnesota: Driving Tours through the History, Geology, Culture, and Natural Glory of the North Star State.* Minneapolis: Nodin Press, 2010.

Wingerd, Mary Lethert. *North Country: The Making of Minnesota.* Minneapolis: University of Minnesota Press, 2010.

Pathways of the Yellowstone

BERNARD QUETCHENBACH

The valley moves. The river flows, sturgeon and paddlefish make their rounds, trout flash in shallow riffles. The air alive with pressure systems, thunderstorms and blizzards, waves of migrant birds. The land itself a continuous writhing of titanic forces, too gradual—usually—to trouble the ridgetop meandering of bears, the seasonal drift of antelope and elk.

The river is alive with time. The floodplain whips between bluffs. And before the river, the shallow seas, home to belemnites and crocodiles; the plains of the brontosaurs; the uplands traversed by hadrosaur herds. Then the mammoths, ancestral horses, outsized bison. Then the Anzick-site Clovis, the "people without iron," the shield-warrior artists of Weatherman Draw.[1] The southbound Athabascans and Kiowa. The Crow longing for the one true place. The Shoshone, Bannock, and Nez Perce, crossing the mountains to hunt buffalo. The Lakota and Cheyenne, the roving Blackfeet. Then Clark's half of the Corps of Discovery, straggling back to the States. The mountain men. The gold seekers. The government expeditions and immigrant homesteaders. The railroad. And the stories and songs, perceptual alchemy of all those human imaginations and sensibilities.

Poet Gary Holthaus, revisiting a history earlier rendered in self-consciously epic poetry by John Neihardt, captures the particular resonance of the Yellowstone country:

> *There is this desire:*
> *Time, motion, and music*
> *In the word*
> *A language like liquid . . .*
> *A river*
> *Yellowstone or Big Horn.*[2]

As we board the Yellowstone Association van to "Celebrate the Marvels of Migration,"[3] our instructor reminds us to focus on "feathers, not fur," redirecting our attention from mammalian megafauna like the two grizzlies that will saunter past the van later this morning, the bighorn band near Tower Fall this afternoon. In Swan Lake Flat, an expansive meadow a few miles south of Mammoth Hot Springs, my classmates and I lug an array of optical equipment from the Bunsen Peak trailhead to Glen Creek, lazy even in spring flood. And there they are—wigeons, pintails, scaup, three kinds of teal, a profusion of migrants gleaming in the gleaming water, birds of passage mostly, mixed with a few newly arrived summer residents.

It is easy to speculate in general terms about why birds migrate. They follow food sources, seek uncrowded breeding or wintering territories. What it all means to the birds as they are swept up in the journey is elusive, though English-speaking birders have adopted from German biologists a word, *Zugunruhe,* for the characteristic urge that spurs migration. At Swan Lake Flat most waterfowl are likely on the home stretch, bound for the sloughs and vernal ponds scattered more thinly than before across the prairie pothole country north of my Billings home, where they will be joined by smaller, perhaps more miraculous, long-distance travelers: lark buntings, longspurs, phalaropes. Like human retirees—snowbirds, we call them—they winter in the American Sunbelt, the Caribbean, Central or South America. But as the days lengthen and the stars wheel around the firmament, they respond to physiological shifts triggered by environmental signals, such as those longer days.

Experiments with a cone-shaped enclosure called an Emlen funnel document *Zugunruhe.* "Inked" birds leave a pattern of footprints on paper lining the cone, itchy feet reflecting equally itchy wings. The goal of Emlen-funnel experiments has generally been to discover how manipulating magnetic impulses or star patterns—by, for example, reorienting a planetarium dome projection—affects the migrants' sense of direction. But along with their scientific purpose, the resulting graphics make in effect evocative artistic expressions of *Zugunruhe,* testifying to the irresistible impulse to move on.[4]

When we talk about animal migration, we might think first of birds, but the Yellowstone region is crisscrossed by the paths of other creatures as well. Beset by climate change and by introduced predators, competitors, and diseases, cutthroat trout still pull back and forth between lakes and streams. While isolation might protect these fish, self-containment is generally bad news for large mammals. Hemmed in by the "islanding" of their home ranges, the region's ungulates trace traditional but flexible routes. Elk move from high country meadows to wintering grounds both within the protected circle of Greater Yellowstone and, increasingly, just beyond, as artificial bounties—fall gardens and prematurely green lawns, for example—draw them toward Cody, Wyoming, and Livingston, Montana. Osborne Russell never mentions moose in his 1834–43 *Journal of a Trapper*, not even in his appendix devoted in part to the animals he encounters. It is inconceivable that Russell, a Maine native, would have overlooked these impressive, familiar, and nutritious cervids had he come upon them with any degree of regularity. Today, however, moose are a much-loved presence in the Rock Creek canyons Russell frequented. Responding to wildfire and other habitat changes, they appear to follow a long-term migration pathway connecting the Yellowstone region with ranges to the south by way of the Green River.

The most noted migrant among Greater Yellowstone's nonhuman mammals is the pronghorn antelope. For six thousand years these sole survivors of a Miocene American lineage have traveled the "Path of the Pronghorn" linking Jackson Hole to the Green River Valley, a route that, though partially protected as the first designated American wildlife corridor, crosses fenced ranches and intensively developed energy fields. Historically, antelope used eight migration corridors across the Yellowstone region, but only two remain open to them. Less well-known than the longer southern pathway is the route from basins north of Gardiner, Montana, across the formidable escarpment of Mount Everts into the park's Northern Range.[5]

The movements of predators are less obvious and predictable, but bears, mountain lions, and wolverines mix populations across or along ridges and mountain ranges. As grizzlies fill available territories and search for food sources to compensate for the reduced trout and fading whitebark pine, they push eastward to reclaim ancestral homes in Wyoming's Bighorn Basin and Montana's prairies. An impressive bear fence surrounds the school playground at Wapiti, Wyoming, and grizzly reports along Montana's Beartooth Front increased from three in 1997 to fifty in 2014.[6] Hikers, myself included, carry bear spray on trails where it did not seem necessary before.

According to "perhaps the most expansive and dramatic Indian migration story ever told," passed on by elderly oral historian Cold Wind to nineteen-year-old Joseph Medicine Crow in 1932 and retold in Medicine Crow's *From the Heart of the Crow Country*, the people who would become the Hidatsa and ultimately the Crow were driven from "tree country," apparently in the Upper Midwest, by unrelenting drought.[7] They pursued game onto the prairies, where some families adopted plains tipis as summer homes. Eventually, they moved again, stopping at Devil's Lake, North Dakota, to seek spiritual guidance. Two leaders, Red Scout and No Vitals (No Intestines, in other versions), received instructions defining future travels and lifeways. No Vitals was to carry a pod of sacred seeds west to the mountains, where his descendants would flourish. Following Red Scout, however, the Hidatsa constructed earthen lodges along the upper Missouri like those of their Mandan neighbors. No Vitals was not at ease. Eventually, as the seventeenth century dawned, he "decided to go westward to plant the sacred seeds and look for the promised land."[8]

Medicine Crow's historiographical method is to painstakingly build a narrative consistent with both Crow oral tradition and the western archaeological record. No Vitals is the key to Medicine Crow's story. Like Moses, his mission was to lead his people to the place of their destiny, but No Vitals had only the seeds to guide him. It is no surprise, therefore, that the journey was long and convoluted—Medicine Crow reports stops in Alberta, Utah, and perhaps Oklahoma—outlasting the lifetime of No Vitals himself. But the "secessionist tribe" finally found the place to plant No

Vitals's sacred seeds, the Yellowstone Basin country, where their descendants live today.[9]

Animal migrations are generally perennial. A typical sandhill crane, for example, will fly between New Mexico and Montana twice a year throughout her life. Similarly, human communities are often transhumant, tracking the seasons from one place to another within a defined territory. Culture-founding journeys like that of No Vitals, however, may prove unidirectional and permanent. The Crow and Hidatsa recognize their historical kinship, and Crow chroniclers find meaning in shared traditions. Medicine Crow's informant Cold Wind had traveled east, consulting with "an old, old man, a tribal historian, who knew stories about the ancestors of the Hidatsa."[10] But relocation transformed Cold Wind's and Medicine Crow's ancestors into an entirely new nation, the Absarokee,[11] "people of the large-beaked bird."

Despite the protracted nature of the Absarokee migration, Medicine Crow concludes that from the moment of departure No Vitals's "band became an instant tribe capable of existing as a separate and distinct entity."[12] He characterizes the transformation as both immediate and complete; when No Vitals and his followers left their Hidatsa community, they "started out afresh as a brand-new tribe without a name" and abandoned the material culture that had characterized their way of life. With the exception of those prescient summer camps when their forebears first reached the prairies, "there was no gradual transition from the earth lodge to the tepee!"[13] N. Scott Momaday's *The Way to Rainy Mountain* describes a similar wholesale transformation. Starting in Yellowstone, Momaday retraces the ancestral Kiowa migration to their new homeland on the southern plains, beyond "the place where they must change their lives."[14]

Many tribes in western North America locate their cultural origins in migration narratives more or less like these. But even the proudly emplaced Nez Perce, whose creation story is keyed to specific landmarks in their original and current Idaho homeland, envision a cosmos in motion, as Nez Perce historian Allen V. Pinkham recounts at the outset of *Lewis and Clark among the Nez Perce*, written with Steven R. Evans:

In movement, life was found. Above the canyons, above the prairies and mountains, the clouds appeared and disappeared, moved by the invisible force of the wind. In canyon bottoms, the creeks and rivers persisted in their incessant rush to the western ocean. In the sky above and the water below, there was movement within movement. As the air moved, insects and birds moved within it. River currents pushed boldly downstream, and the otters swam in the powerful flow, emerging to play along the banks. Geese flew overhead, flying north during *weweey p* (spring season) and south during *sey ní m'* (fall season).[15]

As their title establishes, Pinkham and Evans's subject is the interaction between the Nez Perce people and the harbingers of American westward migration, Lewis and Clark. The Corps of Discovery's captains never ventured to the far frontier again after the expedition's 1806 completion. Meriwether Lewis, most historians conclude, became depressive, ultimately suicidal, perhaps in part due to a debilitating combination of *Zugunruhe* frustration and the sense that his most important contributions were behind him. According to disputed accounts cited by Pinkham and Evans, Sacagawea, on the other hand, returned twice, once to Washington state and then permanently to the Wind River Shoshone community, just southeast of Greater Yellowstone in Wyoming.[16]

Evening sun and shadow angle through sagebrush slopes graced with aspen groves and conifer stands. The bison have begun their rut, bulls rolling dust clouds, rumbling purposefully toward curious cows. This year's calves, still russet-tan, chase antelope and generally cavort. We are at a standstill on Yellowstone's Northeast Entrance Road, buffalo milling across the roadway, vacationers from Indiana and Wisconsin gaping through windows and sunroofs.

I had no idea this morning that we—my wife, Cara, and I—would be here tonight. Today was a day for hiking the high lakes of the Beartooth Plateau. But Cooke City was just twenty-five miles or so from the trailhead. We could follow the Lamar River, a Yellowstone tributary, through the park's Northern Range. Sure, it would be farther, but road construction, to say nothing of the Beartooth Pass switchbacks, impeded the way we had come. Once the suggestion had worked its way into our shared consciousness, it would have been just about impossible not to see Lamar Valley again.

During the fur trade days of the 1830s, Lamar Valley was known, at least by trapper-chronicler Osborne Russell, as the "Secluded Valley," home to a happy village of well-appointed Sheepeater Shoshones, not yet slandered by early park historians and officials as "destitute of even savage comforts."[17] Russell returned repeatedly, drawn, he said, by "something in the wild romantic scenery of this valley which I cannot nor will I, attempt to describe."[18] Reeled back to the "Yellow Stone" region whenever his wandering took him too far—say to the Bighorn Mountains or to Great Salt Lake—Russell didn't need an official national park designation to feel the place's centripetal attraction. Though he had a long, sometimes prosperous stay on the West Coast after the trappers' ephemeral lifeway dissolved, it was those nine years as a mountain man he chose to memorialize, *Journal of a Trapper* his one lasting legacy.

A. Starker Leopold famously characterized the national parks as presenting "a vignette of primitive America."[19] While his managerial goal may seem arbitrary or chimerical today, the story of the buffalo does lend the vision behind it a measure of credence. Exterminated from much of North America in the nineteenth century, wild bison hung on in remote reaches of Yellowstone's backcountry. They were supplemented by animals from private herds (in a remarkable stroke of good luck, the imported bison were apparently devoid of domestic cattle genes). Yellowstone buffalo could presumably reclaim more and more of their historic range if allowed to reestablish former migration routes, but though a few wintering areas have been opened to them in recent years, wild bison are still largely restricted to the park and its immediate surroundings.[20] Along with rewilding organizations, Native American tribes seeking cultural revitalization lobby to add "excess" Yellowstone bison to burgeoning private herds. Masked by concerns over disease, property damage, and grazing competition, what leads organized foes of free-ranging bison—sometimes sporting red-slashed NO BUFFALO buttons—to foment outrage at public meetings may be a sublimated fealty to Manifest Destiny.

Visitors to Lamar Valley can indeed catch a glimpse of something like presettlement Wyoming behind the exuberant vacationers and worried rangers. Leopold's pastoral illusion combines with volcanic world-in-the-making geology to give the park and its environs an aura of, if not exactly timelessness, time layered into a palimpsest of Earth and human history. Amid the palpable presence of shifting continents and rising and collapsing cultures, camera-toting tourists are just another wave.

The link between Leopold's "primitive America" and the buffalo has been recognized ever since the mountain men intuited their own demise in the bison's depletion. The late-nineteenth-century Ghost Dance sought a restoration both of Native American lifeways and the lost herds they depended on. "Home on the Range" morphs across human generations into bluesman Keb' Mo's "I wanna go / Where the buffalo roam / I'm just a city boy / Looking for a home."[21] Lamar Valley, where the buffalo still roam at least a little, moves the American soul like the echo of a lost paradise.

Lewis and Clark and Osborne Russell heralded the nineteenth-century American obsession known as "westering," a sustained migration that displaced Native peoples, irrevocably altered the North American landscape, and birthed a heroic and tragic national narrative central to countless films, elegiac paintings, works of fiction, and poems. Norman Lock's 2015 novel *American Meteor* testifies to the persistence and multifariousness of this cultural type. Protagonist Stephen Moran embodies the standard frontier trope of the young roustabout who, having killed a man, escapes legal jeopardy and vengeful relatives for a new start in the West. But most westerners did not leave poorly hidden corpses behind, and the promise of boundless mineral wealth was, it must have been obvious even then, a long shot. Something analogous to the birds' *Zugunruhe* infected multitudes from small farms and bustling eastern cities with an intolerable itch to go west, wealth and opportunity more a rationalization than an actual motivating cause. To the question of why someone would join the westering throng, Lock's Moran explains, "Men would say,

'To get a piece of land,' 'To get rich,' 'To get away from my wife and family,' 'To get the bit out from between my teeth,' 'To get closer to God,' 'To get out of His sight.' Or they would say nothing, looking you fiercely in the eye or at thin air or the dirt at their feet. I suppose the best answer—meaning the most truthful—was . . . 'I don't exactly know.'"[22] Enabled by no less an American than Abraham Lincoln, the railroad took over from the riverways and wagon roads in much of the interior West. In *American Meteor* the Union Pacific provides Moran, the no-prospects son of Irish immigrants, a way to negotiate not only the geographical spaces of the West but also the nation's class structure. Moran parlays his limited and partly fabricated Civil War experience into a medal from Ulysses S. Grant and a gig as bugler for the Lincoln funeral train—he is recommended by a certain poet he encounters at a Washington hospital, whose *Leaves of Grass* he carries throughout his travels. After the procession reaches Springfield, he, along with Lincoln's funeral car, is taken up by railroad magnate Thomas Durant. Eventually, as apprentice to legendary frontier photographer William Henry Jackson, he tags along on Jackson's quest to record the "stark forms of existence" at work camps and a destitute Ute village.[23] Perhaps inevitably, Lock steers his protagonist into a Yellowstone Basin encounter with Custer and Crazy Horse at the Little Bighorn. In keeping with frontier jeremiad tradition, Moran is left embittered and alienated by the decadence of Durant's ostentation in the face of unheralded Chinese labor; Jackson's brilliant but cold drive; and the wanton destruction of the buffalo, the Native Americans, the land itself.

Railroad money and publicity were instrumental in generating the political will to bring Yellowstone National Park into existence, and early tourists reached Mammoth Hot Springs by way of rail vacation packages. But tying fortunes to established or anticipated tracks was risky. Northeast gateway community Cooke City was named for Northern Pacific financier Jay Cooke, Jr., whose efforts to expand rail capacity, along with his attempt to peel off Lamar Valley for a railroad corridor, ultimately failed. Downstream in the Yellowstone Valley proper, the lost community of Coulson welcomed the Northern Pacific with open arms, only to have the tracks bypass it for cheaper land a mile away; Coulson withered, while Billings grew into the "Magic City."

Pass through Billings today, and the mark of the railroad is inescapable. From frontiersman Yellowstone Kelly's grave on the rimrock bluffs—the historically dubious inscription reads, "HE ASKED TO BE BURIED HERE, OVERLOOKING HIS BELOVED YELLOWSTONE VALLEY—you might see mile-long coal trains blocking either side of the Yellowstone River, a barrier to wildlife and, as anyone who has driven through downtown Billings knows, to north-south traffic as well. But for east-west travelers the rails, like the river itself, empower movement. Billings writer Doug Oltrogge, a recent graduate of the department in which I teach, quotes an uncle who took to the hobo life because "the trains were always rolling by."[24]

Contemporary poet Tami Haaland's "Kathy Catches a Train" portrays the rails as both impediment to and enabler of mobility. The poem begins with the speaker waiting at the Twenty-Seventh Street crossing, a familiar circumstance in Billings, bound for a lunch date. On the other side of the tracks Kathy, inspired by a sudden impulse to overcome the obstacle presented by the stopped train and an abetting circumstance—the train starts moving—surrenders to *Zugunruhe*. The still-stationary speaker projects a future conversation in which "I'll tell her how she looked that day, boldly impatient / when her road was blocked, the machine taking her from her settled life."[25]

Set by waterways and mountains, lines of travel have brought various human communities together throughout the Yellowstone country. Plains tribes met Shoshone and Nez Perce hunters. The Kiowa passed through on their way south, their journey echoing earlier migrations of Athabascans en route to new lives as the Apache and Navajo of the Southwest. Mountain men from Canada, Scotland, and the United States made their brief but resonant mark on American history, and homesteaders scattered Norwegian names across the plains north of the river. Ken Egan Jr. reminds us that the Bozeman trail along the Yellowstone was pioneered in part by prospectors coming from farther west.[26]

With all of this crossing of paths, it is not surprising that conflict-ing American impulses to exploit and conserve, to seek material and spiritual treasures, have come to a head, and continue to do so, in the Yellowstone country. Migration and relocation catalyze and exacerbate those conflicts. Bison and grizzlies radiate out from the park toward private property to reclaim historic ranges—lost parts, if you will, of their ancestral stories. Mineral and energy cor-porations pursue new territories, extending the capitalist legacy of fortune seeking and environmental degradation. Like wilderness preservationists, tribes and ranchers aim to "keep it as it was," albeit at different points in history. For good reasons environmentalists favor Wendell Berry's admonition to "stay home,"[27] fostering dura-ble attachments to beloved and well-understood homelands, but movement is inherent in nature and in human nature specifically. Even the nonmigratory Nez Perce traveled considerable distances, and still do, to hunt buffalo; tribal leaders assisted Lewis and Clark to cement a useful alliance, but the prospect of new horizons must have appealed to the individuals who served as guides.

If the convergence of various migrations around Yellowstone is not preordained, it certainly is appropriate. Like the cosmos of Oglala spiritual leader Black Elk's great vision, the Yellowstone country's pathways are three dimensional, avian skyways overlying volcanic channels to the depths of the earth. Given a generous helping of time, the fourth dimension, tectonic surges reach the surface, to be gradually or abruptly fed into mountains and rivers. The Beartooth, Bighorn, and Pryor Mountains are products of the great earthshrug of the Laramide orogeny. The lava fields of Idaho and the jagged Absarokas and Tetons mark more recent upheavals. Ongoing geologic pressures power the boiling pools and blasting geysers of the park.

Looking at a relief map centered on the Yellowstone caldera, one can trace the human and animal travel corridors crisscrossing that titanic upwelling. Rivers course away from the mountains surround-ing the volcanic core in all directions, draining a large portion of the North American interior. The Yellowstone flows into the arc-ing Missouri. Two of the three forks—the Gallatin and Madison—

that meet to make Big Muddy are born in Yellowstone Park, and the Jefferson, the third fork, rises in the mountains of Greater Yellowstone's western rampart. The Green, flowing south, joins the beleaguered Colorado, which for better or worse has bestowed on the country the urban and agricultural behemoths of the modern Southwest. The Snake hooks first south and then northwest to the Columbia. The plateaus at the head of the Yellowstone Valley rise as if from the center of the earth, shedding water and stories.

A couple of years ago I participated in a writers' conference that culminated in a picnic-style banquet at the Jackson Hole Arts Center. It was a cool evening following a stormy afternoon. Sitting at my table was a freelancer who was departing the next morning to write a *National Geographic* feature on Mongolia. He loved Mongolia, had been there several times before. But he said he'd always come back to Yellowstone. It's a place with a certain edge, he told me, a place that will keep you alive. I knew what he meant. In 2006, after eleven years away, I, too, was drawn back to the Yellowstone area. We had built a comfortable life in central Florida, where I worked at one of the most beautiful campuses in the country, featuring the world's largest installation of Frank Lloyd Wright buildings and a lake sprinkled with egrets and spoonbills. It wasn't easy to explain why I was giving all that up for a lateral career move leading not to my birthplace in Upstate New York but to the region of my first teaching job, which had lasted just a brief four years. Something like *Zugunruhe*, incorporated in the notion that "Yellowstone will keep us alive," had no small part in it.

I have come to believe that each of us constructs a kind of legend we tell ourselves to make sense of our random and chaotic life experiences. Some fortunate narratives are rooted in an enduring fealty to a certain locale, a Wendell Berry farm or a Nez Perce creation site. For a variety of reasons, some apparent and some more mysterious, *Zugunruhe* takes the lead in other tales. Lacking the mythic depth of No Vitals's quest, Russell's intrepid adventurousness, and Kathy's instinctive grasp of destiny, my own story must thread its unheroic way through a loosely knit series of places and situations. Wherever I have gone, I have carried an undiminished sense of gratitude and loyalty to my original home along the shore of Lake Ontario and the friends and family I left behind there and at other points along the way. But I can't help but feel that something important, some elusive but palpable resonance, would be missing from my story had the pathways of the Yellowstone not called to me.

Through the air they come, the avian migrants. You can hear them at night, pouring south to north, north to south, their shadows the paths of antelope and elk, bison and moose. Human memory equips the rivers with bullboats, canoes, and keelboats—carrying, among others, the Corps of Discovery—watched from the past by No Vitals, from the future by Osborne Russell and Joseph Medicine Crow, from rimrock bluffs by bears and lions, by Yellowstone Kelly dreaming in his grave above the rails and highways. The paths of living things converge and divide, a mere surface scratching over the basement granite, the intrusions of rhyolite and basalt. The landscape itself slides and buckles its way across the molten hotspot, a journey etched into the lava flows of Idaho's Nez Perce country, the region's steaming springs its passing campfires.

Why wouldn't those titanic creative forces that shape the planet sometimes put bird or bear in motion? Or erupt into a people's story of itself, taking shape as a mythic purpose or triggering a poet's imagination? Along and across the Yellowstone country the *Zugunruhe* that informed the mission of No Vitals and the wandering of Osborne Russell continues to course through the migrants of Swan Lake Flat, to draw pilgrims to Lamar Valley's buffalo herds, and to inspire literary manifestations like Stephen Moran's westering and Kathy's spontaneous freight hopping. When such a deeply seated impulse comes to the fore, there may be no choice but to get caught up—one way or another—in that compelling flow.

NOTES

1. The Anzick site, located near Wilsall, Montana, is the only Clovis-age burial site yet found in the Americas. The "people without iron" is an oft-repeated Crow description of the Bighorn Medicine Wheel's creators. Weatherman Draw is a rock art site near Bridger, Montana.
2. Holthaus, *Circling Back*, 4.

3. Yellowstone Association Institute, May 9–10, 2015, Katy Duffy, instructor.

4. Hughes, *Migration of Birds*, 129–31; Friederici, "Star Trek."

5. See "Pronghorn Migration"; and Ostlind, "Perilous Journey."

6. Custer Gallatin Facebook page.

7. Medicine Crow, *From the Heart of the Crow Country*, 16–17. A larger-than-life centenarian whose remarkable experience included much-honored service in World War II—to complete the four battle deeds required for distinction as a Crow warrior, he even stole some German horses—Medicine Crow was the last Crow war chief and the first of his tribe to complete a master's degree (University of Southern California, Anthropology, 1939). His 2016 funeral was attended by hundreds of mourners. Barack Obama, who had presented him with the Presidential Medal of Freedom, issued an official White House response to his passing.

8. Medicine Crow, *From the Heart of the Crow Country*, 20.

9. Medicine Crow, *From the Heart of the Crow Country*, 20.

10. Medicine Crow, *From the Heart of the Crow Country*, 18.

11. *Absarokee* is how the name appears in Medicine Crow's text. More recent sources prefer *Apsáalooke*. "People of the large-beaked bird" is the standard English-language translation and the source of the tribe's common English name.

12. Medicine Crow, *From the Heart of the Crow Country*, 21.

13. Medicine Crow, *From the Heart of the Crow Country*, 21, 23.

14. Momaday, *Way to Rainy Mountain*, 7.

15. Pinkham and Evans, *Lewis and Clark*, 1.

16. Pinkham and Evans, *Lewis and Clark*, 251–53.

17. Hiram Chittenden, quoted in Loendorf and Stone, *Mountain Spirit*, 3. Early Yellowstone Park managers belittled the Sheepeaters, or Mountain Shoshone, to justify their removal from the park.

18. Russell, *Journal of a Trapper*, 46.

19. See Leopold, "Wildlife Management."

20. In December 2015 Montana governor Steve Bullock designated a limited area north and west of Yellowstone Park as the state's first year-round territory open to free-ranging bison in a century. He continues to stress population limits to contain the Yellowstone spillover.

21. Keb' Mo', "City Boy."

22. Lock, *American Meteor*, 137.

23. Lock, *American Meteor*, 125.

24. Oltrogge, "Trying to Understand," 25.

25. Haaland, *When We Wake in the Night*, 91.

26. Egan, *Montana 1864*, 167–68.

27. Berry, *Selected Poems*, 101.

BIBLIOGRAPHY

Berry, Wendell. *The Selected Poems of Wendell Berry.* Berkeley: Counterpoint, 1999.

Custer Gallatin National Forest Facebook page. Accessed January 9, 2017. https://www.facebook.com/Custer-Gallatin-National-Forest -1448408995440670/.

Egan, Ken, Jr. *Montana 1864.* Helena: Riverbend, 2014.

Friederici, Peter. "Star Trek." *Audubon,* March–April 2015, 48–53.

Haaland, Tami. *When We Wake in the Night.* Cincinnati: Word Tech, 2012.

Holthaus, Gary. *Circling Back.* Salt Lake City: Peregrine Smith, 1984.

Hughes, Janice M. *The Migration of Birds.* Richmond Hill ON: Firefly, 2009.

Keb' Mo'. "City Boy." *Keb' Mo'.* Sony B000002915, 1994, CD.

Leopold, A. Starker. "Wildlife Management in the National Parks." *National Park Service,* 1963. Crater Lake Institute. Accessed July 2, 2016. http:// www.craterlakeinstitute.com/online-library/leopold-report/complete .htm.

Lock, Norman. *American Meteor.* New York: Bellevue, 2015.

Loendorf, Lawrence L., and Nancy Medaris Stone. *Mountain Spirit: The Sheep Eater Indians of the Yellowstone.* Salt Lake City: University of Utah Press, 2006.

Medicine Crow, Joseph. *From the Heart of the Crow Country.* Lincoln: University of Nebraska Press, 1992.

Momaday, N. Scott. *The Way to Rainy Mountain.* Albuquerque: University of New Mexico Press, 1969.

Oltrogge, Doug. "Trying to Understand Freight Riders' Desperate Freedom." *Last Best News,* September 3, 2015. Accessed July 2, 2016. http:// lastbestnews.com/site/2015/09/trying-to-understand-freight-riders -desperate-freedom/.

Ostlind, Emiline. "Perilous Journey of Wyoming's Migrating Pronghorn." *High Country News,* January 4, 2012. Accessed July 2, 2016. https://www .hcn.org/issues/43.22/the-perilous-journey-of-wyomings-migrating -pronghorn.

Pinkham, Allen V., and Steven R. Evans, *Lewis and Clark among the Nez Perce.* Washburn ND: Dakota Institute Press, 2013.

"Pronghorn Migration on the Path of the Pronghorn." *WCS North America.* Accessed July 2, 2016. https://programs.wcs.org/northamerica/wild -places/yellowstone-and-northern-rockies/pronghorn-field-program /pronghorn-migration-path.aspx.

Russell, Osborne. *Journal of a Trapper (1834–1843).* Edited by Aubrey Haines. Lincoln: University of Nebraska Press, 1965.

The Proximity of Far Away

Climate Change Comes to the Alligator

RICK VAN NOY

March 1. By now my family has usually heard a few spring peepers, high, tinny bell ringers, in the marsh across the creek from where we live in Virginia's New River Valley. A few individuals emerge first, and by mid-March their singing rises, at dusk, to a full crescendo. Winter has had a firm grip on the East Coast this year, so they are at least a week late.

Like a well-known Concord naturalist, I have been keeping a record of the first spring peeper in our marsh. A meticulous note-taker, Thoreau recorded the date ice disappeared from the middle of Walden Pond, the ice-out date, in his journal from 1846 to 1860. The average date for the fifteen-year period was April 1. More recently, volunteer students from Journey North and park rangers at the pond have made note of the same event. Since 1995 (throwing out 2010, when the ice never came in, though it was sixteen inches thick in Thoreau's time), the date is around March 17, a full two weeks earlier.[1] We know what's going on. We know why. But why is this information not connecting to people and their actions?

Those peepers are responding to their circumstances and environment, heeding an ancient call for survival. The ground is mostly unfrozen (though they can survive if it freezes again), the days longer, and the males try to outdo one another in song. Called "pinkletinks" on Martha's Vineyard, "tinkletoes" in Canada, they are small enough to fit on a fingertip, but man can those frogs make some noise.

When those peepers begin to call, something is changing in me as well. I'm (almost) ready to put away my skis and usually feel an urge to plant something—tubers, greens—in the soil. Warmer days and the return of light, the sap starts moving in us, spring fever. The oldest part of our brain, which evolved some 200 million years ago, is often called the "reptilian brain," and we share it with frogs and birds. It controls life functions such as breathing and heart rate but also our fight-or-flight mechanism. Lacking language, its impulses are instinctual, ritualistic, concerned with survival. The basic ruling emotions of love, hate, fear, lust, and contentment coil up through this first stage of the brain. Over millions of years of evolution, layers of more sophisticated reasoning have been added to it, can override it, but it gets first call.

The climate crisis is global, but the effects are felt most intensely as place based and local. Between the disasters—the droughts, the hurricanes—are the early-blooming orchids, the thin layers of ice, the early arrivals of spring peepers, the late departure of migratory birds. Noticing these small changes requires knowing a place deeply, the kind of local knowledge that is passed down over time. Surely the ability to recognize patterns is also evolved into us. The hunter sees a deer on a particular path and might expect that deer again. Such skills in pattern recognition also keep us safe from lurking dangers.

The ability to mark small changes unfolding over time is lost to many of us living in a harried, frenzied now, with a short attention span news cycle. Climate change is, however, the inevitable effect of past actions not only on the present but on the future. The patterns and trend lines are there, but a series of severe storms does not a climate change make. Unless linked to particular disasters—and scientists warn against it—climate change does not make great TV news, nor does it seem to rouse many people from their torpor to move on the issue of global warming. No "sufficient catalyst" has yet occurred to change the tide on climate change, though the ocean tides are rising: not the BP oil spill, the warmest decade in history, Superstorm Sandy, or the droughts in California.[2] If climate change were a war, there has yet to be a Pearl Harbor.

At one time environmentalism could afford to be intensely local. It was Thoreau fishing his pond, Edward Abbey picking Kleenex out of cliff rose and cactus, Rachel Carson documenting the effects of DDT on local communities, right down to the very worms. As Adam Rome shows in *The Genius of Earth Day*, the early environmental movement also consisted of suburban mothers who wanted to protect their children from the immediate threats of contaminated air, water, and food. The danger of global warming, caused by an invisible, naturally occurring gas, has been less local and seemingly less direct in its impact.

It is possible that more and better data could win over climate change skeptics. We have maps of the arctic ice sheet that show how the ice is contracting on the surface, but geophysicists are also showing how it is melting on the bottom, decreasing in thickness. And while most discussions of global warming focus on the air temperature, about 90 percent of the heat generated by the greenhouse effect is warming the oceans, according to the Intergovernmental Panel on Climate Change (2007). Oceans are also acidifying as a result of increased carbon dioxide, impacting wildlife and habitat, phenomena that can be measured but hard to capture in a picture or map. I imagine some webcam or drone that could give a "real time" perspective on the changing climate, like the popular wildlife cameras, but the overall effects of climate change are too slow moving, especially as they impact our lives.

We have good pictures and data points. We see ice caps calving and glaciers retreating. We have maps that show projections of storm swell and the low-lying areas that are drowned by sea level rise. What we don't have is global action.

A 2013 poll by Yale University found that while 68 percent of Americans say that climate change will affect future generations, only 38 percent think it will affect them personally.[3] Though a good deal of the skepticism could be attributed to the doubt sowed by energy companies and their lobbyists, perhaps something more is going on, something the ideal of a global imagination may fail to account for.

In his 2014 book, *Don't Even Think about It*, George Marshall discusses some of the science behind climate change denial. He surveys the work of psychologists such as Daniel Gilbert who argue that we evolved to respond to more immediate, abrupt, and direct threats than the gradual, distant one of climate change, at least in terms of its eventual magnitude and effects on our personal lives. Addressing it requires making sacrifices now in order to prevent unclear costs in the far-off future, which humans (and their elected officials) are not good at. And there is no clear enemy, except you and me and everyone we know. Although Admiral Samuel J. Locklear III, the commander of the United States Pacific Command, has said that global climate change is more dangerous than terrorism, our reptilian brains respond more to the terrorist threats.

Trying to make sense of the lack of urgency, I wondered if we should see more response, less denial, among people in places most affected by climate change. After all, for certain low-lying areas climate change is not just theoretical but a direct assault on their property and place. While the peepers were ending their spring call, I traveled to Norfolk, Virginia, one of the largest metropolitan cities vulnerable to sea level rise, second only to New Orleans. Norfolk is facing a double whammy: rising seas and sinking lands, or subsidence. Michelle Covi, a member of the Mitigation and Adaptation Research Institute at nearby Old Dominion University, told me the city used to experience two days of tidal flooding per year. Now they get ten. I somewhat expected residents to be well attuned to the effects of climate change, but some thought the flooding they were experiencing was not a matter of global patterns but merely a matter of city maintenance. Over oysters and beer one resident told me the city just needs to clean out drains. Some older neighborhoods, such as Chesterfield Heights, are built near "legacy creeks," former wetlands that were filled in or developed. Skip Stiles, the executive director of Wetlands Watch, told me "a creek wants to be a creek"— it's where the water wants to go when it floods.

Stiles's group has pivoted from saving and protecting wetlands to saving and protecting communities—not just the marsh but the coast itself. And when he talks to gatherings and uses the words *climate change*, he meets resistance. The reptilian brain throws up defenses. "It's about how you frame it," he told me. When he first talked to local community groups, he talked about climate change and showed maps of sea level rise, but those efforts went nowhere. Pictures were more effective. He would show a stump sticking out of the water, evidence of saltwater flooding. Someone in the audience would recognize the place: "I used to hunt there."

I also sought out people on the Outer Banks of North Carolina. On the weekend I went—the last in August—the National Weather Service map of the United States showed little activity anywhere. It uses colors to show weather events, but the country was unshaded, showing only the colorless grids of county and state lines, except for a magenta section of eastern Washington, a red flag warning for wildfires, and most of Idaho was shaded in gray, air quality alert. Then in that small bulge of North Carolina that juts out into the sea, a pale green flood advisory. What better weekend to go? I ignored the advisory and packed my gear. After all, it was just a representation of a flood, not actual water lapping at my tent.

My day started with a walk to the beach, but at this beach access, near the Black Pelican in Kitty Hawk, there was little beach, only a small area between waves and a massive, man-made dune. The dune was a form of "beach nourishment," where sand is pumped or dumped, not really stopping erosion but giving the waves something to chew on for a while. A few gulls wandered along the wrack line.

Then to Ten O Six, a "beach road bistro." The owner, Toby Gonzalez, wears a white, stained T-shirt, emerges from the kitchen with a good cup of coffee and an even better breakfast burrito. He tells me he has lived there his whole life, so I ask him about changes to the island, especially related to sea level rise. He said he hadn't really noticed any but that it was "hard to argue with the numbers." Still, the numbers did not seem to be convincing him. I think he said this for my benefit, perhaps a nod to my being a patron.

Another customer came in, another lifelong resident, from the northernmost town, Duck, and Toby asked him about changes. "Tide comes in," he said. "And tide goes out." They laughed. I asked about projections of sea level rise up to three feet by the end of the century. "I won't be here," new customer Dave said. And Toby started riffing. "If it does rise, I'll have to charge more for my sandwiches," he said with a wink. "Beach front property." "Damn Atlantis," he went on, smiling, "trying to claim our women."

According to a report from the Yale Project on Climate Change Communication begun in 2008 and updated yearly, there are "six Americas" when it comes to perceptions of the impact of global warming: alarmed, concerned, cautious, disengaged, doubtful, and dismissive. The comment about the tides coming in and going out seemed to come from the perspective of the doubtful, and the comment about it being "hard to argue with the numbers" seemed cautious. And while the jokes would seem dismissive, I detected a bit of "concern" in them. Global warming is happening but is still a distant threat. While he lingered, Dave from Duck added, "We keep fucking with this planet, Mother Nature is going to do something." But his main solution was more sand fence. He pointed to a picture hanging on the wall of a fence halfway buried by a dune.

I told them I was headed for the Alligator National Wildlife Refuge area because they are already seeing evidence of sea level rise. Dave from Duck said some of the land there he used to hunt on "floats." I couldn't tell if we were having a problem communicating. Floating land? Was Dave floating on something when he hunted? But then I remembered that much of the land in the "Alligator" is peat, spongy. Christine Pickens, of the Nature Conservancy, later told me that indeed, in parts of the Alligator there are sections of marsh and vegetation that float, not unlike mangrove islands. They are tricky to walk on. Step through and beware of what lies in wait below—gator.

Before heading east across the bridges to the mainland, I stopped at Jeanette's pier, once wiped out by Hurricane Isabel, wood replaced by concrete. Owned by the North Carolina Aquarium Society, the pier focuses on education about fish, marine science, and resource conservation. The parking lot is made of porous pavers to help with flooding. On that day they were holding a surfing tournament. A few surfers were putting on wetsuits and readying their boards. I asked if sea level rise would affect their sport. Both were "doubtful" it would, but neither did the loud music and promotional banners lend toward reflection.

Part of the reason I wanted to visit the refuge is that according to a 2005 report, it had a higher density of black bear than any place on the East Coast, three per square mile. Also, it had a population of red wolves, which I didn't even know existed in the East. I met up with the refuge manager, Mike Bryant, and the wildlife biologist,

Dennis Stewart. Mike is a fit fifty and wears gray stubble. Dennis is taller, closer to retirement, and has been with the refuge since it was established thirty years ago.

In a conference room at the center I pull out my map of "sea level rise vulnerability" in the Albermarle-Pimlico Estuarine Systems, trying to get oriented, trying to figure out what's going on. Most of the land is red, "severe" vulnerability, according to our key (less than half a meter), with a few moderate splotches (over two meters).

My map represents a "bathtub model," visualizing water at a constant elevation. Right away Stewart points out how the yellow hummock is misleading because it is a peat mound, a mound of decayed vegetation. If sea level started to rise, it would degrade the peat. Peat accretes faster than it decays under normal conditions, but if it becomes saturated with salt water or overly dry and exposed to air, it breaks down and looks like "coffee grounds."

Stewart talks about how the refuge was once a healthy forest of cypress, black gum, and pond pine, or pocosin pine, found all along coastal marshes. But lately tree mortality has risen dramatically due to increased saturation and salinity. Stewart sees what he calls a "wedge of change," where salinity has crept in. It attacks one specific place and fans out from there, attacking species that are not salt tolerant, like the trees. The effects of salinity are particularly bad near some of the ditches, or sloughs. These were often created to make roads. Material was dug out of the system to elevate the road. Now they carry some of the salinity from the rising sea.

The forest is a kind of frontline community. But due to the rising sea, the pines are dying, transitioning to shrub, and they are giving way to marsh. "Where there was forest, there's now marsh." Bryant uses an analogy of placing coins under the table. We may not notice the change; it is subtle, but it is there, and he is hoping to forestall it. "We're not gonna stop sea level rise but want to create some resilience," especially for the creatures who depend on the refuge, like migrating waterfowl. Christine Pickens told me something similar: "We are not going to stop the change, but we might preserve function for as long as possible."

One of the things they are doing at the refuge, in consort with

The Nature Conservancy, is creating oyster reefs off the shore to slow the rate of erosion. The reefs slow the wave energy before it reaches the shoreline. Pickens tells me they measure erosion on the shore both where there is a buffer and where there is none. Erosion is 25 percent less with oyster reefs, and 50 percent slower when they use marl, a lime-rich mud, embedded with oyster shells. Pickens and The Nature Conservancy have also put check valves in some of the sloughs to reduce the amount of salinity brought in during floods.

Some of the traditional fixes to shoreline erosion are to install bulkheads, walls made of rocks or wood to stop erosion. But barrier islands have complicated dynamics. They migrate and move. In a process known as barrier island rollover, some of the sand on the coast rolls over the other side and eventually feeds the marsh. The wind comes in from the west, sometimes bringing sand back. By building up the shore, we are actually hurting the natural process, and North Carolina is losing about three feet of shoreline per year.[4]

The response on the part of some of the beach communities is roads and engineering solutions first, and when Dennis and Mike have advocated for the wildlife or for solutions that work with nature, they are met with resistance. The piping plover? "How does it taste?" said one group. In the politics of the seashore there are the "from heres" and the "come heres," and they are often distrustful of one another. This comment led to a discussion of North Carolina politics.

The North Carolina Coastal Resources Commission, which regulates land use in the state's twenty coastal counties, asked a science panel to assess their vulnerability to sea level rise. The panel reviewed the scientific literature and projected thirty-nine inches of rise before the end of the century. Roads would be underwater. Properties would have to be abandoned or moved. Money, a lot of money, would be needed. A member of the science panel, coastal geologist Stanley Riggs, said the islands will soon resemble a "string of pearls" separated by shoals unable to support a fixed highway.[5] The twenty coastal counties and many realty companies complained. The report was scaring people, especially tourists. So the governor appointed a new commissioner, Frank Gorham, an oil and gas man who announced that the panel must limit their study to a thirty-year projection. The model for sea level rise didn't change, just the timeline. A one hundred–year forecast, said Gorham, lacks credibility. We agreed it was a Scarlett O'Hara moment: "Oh, I can't think about this now! I'll go crazy if I do! I'll think about it tomorrow."

"The main problem they have is fear," Michael Orbach, a marine policy professor at Duke University, told the *Washington Post*—especially fear of damage to the coastal economy. Something is threatening what they hold dear, and the amygdala is activated. But it's an old part of the fear center, one motivated by a different kind of survival, an economic one. This fear is driven by ideology—"motivated reasoning," the social psychologists call it—and facts and evidence have a hard time trumping it. These people lie mostly on the far end of the "six Americas" spectrum, dismissive.

What is very difficult to communicate to such groups is how their self-interest should involve long-term planning. The piping plover is a surrogate species, one of the many in the history of environmentalism—spotted owl, polar bear—that would suggest to some an interest in valuing species over human communities. But they are often a dying canary in a very dangerous coal mine. Working to save the Alligator is working to save a possible source of fish, game, clean air, and clean water. The alligator in that refuge are at the northernmost end of their habitat. A change in temperature, or salinity, could drive them out. They control the population of small mammals, which feed on wetland grasses, which control erosion. Without alligator, less and less Alligator.

Before I left, I wanted to paddle in the refuge. I put my kayak in at Milltail Creek, slipped out into a bigger lake, and then floated into a narrower stream. A slight breeze came up, and I enjoyed the sound of the water lapping against the boat, the wind whisper through the grasses and trees. I heard the twangs of a few bullfrogs and the calls of birds. I spied an osprey, big and graceful, and scanned the shore for bears or wolves. I thought of howling but didn't want to disturb the calm.

I stayed in the middle of the creek, avoiding the floating grasses and the few logs sticking out from shore, although there was really no clear border, no firm shoreline. In a way, no map. I thought a tree branch to my left, brown, wet bark, might have been an alligator, and then another paddle stroke, just as I was chastising myself for letting my imagination play tricks, a boil of tannin-colored water and tail. I saw it. It was only six feet away and maybe that long.

Famously, the earliest of European explorers to encounter the alligator in the New World were so awed by what they saw it summoned hyperbole and inaccurate representations. In his *New Voyage to Carolina* (1709) John Lawson said the alligator "sometimes exceeds seventeen Foot long. It is impossible to kill them with a Gun, unless you chance to hit them about the Eyes." He claimed that "against bad Weather" "they roar, and make a hideous Noise."[7] William Bartram also noted their roar in his "Battle Lagoon" passage of *Travels* (1791). The alligators threw his "senses into such a tumult." After watching them feed on fish, "shocking and tremendous," he found he could barely sleep and was unable to suppress his "fears and apprehensions" of being attacked. One alligator rushed out of the reeds, and "with a tremendous roar came up," darting under his boat "as swift as an arrow," then "belching water and smoke that fell upon me like rain in a hurricane."[8] In both passages the alligator is associated with weather: both, it seems, were difficult to predict or know.

My alligator went underwater without a roar, but my kayak had to pass over the spot it had recently lurked. I didn't expect to see an alligator, but now it was eyes everywhere. I was going to paddle all the way out to the Intracoastal Waterway, a few hours, but I turned around after another thirty minutes. I was hypervigilant, but I didn't see it again, until I did. On the way back a set of eyes on that bridge of the forehead emerged just above the surface, spied me, and then disappeared. Again, I had to cross its water path to get where I was going. He had certainly increased the activity in my adrenal gland and in my reptilian brain. I was ready to fight if it came to that. I had firm grip on my paddle, possible weapon. I also told myself all the things the frontal cortex tells you, the thing that says "It's only a movie" or "It's more afraid of you than you are of it."

At the time I was going over the day's notes in my head and looking for an ending, but "leg gruesomely ripped off by massive reptile" was not it. Neither was "parts of professor's body found floating in lake." But what a rush. Like climate change, the gator is a thing that can't quite be controlled. And when it vanished, I thought of how in matters of climate change, and reptiles, it's that thing you can't see that can kill you. I was ready to engage it if I had to, and if people in the doubtful-dismissive zone felt the direct presence of a climate change threat, they would too. For all our models and projections, to really know what is happening, it may be best to see changes (and make measurements) in the field.

My wife and teenage kids teased me when I got home. "I saw an alligator," I tell them, a fish story hard to believe in the Virginia mountains where we live. "What did you expect?" they say. "You were visiting a refuge called Alligator." Only I didn't expect it. I read that it was a possibility, but some representations lie to us. Some maps do too, or we lack some kind of spatial and temporal understanding to grasp how the models on them really impact us. All the climate change maps and models predict some pretty bad things, so bad that an understandable response is resistance. Back people into a corner, and they want to fight back in some way. The alligator gave me a way out. And then it dove deep down below into the darkness.

Darkness is one way this story could go. Nearby the Alligator is Fort Raleigh on Roanoke Island. It tells the story of the Lost Colony. In May 1587, in the time of Shakespeare, Sir Walter Raleigh sent John White with three ships carrying eighty-nine men, seventeen women, and eleven children to set up a permanent English settlement. Although intending to settle near Chesapeake Bay, the settlers were forced to locate on Roanoke Island in late summer, with little time for planting. Virginia Dare, named for the Virgin Queen, was the first English child born in the New World, but the community had a difficult time. White returned to England for more supplies, but the Spanish Armada tied up shipping. He did not return until August 1590 and found no trace of the colony, only the word *Croatoan*, the name of a local Native American group, carved on a tree. This seemed to indicate the colony had moved to a nearby island called Croatan (now Hatteras), but storms prevented investigation, and White returned to England without ever knowing what had become of his family or the colony. One explanation for what doomed it? Climate change. The archive of tree ring analysis on bald cypress shows that the worst drought in eight hundred years occurred between 1587 and 1589.[9]

Of course the climate is always changing, but the rate of change is accelerating now. Without the resilience to adapt to the changes, like that of the Native American communities at the time, the colony was lost. Our colony could be again now. But there's another way the story can end. Several miles to the east is another National Park Service exhibit, that of the Wright Brothers, who relied on teamwork and an application of the scientific process, along with close observation of what was happening in nature and bird wings, to fly.

Much of the climate change news is dark, so dark it can lead to despair. In dim rooms at conferences I have watched presentation after scientific presentation showing graphical projections of carbon dioxide and temperature and their likely effects. Yet too often the graphs and data and manner in which such presentations proceed fails to speak to something deep within us, something primitive: a need to survive. The alligator can live in that darkness, but we can't. Despair for the dying patient does not lead to rescue.

Navy SEALS are said to undergo a test in which they use SCUBA gear underwater for twenty minutes. Then someone ties a knot in their tubing, activating the fear response. The reptile brain shrieks. The candidate can't breathe. Most give in to their fears and swim toward the surface, but some set goals: untie the knot. The amygdala screams, "Breathe! Get away from the thing trying to kill you!" But others quiet that part of the brain, and they execute. They plan, and then they come up toward the light.

What they are doing in the Alligator is noting the small changes on the ground, the changes that signal bigger ones to come. They are noting those changes and designing strategies, with nature in mind, to reduce the impact of climate change. For most of us there is no direct tangible experience of an ocean that is more acidic or a sea level rise that has yet to occur. For climate change to resonate with people, it must be proximate and present, not only general and global but also micro and immediate. To save the Alligator we will have to engage that part of us we share with the alligator, that protective instinct, and also that very human part of us, language, that allows us to tell stories. Those stories should involve how climate change affects something very near and dear to each of us until they make a chorus of voices, no longer dismissed or ignored. Peepers, relatives of alligators, come out of the dark ground in spring, singing, "The earth is warming up." It is time to get a move on.

NOTES

1. At Lake Winnipesaukee locals have kept records of when the "MS *Mount Washington* can make it to every one of its ports" since 1887. In the 1880s the date was close to May 1. In the 2010s the ports are open closer to April 1. Conservation biologist Richard Primack has also used Thoreau's data to show evidence of climate change on the arrival of spring flowers.
2. Murphy, "Pessimism, Optimism, Human Inertia," discusses the "sufficient catalyst."
3. See "Climate Change in the American Mind."
4. See "Oceanfront Construction Setback Factors."
5. Riggs et al., *Battle for North Carolina's Coast*, 104.
6. Montgomery, "On N.C.'s Outer Banks."
7. Lawson, "From *A New Voyage to Carolina*," 107.
8. Bartram, "From *Travels through North and South Carolina*," 108–9.
9. Stahle et al., "Lost Colony."

BIBLIOGRAPHY

Bartram, William. "From *Travels through North and South Carolina, Georgia, East and West Florida . . . 1791*." In *Reading the Roots: American Nature Writing before Walden*, edited by Michael P. Branch, 184–90. Athens: University of Georgia Press, 2004.

"Climate Change in the American Mind: Americans' Global Warming Beliefs and Attitudes in November 2013." Yale Project on Climate Change Communication. http://environment.yale.edu/ climate-communication /files/Climate-Beliefs-November-2013.pdf.

Lawson, John. "From *A New Voyage to Carolina*." In *Reading the Roots: American Nature Writing before Walden*, edited by Michael P. Branch, 105–9. Athens: University of Georgia Press, 2004.

Marshall, George. *Don't Even Think about It: Why Our Brains Are Wired to Ignore Climate Change*. New York: Bloomsbury, 2014.

Montgomery, Lori. "On N.C.'s Outer Banks, Scary Climate-Change Predictions Prompt a Change of Forecast." *Washington Post*, June 24, 2014.

Accessed July 4, 2016. https://www. washingtonpost.com/business
/economy/ncs-outer-banks-got-a-scary-forecast-about-climate-change-so
/2014/06/24/0042cf96-f6f3–11e3-a3a5–42be35962a52_story.html.

Murphy, Patrick D. "Pessimism, Optimism, Human Inertia, and Anthro-
pogenic Climate Change." *ISLE: Interdisciplinary Studies in Literature and
Environment* 21, no. 1 (2014): 149–63.

"Oceanfront Construction Setback Factors." N.C. Division of Coastal Man-
agement, Policy & Planning Section, 2014. http://portal.ncdenr.org/web
/cm/oceanfront-construction-setback.

Riggs, Stanley R., Dorothea V. Ames, Stephen J. Culver, and David J. Mal-
linson. *The Battle for North Carolina's Coast: Evolutionary History, Present
Crisis, and Vision for the Future.* Chapel Hill: University of North Carolina
Press, 2011.

Rome, Adam. *The Genius of Earth Day: How a 1970 Teach-In Unexpectedly Made
the First Green Generation.* New York: Hill & Wang, 2013.

Stahle, David W., Malcolm K. Cleaveland, Dennis B. Blanton, Matthew D.
Therrell, and David A. Gay. "The Lost Colony and Jamestown Droughts."
Science 280, no. 24 (April 1998): 564–67.

What You Take from the Sea

MARY SWANDER

The helicopter buzzed over my cottage, flying low, the noise so loud that I stopped my work and glanced out the window toward the Atlantic Ocean, the waves, a steady green unwrinkled blanket rolling out to Inishbofin Island, Ireland. The helicopter blades whirled and twirled through the bright blue Connemara sky, droning south toward Omey Island on the other side of the peninsula. I was accustomed to these kinds of flights over my acreage in Iowa in the States. Every summer helicopters churn above my garden, searching (so the common wisdom says) for marijuana plants. Mmm, I thought, they have drug agents in Ireland too.

Yet five minutes later a plane flew over with the word RESCUE painted on its side. Still, I wasn't lulled out of my peaceful morning writing at the dining room table. I was listening for the ring of the phone. The day before I'd ridden out across the strand at low tide on my bicycle to Omey Island. The sand was wet but firm beneath my tires—a clean, fast spin to the tires. I visited the graves of my ancestors in St. Brendan's Cemetery, one stacked on top of another in a small common grave, their remains sinking into the Atlantic Ocean.

I headed back home shortly before the tides were tabled to roll back in, engulfing the strand in water. I hit the dock with a whack, and my rear tire blew. I dragged the bike a mile and a half home. The man from the bicycle shop in Clifden drove out to my cottage near Claddaghduff, picked up the bike, and promised to repair and deliver it again the next morning. I was patiently waiting for him, hoping to take off again in the afternoon on another trip across the strand.

I had come to Ireland to find my mother's family farm—a rocky strip of land on the ocean near Claddaghduff in Patches Township. When I stood on the edge of the farm on the edge of the sea,

I looked right over to St. Brendan's Cemetery on Omey Island. Large Celtic stone crosses rose up above the graves into the gray-green mist. I had come to Ireland for this extended visit because I could feel the pull of the diaspora with the push of late middle age. I had hoped to connect with the cousins who still grazed sheep on the farm, but above all I had come to experience the spirit of the place—the landscape, flora and fauna, the culture and backstory to my own existence.

I had traveled to Ireland several times in the past, had hitchhiked throughout the whole country as a youth, my tattered yellow backpack thrown over my shoulder. I drank Guinness, danced, sang ballads, and had a little fling with a pub owner. But I was ever the visitor, the tourist, the Yank running to catch the next train or the plane back home. Now I wanted to get off the road and sink down into this place, into whatever sentiments and secrets I would find here. I wanted to come face-to-face with the fierce wind, the fierce ties that knit together these interrelated, joyful, grief-ridden families surrounding me, the ghosts of a political and religious past that severed those ties, forcing my grandfather and three siblings to set off for America on the waters of an unbound future.

The sun shone down on the rocks that scattered themselves from the cottage to the sea. A mile of wildness unfolded in front of me, tangles of fuchsia bushes lining the small, black-topped road leading to Rossadilask. From the dining room window I'd watched mink jump out of the fencerow and scurry away over the granite rock, seemingly oblivious to the thorns on the blackberry vines spreading out over the landscape. Little dashes of brown rushes burst forth on the flat, treeless horizon. Gorse was the tallest plant on the vista, a beautiful but treacherous shrub, its yellow flowers just opening, its thorns helping to protect nesting birds—linnets, European stonechats, and Dartford warblers.

The helicopter circled overhead again. Happy, the landlady's border collie, rose from her warm spot near the turf fire and stretched, her powerful hind legs straightening, her nails digging into the red woolen rug. Then the dog ran to the back door and pawed to get out when she spotted Barry, the landlord. Barry stood at the door with a trowel in hand and an armload of bedding flowers for the planters along the south side of the house.

"Two fishermen have gone missing," Barry said. "They're searching for the bodies now."

Barry explained that someone had spotted an empty currach washed up on the rocks on Omey Island. A rescue crew had been called in, and all in Claddaghduff were anxiously awaiting the results, and all in Claddaghduff knew that neither man could have survived. Traditionally, few men in Connemara know how to swim, fewer still wear life jackets. The sea is so wild and rough there that swimming would do little to save your life. It's better to go down fast without struggle, the fishermen reason.

So the wait began. Through lunchtime and on into early afternoon. Even though I did not know the fishermen, I could imagine the head count in the village, the determination of the names of the missing, the slow flash of denial through the minds of their loved ones, then the yearning, the desperate hoping that somehow, somehow, their men would still be found alive. Out the window the sea was still placid. Not a wave, not a spray of foam threatened the view. Shortly after one o'clock, the owner of the bicycle shop called.

"My son won't be able to fix your bicycle right now," Mrs. Mannion said. "It may be a few days yet." She explained that her son doubled as both the local bicycle repairman and the undertaker. The bike would have to wait.

Around three o'clock Geraldine, the landlady, stopped by. "They've found one body, and they are still searching for the other," she said. She hoped that they would indeed find the second body. "It's so hard for the family," Geraldine said, "when they have no remains."

For the next two hours the helicopter and the airplane made continual passes over the house. Cars sped by on the road. I thought of J. M. Synge's play *The Riders to the Sea*. In the opening of the drama two sisters examine a bundle of clothes that had been taken off a drowned man who'd washed ashore in Donegal. The priest had asked them to determine if they belonged to their missing brother, Michael. The sisters don't want their mother to see the clothes for fear grief will completely overwhelm her. Maurya, the mother, has lost her husband, father-in-law, and four sons to the sea, some of them found and some of them not. The sisters hide the bundle in the turf loft.

At five o'clock the noise from the helicopter and the airplane stopped. Geraldine swept by the house again.

"They've found the other body," she said. "They're taking them both to Galway now for autopsies. 'Tis a real tragedy. One drowned fisherman has already lost a brother. The other fisherman has lost three brothers to the sea."

In Riders to the Sea Maurya leaves the house to bring Bartley, her remaining son, a bit of bread. But she soon returns, having seen an apparition of not only her dead son, Michael, but of Bartley. Bartley, too, has drowned. A gray pony knocked him into the sea. With all her men gone, Maurya tells her daughter to call in the coffin maker as she will surely not have long to live. *They're all gone now, and there isn't anything more the sea can do to me.* Then Maurya begins to keen for all her losses and the losses before them. *No man at all can be living forever, and we must be satisfied,* she finally concludes.

The houses of the drowned Claddaghduff men were just behind my cottage. I imagined their wives, having identified the bodies, walking slowly back from the pier. Yes, those were their clothes. Yes, those were their men, the fathers of their children. The women stood on the edge of the ocean, on the westernmost tip of Europe, and watched their loved ones loaded into the helicopter to make the trip to Galway City. Pulled from the depths of the sea, their bodies were now lifted up, up, up, into the sky. I heard the prayers, the cries of lamentation they must have uttered to each other on their sad shuffle home. And just when they wanted to sink their heads into their hands at their kitchen tables, their children gathered around them, presences who do not allow a parent the luxury of collapse. *No man at all can be living forever, and we must be satisfied.*

That night Sweeney's Pub was filled with men from the village. The tables by windows were full of fishermen, drinking draws of Guinness and quietly staring out at the sea. The stools circling the bar were filled with men pretending to watch the soccer game on the large flat-screened TV. The booths in the back of the room were filled with men pretending to watch a game show from a second television hanging down from the ceiling. At nine o'clock the bartender turned both televisions to the news.

"I don't want to watch the news tonight," a man in a booth said. He stood up and walked out of the pub.

The rest of the men watched the broadcast, the announcer piecing together the little bits of information that were then known. The fishermen had left Aughrus Point in a currach sometime in the early morning to check their lobster traps. By all reports the sea was calm. Then around eleven o'clock someone sighted their boat hung up on the shore of "Omney Island." The announcer mispronounced the word, and the whole room groaned. After an extensive search, both bodies were found. The men were neighbors, not father and son.

But what took the two men down? No one knew. They could only guess. Perhaps a swell came up and blew the currach into the rocks. Perhaps the currach flipped over. When you check lobster pots, one man must stand in the currach and pull up the ropes. The other has the tricky task of keeping the boat from tipping. It's not a job for the inexperienced, and the younger man was inexperienced. But surely the older man. *Surely, surely.* At least they weren't father and son.

"If a father and son are in a boat in this bay," my neighbor Hugh told me, "one won't save the other. Remember, neither can swim, so if one jumped in after the other, they would both drown. And they think it's better to have at least one breadwinner in a family. And the people here have a very superstitious relationship to the sea. If you go overboard, they won't pull you out, even if you aren't related. They're fearful of the sea coming back after you. They have a saying: *An Ze a Caileas an Farrize Geoblas.* That translates literally to "A person that the sea loses it will take," or more fluently, "What you take from the sea, the sea takes from you."

During the next couple of days the stories grew and changed about what the sea had taken from Claddaghduff. The older man was fifty-eight and hadn't been in a currach for a long time. The other man was forty-nine and was an expert fisherman, at it all his life. The older man had three young children, the baby just six months old. The younger man had one child, a newborn, just three weeks old. The men were on their way down to Galway Bay, where they had lobster pots. The men were tending their lobster pots right there off of Aughrus Point. They hadn't gone far when they died.

The only thing for certain was the pronunciation of *Omey Island*. The newscaster corrected himself on a later broadcast.

"Altogether, the two drowned men left seven children in this school," the elementary school principal told me. "That is for certain. And all the other children, of course, are cousins and relatives. One day they are doing really good, then the next, they slump down in the desks."

On the bulletin board in the school, just inside the main door, the principal had handwritten a sign in big, bold, black letters: SWIMMING LESSONS BEGIN APRIL 30.

The preparations for the funeral began in Claddaghduff on April 24. First, the fishermen's currach was burned. No one would use a boat that had caused the death of others. A currach is a traditional Irish canoe, fashioned from an intricately designed wooden slatted frame. In the past animal skins were stretched over the slats, but now canvas is used as a covering. Once the canvas is in place, the whole boat is waterproofed with several layers of tar. The currach design uses little precious wood in this treeless landscape and has a long seafaring history. Julius Caesar first mentioned it in writing, reporting having seen currachs roving the North Atlantic. Saint Columba is said to have used a currach, and in the sixth century Saint Brendan may have made the first transatlantic voyage to the Americas in a currach.

Currachs are tipsy. In *Riders to the Sea* Maurya remembers one of her lost sons: *There was Patch after he was drowned out of a curagh that turned over.* But the small, light currach was said to navigate the rough seas better than a larger vessel. And in a poverty-stricken land where well into the twentieth century the roads were cow paths, a small, handmade boat was often the best option for transportation.

The news of the autopsies drifted onto the Claddaghduff shore. One man was drowned outright; the other had a blow to his head that had knocked him unconscious before he drowned. Their bodies were embalmed, then taken back to their homes—just yards from each other—for the wakes. Thirty men went to St. Brendan's Cemetery on Omey Island and dug two graves—one for the older man in the older part of the cemetery, the other for the younger man in the new addition to the plot—their spades cutting down into the sandy soil, sinking down into the earth until they hit another coffin.

Early Thursday evening I watched people stream in and out of the dead men's houses for the wake. The visitors, dressed in black, often carried sympathy cards or dishes of food. I knew the scene well from all the wakes I'd attended of my mother's relatives. First, before the body and the visitors arrived, there was a mad effort to clean up the house. The women in the family yanked themselves out of their grief to find dustrags and brooms. They tied the rags around the end of the brooms and knocked cobwebs from the ceiling with fierce, sweeping motions of their arms. They scrubbed down the bathroom, then gathered together every bit of clutter—newspapers, magazines, mail—and threw it all into a big box in the closet.

Surfaces were dusted and the rags stuffed back into a drawer just in time for the hearse to pull into the drive. Car doors swung open, slammed shut. The mouths of men emitted short, breathy groans, their biceps straining, carrying the casket up the front steps. Furniture was rearranged—the sofa shoved to the far end of the room—to accommodate the casket. Clean, dressier clothes were pulled from the closet, good shoes wiped of dust, combs run through hair. The next-door neighbors were the first to arrive with biscuits and cakes. They headed to the kitchen, the women orchestrating the refreshments, brewing tea, arranging cups, saucers, napkins, and silverware. Men began to pool outside on the front steps, here and there a bottle of stout in hand. More visitors streamed up the walk, heading straight into the living room. *I'm sorry. I'm very sorry.* They took the hands of the widow. Then turned to the deceased, rosary beads wound through his hands. They stared down at the fisherman—brother, cousin, friend, neighbor—uttering a prayer. *Lord have mercy. Christ have mercy.*

More and more mourners poured through the door. They moved back and forth between the two houses, paying their respects first to one family, then other. The houses filled with dark clothes, with sobs and handkerchiefs. The houses filled with sandwiches half-eaten on plates, with chatting, one villager engaging another. The houses filled with the rattling of teacups, with the thread of a story, a story about the deceased, a happy memory whose telling moved from neighbor to neighbor, each contributing part of the plot. The noise in the room swelled, then burst into laughter, laughter that shattered the air that held a faint smell of formaldehyde.

The next morning the early air was damp and misty. I opened the front door of the cottage, and my bicycle rested against the stoop, the tire fixed. Through the lens of a pair of binoculars, I could see waves lapping at the Inishbofin Island shoreline, spraying bits of foam into the air. The early ferry sped across the water toward Cleggan harbor and the Pier Bar, where several smaller craft were docked, their red bows bobbing in the water. Several dozen lobster pots were stacked high on the pier, blue marine lines woven through the wire mesh. Eventually, each one would be let down by rope into the water to settle on the ocean floor.

Around eleven o'clock Happy plopped down on the floor beside me. The sun came out, and the day turned bright and clear, the sky cloudless and blue. We sat at the dining room table again and watched the traffic on the road. First, one vanload of people, then another, a car filled with five or six family members, then the first hearse. Then the second sped by. The funeral was scheduled for noon, when the sea was at low tide, the water receded enough to open the strand to Omey Island.

Just before noon Happy and I hiked up the hill to Claddaghduff. From the stone wall overlooking the ocean, I glanced down at the Catholic church just on the edge of the sea. My family had donated the land and helped build Our Lady Star of the Sea, and now families from all over the country of Ireland were pressing inside. Two rows of well-worn pews flanked either side of the nave, with the altar taking center stage in the chancel. With trees scarce in this part of Connemara, the pews and the curved ceiling beams were carved of driftwood. The sun poured through the stained-glass windows recessed into the walls, illuminating simple, bold likenesses of Saint Patrick and Saint Brigid.

Five priests awaited the caskets that were being carried the short block from their homes. And over five hundred people, unable to squeeze inside, milled around the churchyard of Our Lady Star of the Sea. They stood there waiting to hear the funeral mass through the opened windows and doors. Fathers and sons, mothers and daughters, husbands and wives—some were dressed in suits and ties, others in jeans, most in sport coats, both the men and women in slacks.

It was the biggest funeral ever in Connemara, the villagers told me, but the numbers were a bit of a misrepresentation. Many Dubliners had read Feichin Mulkerrin's obituary, then jumped in their cars, driving to Claddaghduff for the funeral. The Dubliners had no idea that the village boasts at least three Feichin Mulkerrins. The Dubliners were shocked when they gazed into the church and found their Feichin alive and well, sitting in one of the pews.

Whether in attendance for the proper Feichin or not, the mourners all remained in place for the funeral, which lasted nearly an hour and a half. At 1:15 p.m. about thirty people seeped off of Omey Island, slowly edging their way across the strand toward the church. At 1:30 the pallbearers carried the caskets out of the church and into the two black hearses. The immediate families of about fifty people followed behind, winding their way down the narrow pathway toward the strand, open and clear of water for several miles in each direction. Hundreds of people followed the families, most on foot, some in cars and motorbikes. The sky had turned aqua, with big foamy cumulus clouds hanging on the horizon. The sea splashed at the edges of the strand, a reminder of its presence, its ever-changing nature, its power to engulf.

Then the funeral procession moved out through the parted sea, a procession emblematic of processions that have been repeating themselves here in this place for centuries, processions that carried the bodies of the young and the old, of those who had come home prepared to die, of those who had called this home all their lives but had been unprepared. I keep the obituary of my great-grandmother Mary King Lynch in a shoebox on a shelf in my home in Iowa. Born into the Great Famine, she lived to old age here on this peninsula. The funeral mass was said in Our Lady Star of the Sea, the newspaper clipping said, then the body was carried across the strand to the family plot on historic Omey Island. Now I was watching a re-creation of my great-grandmother's funeral and all the family funerals that had embarked for over a century from Our Lady Star of the Sea Church.

The black hearses moved across the strand, slowly, inching forward, their outlines tapered and curved as if they were beached whales, as if they were the very boulders on the sand, on the bottom of the sea. The Omey Island inhabitants—just a couple of people—met the procession and fell into line behind them. Soon the procession stretched the length of the strand, at least a mile and half, the mourners little black dots against the white sand. Inside the hearses the caskets were covered with flowers—roses and carnations—the one splash of color in the black-and-white scene.

One stride, then another, the families took direct, steady steps, all staying in sync, leading the other mourners in a rhythmic slow march, a silent meditation on the lives of their loved ones, of the dangers of the sea that has provided an unreliable but necessary income, a sure but perilous means of transportation, a magnificent but wild backdrop to their existence. What is it like to live with the history of so many accidents, so many loved ones lost to the sea? How does that constant anxiety become internalized? Passed on from mother to daughter, father to son? Will these families ever reach the quick acceptance of a Maurya from *The Riders to the Sea*? In her final speech in the play she states simply: *Michael has a clean burial in the far north, by the grace of the Almighty God. Bartley will have a fine coffin out of the white boards, and a deep grave surely.*

No one will ever know the cause of these deaths. But all who live in this western tip of Ireland know the anxiety of trying to eke out a living on this landscape of rocks, bogs, and sea. All know the stark beauty of this place but also the shadowy undertow. The word *Claddaghduff*, after all, means "dark shore." All know that fate may sweep through a family not once, not twice, but four different times. How does one live in opposition to such a threat? How does one engage in life with hope in the face of such peril? How many centuries have these people, my people, walked across this strand carrying this burden in a box?

The procession trailed up the hillside into the newer part of St. Brendan's Cemetery. They let the ropes of the younger fisherman's coffin down into the shallow grave, the priest reciting the burial rite, the mourners, buoys, around the grave. The male relatives of the fisherman each took a turn with the shovel, dropping chunks of dirt onto the casket, one scoop and then another. *Ker-plunk.* After the relatives the fisherman's neighbors took up the tasks. *Ker-plunk.* And after the neighbors, friends. When the grave was filled over with dirt, chunks of sod were placed over the four-foot-high mound. Bouquets of flowers were laid on top of the sod, then a fishing net was cast over the whole burial site, holding down the flowers and sod from the fierce wind.

Slowly the procession moved to the older part of St. Brendan, past the O'Toole plot, with the tiny replica of a currach and lobster traps encased in plexiglass, to a family plot very near our family's gravesite. This part of St Brendan's was marked with family names. Lacy, Feeney, Lynch. Here the older fisherman was buried near his mother and brother. *Ker-plunk.* The priest's prayers rose into the air, the mourners murmuring the responses. The dirt filled the hole. The sod covered the casket. The flowers covered the sod. And the net, the net trapped all.

The crowd made their way back across the strand—the empty hearses followed by the bereaved families. Cars and motorbikes zigzagged around the procession to reach the mainland ahead of those on foot. And when the last had come ashore, the families returned to their houses, the visitors to their cars, and the villagers to the pub. Slowly the tide began to rise, lapping at the edge of the strand then little by little making a gradual slide over the strip of land, the thin filament that anchored one island to another. The sky held onto its blue radiance, and the sea rose higher, matching the hue. On the horizon sky and sea became one, St. Brendan's Cemetery adrift in the Atlantic Ocean. The water rose even higher, the strand completely covered, and Omey Island was an island again.

Recontinentalizing Europe

Terrestrial Conversion and Symbolic Exchanges at Europe's Mediterranean Frontier

EMILIO COCCO

"The sea has disappeared into our heads," although the greatest share of international trade depends on thousands of giant cargo ships crossing the ocean every day and tons of minerals being extracted from the depth of the high sea bed for energy supply.[1] Over 10 percent of the world's population lives on islands, and 60 percent of the world's population lives along or near the coast.[2] The oceans are vast, and most of them fall outside state control: these are "Marine Areas beyond National Jurisdiction" (ABNJ) for which no one nation has sole responsibility for management. The "common oceans" make up 40 percent of the surface of our planet, comprising 64 percent of the surface of the oceans and nearly 95 percent of its volume. In contrast, about 80 percent of all marine pollution originates on land and not necessarily only from coastal states.

As a result of these facts, a growing number of people are directly affected by the use and abuse of the ocean's resources, but only a small percentage of the world's population has a direct experience of the ocean's materiality.[3] It is not surprising, then, that even social science experiences a sort of terrestrial bias, despite a number of theorists recently warning us that "[we] should be thinking with water—including oceans."[4] In a recent contribution on the theoretical implications of maritime sociology,[5] I also claimed that such a terrestrial bias has a deep effect on paradigms and disciplinary trends. Particularly, one could match such a terrestrial bias with the long-standing influence of methodological nationalism (to be, maybe, renamed "terrestrialism") and of a state-centered understanding of society.[6] Eventually, a land-borne orientation tends to locate oceans, seas, and any mass of water at the intersection of both political spaces and academic specializa-tions.[7] The result: a de facto marginalization of the ocean both in public and scientific debates.

Interestingly, Adrian Favell, commenting on recent trends in global sociology, reached similar conclusions through somewhat dif-ferent considerations.[8] Favell discussed Nikos Papastergiadis's work on migration and his central organizing metaphor of "turbulence," which contrasts grounded social structures to the fluidity of trans-border dynamics. Papastergiadis, according to Favell, thinks that tra-ditional sociology has been trapped within a nation-state-centered framework of discrete societies that misleadingly pictures a world of stable and bounded national cultures able to reproduce their social structures endogenously. However, there is still little knowl-edge about the impact of turbulent social dynamics, transnational and global in their nature, on the basically sedentary structures of the vast majority of the world's population who do not migrate and who do not live transnational lives. In the same way, the ocean—the primary *medium* of a globalized society—does not hold a prominent position within contemporary social science in spite of a renewed interest among some North American scientists who established a new scholarship of "thalassology," or sea studies.[9]

Thus, in spite of a general and visible neglect, the new thalasso-logical trends have provided fresh and inspiring perspectives for the analysis of territory, environment, and space. Particularly, they engender interdisciplinary approaches that combine micro-macro dimensions and cut through established divides between ethnicity, culture, biology, and economics. Back in 1989, Frank Boeze, investi-gating humanity's relations to the sea, pointed at the cross-sectorial and multifold nature of such relationships, which he broke down into separate categories, including the use of the sea for natural resources, for transporting goods and people, for power projection, for scientific explorations, for leisure, and for cultural inspiration.[10]

More recently, Stefan Helmreich approached the matter from an anthropological perspective on the work of marine biologists and provided an original insight into the constellation of nature, culture, and seawater.[11] To Helmreich seawater is not just a symbol (as it often is in anthropological theory) but also works as a theory machine because water in nature "moves faster than in culture" and needs to be channeled and exploited for human purposes. That is to say, water needs to be "landed" and used for cultivation, both in material forms of agriculture and symbolic aspects of culture. Thus, flexibility and mutability in nature bring about the same features in the cultural field, providing a common ground for meaning constructions. As a result, what we call globalization could also be approached in terms of "oceanization," although such a fluid ontology quite often reflects a culturally specific vision: a representation of an unbounded wild ocean to be closed in cultural forms, which eventually reminds us of colonial projects of keeping the high seas "free," outside sovereign territorializations.

As a matter of fact, Western constructions of the "nature" of the sea as "fluid" and "protean," or as "another world . . . without human culture," in contrast to the grounded "culture" of land, are not universal.[12] On the contrary, how that "space" is imagined is relational, and what matters most in Helmreich's perspective is that in a "global" imagination of the ocean, which poses oceans as units of cultural analysis, the sea operates as a theory machine for re-narrating sociality. Eventually, such accounts do not separate meaning and materiality because this division would only bring us back to the old nature/culture distinction. Conversely, seaborne narratives could help the establishment of relational and material perspective on newer representations of space in a global context. Given these observations, I propose moving beyond the "terrestrial bias" and developing a maritime reading of continental macrospace, using a 2009 essay titled "Recontinentalizing Canada: Arctic Ice's Liquid Modernity and the Imagining of a Canadian Archipelago" as my foundation.[13] The article is quite thought provoking and particularly salutary for my aims: I intend to concentrate on the representations of the European continent and the European Union from their southeastern maritime frontiers. Also, I wish to spotlight the concepts of borders and mobility from a maritime perspective.

The authors of "Recontinentalizing Canada" focus on mobile actor networks of moving people, images, and discourses in changing time-space frameworks as a way to understand relatively neglected dynamics of mobility from a "material-relational" perspective. In other words, they think that the glacial shifts induced by the Arctic ice melting are not merely natural phenomena that provide the physical background for social dynamics. Rather, from their relational-material perspective the movements in landscape are deeply connected and dependent on human mobility, to the point that the two aspects should not be thought of as separate processes. In fact, social and material transformations in the Arctic articulate a unique process of recontinentalization that de-emphasizes the land and highlights the marine dimension of space. From this standpoint to look at the changing land-ice-ocean mass would mean to reconceptualize boundaries and meanings of the Canadian continental macrospace, assuming that materiality, temporality, and sociality produce themselves together.[14] So, to re-territorialize Canada is also an intellectual endeavor to leave the dominant terrestrial representations that shelve the aquatic element and move toward a progressive consolidation of a new seaborne Canadian identity, which is more deeply connected with a large and growing coastal and insular gravitational center

Thus, following the thalassological suggestions of the article, we need to change perspective to work out alternative, post-terrestrial macrospatial ideas about Europe's identity and its continental representations—especially in a time when social science struggles to critically revise the grip of powerful spatially frozen metaphors such as "fortress," "prison," "cage." Interestingly enough, what is central to this metaphor, in which "the sea is absent from our minds," are the concepts of borders and frontiers. Over the last decades an extensive body of scholarship has started to treat borders and frontiers as specific social phenomena to be studied and understood according to appropriate frameworks and methodologies.[15] Actually, *borders, frontiers,* and *boundaries* are the most typical words used to describe something to be represented spatially by lines. The same types of words can be found in many European languages, and in most cases they tend to be interchangeable. What is common to all of these terms is that they usually describe a line that possesses an outer orientation that is closed and fixed but that sometimes tends to be "permeable" and "moving."[16]

Lefteris Topalogou reminds us, however, that another current perspective studies borders through a dialectic relationship between a totally "fixed border line" on the one side and that of the "vague border" on the other.[17] In Eastern European languages, for instance, there are words that defy geographical linearity and fixity of borderness and refer to a different semantic, whereby borders are represented more as place-based and socially shaped institutions.[18] Terms such as the Polish *kresy* describe a limitrophic, open, and dynamic "open frontier" region; or the same word, *ukraina*, which expresses an open-ended "contact area," "edge," or "corner." Both are quite different things from the stable territorial division denoted by the word *granica*.[19] Given this linguistic data, in an attempt to examine the future of the European Union's borders, Jan Zielonka suggests two potential models: the "Neo-Westphalia Super State" and the "Neo-Medieval Empire."[20] In the first case borders are strictly defined, and they outline a homogeneous socioeconomic and cultural reality by exhibiting a hierarchical and unitary authoritarian system. In the second case, however, borders are unstable and engulf various cultural models as well as coexisting socioeconomic models in which the regions and the various networks play a major role at a local level. According to this perspective, the strict definition of a borderline in space loses much of its traditional symbolism.[21]

Over the last decades an extensive body of scholarship has started to treat borders and frontiers as specific social phenomena to be studied and understood according to appropriate frameworks and methodologies.[22] Specifically, in the last decade of the last century, border studies have focused on a number of strategic issues such as the natural versus artificial nature of boundaries, the impact of borders on individual and collective identities, and more importantly for us here, the interplay between spatial and social dimensions of reality. Accordingly, some authors openly argue that borders are neither just social institutions nor the simple geographical expression of political systems. On the contrary, they represent elements of an everyday procedure that lies deeply embedded within society.

For instance, Sarah Green evokes the suggestive metaphor of "tide-mark" to grasp the complexity of border-ness because "tidemark combines space and historical time, and envisages both space and time as being lively and contingent. Borderli-ness in that sense concerns *where* things have got to so far, in the multiple, unpredictable, power-inflected, imagined and visceral way that everyday life tends to occur."[23] Reflecting on these perspectives, I believe that border studies provide an added value to push social science beyond ethnocentric schemes and methodological nationalism, toward a perspective that could bring together social and material exchanges between the sea and the land.[24]

EXCHANGES AND CONVERSIONS
BETWEEN THE SEA AND THE LAND

An inclusive look at borders cannot but embrace the wider set of social relations that allows their social construction: borders are plural and relational concepts that change in the temporal, material, and social dimensions.[25] Therefore, it should look quite inappropriate to reify the concept of border into a frozen structure (i.e., "Fortress" Europe) and label it as the social expression "a line drawn on the land."[26] At the same time, it is probably not enough to provide a postmodern picture of the border as the sum of individual psychologies and personal accounts that create a constellation of points and trajectories in an empty, smooth space.[27] I think that such a dilemma is the result of an oversimplification, which is strictly depending on the "disappearance of the sea into our heads." In other words, the cognitive lack of a liquid dimension in the understanding of social processes affects the understanding of the nature of borders.[28] As a result, borders inevitably become either a matter of soil partition or the potentially never-ending expression of cultural distinctions without any material reference. Conversely, I suggest that to rethink borders from an ocean-borne perspective on the global society in which they work would enable exchanges and conversions between the land and the sea, both at real and imaginary levels.

As a matter of fact, sometimes people, things, objects, places, or beliefs travel across borders and are exchanged, dislocated, and relocated. In other cases the borders can affect movement—stopping, delaying, diverting, or hastening. Finally, the same borders can move, and such movements make things domestic or alien to the people who remain there, watching borders moving above their heads many times during a single life span. However, in spite of all the mobility involved, what really makes the difference is the point of view of territorial states that require borders to be "sacred cows": fixed, untouchable, and, possibly, perennial.[29] The first and most important reason is that states claim to be the only organizations that can couple cultural identity and territorial borders, by acquiring what G. Simmel defined as a sort of spatial exclusivity (*Ausschließlichkeit des Raumes*).[30] This is the reason why nation-states historically emerge as specific social organizations that can communicate mutually exclusive identity through the *medium* of territoriality. Accordingly, it is politically impossible to have two sovereign nation-states acting over the same territory because the latter should belong exclusively to either one or the other.

Even cities or regions with a recognized multinational or multiconfessional identity have to fit within a single political-administrative framework and, often, become part of single national imaginaries and cultural heritages. For instance, the rich and diverse cultural heritage of Mediterranean port cities, where several religious and ethnic communities coexisted for centuries, becomes the exclusive legacy of a single nation-state that reduces "diversities" to "minorities." As a result, the alignment of a complex set of memories with dominant value positions marginalizes or dismisses minority groups and subordinates narratives.[31] Thus, in cases where identities are contested and spatial references are overlapping, the role of borders is precisely to separate and clarify different realms of political and cultural homogeneity, to the point that even geographically defined areas such as islands sometimes undergo processes of political partition among different nation-states. One can think of the controversial history of islands such as Ireland or Cyprus but also at the political partition of traditionally united regions such as Tyrol (Italy-Austria), Istria (Croatia, Slovenia, and Italy) or Macedonia (Greece and the former Yugoslav republic of Macedonia). Finally, a similar experience is common to "divided" cities such as Berlin, Rome, Jerusalem, or Sarajevo.

In maritime border regions such as the southeastern Mediterranean, the border-making process usually fuels a spatial tension between the dimension of national identity, involving ethnocultural contents, and the one of state identity, involving territorial and institutional elements, that are rarely coincident in areas where the nation-state is a latecomer. Moreover, the Mediterranean Sea has been socially constructed with an ambivalent status.[32] On one hand, as Steinberg remarks, Mediterranean peoples historically constructed the sea "as a non-possessible space, but one in which and across which state power legitimately could be asserted in the interest of stewarding its bounty."[33] On the other hand, nation-state-building processes have been radically "terrestrializing" (with land-based infrastructures) a multicultural environment that was deeply rooted into a sea-oriented social world. This Mediterranean maritime world is well described by F. Braudel, who points out the interlocking role of Mediterranean coastal cities, otherwise named "mirror" cities, thriving on the movement of people and freight. In this picture the Mediterranean appears as a moving space produced by the interpenetration of sea-bound and land-bound opposite but concurrent trends.

Those port cities were veritable hubs fed by the activity of mobile and cosmopolitan communities of maritime-oriented people. Jews, Armenians, or Greeks, among others, represented intense social networks that circulated ideas and practices.[34] Thus, their economic and social performance had the effect of binding together social strata and geographical sites that were quite separated and were not necessarily part of the same diaspora.[35] The involvement of diasporas in some specific sectors of trade, administration, finance, and craft eventually strengthened the connections between nobility, traders, peasants, and bureaucrats. In other words, their role of mediation enhanced the creation of a functionally connected regional space and at the same time introduced some degree of heterarchy. Certainly, all European diasporas developed autonomous cultural subjectivity as they were simultaneously experiencing the interdependence of wide trans-European connections. However, those networks and connections progressively disappeared, and Mediterranean port cities are now firmly tied to bounded land and national cultures.

In other words, following nation-state-building processes, the Mediterranean cities lost their role of transcultural maritime hubs and were progressively nationalized. They are now connected with railways and highways to their national inland, their seaborne financial and cultural capitals moved to continental capital cities. The best example is probably the city of Venice, which symbolically lost its insular identity and maritime inclination once it was connected with a bridge to the peninsular inland (a bridge ironically named "liberty bridge"). So, what used to be a maritime power with a strong archipelagic identity, stretching toward the Eastern Mediterranean, has become a tourist hotspot and an administrative center of a continental region (Veneto). Venice, in many ways turned its head away from the sea, which now mostly remains as a place of memory for tourist consumption and leisure activities. Accordingly, looking at the map, all the capital cities of the Adriatic Sea states are far away from the sea. The prominent cities of what used to be the "Gulf of Venice," such as Venice itself, Trieste, and Dubrovnik, are now coastal peripheries of national states well settled inland. As a result, an important portion of the Mediterranean space such as the Adriatic region is progressively fractured and partitioned into sovereign spaces of land-oriented continental states, which convert the national space into a fluid environment and enable the emergence of ethnic islands, enclaves or archipelagos surrounded by the "liquid land" of the national culture.[36] The latter makes the horizontal space of the nation, which, in spite of all possible internal plurality, is made homogeneous by a shared ethnocultural affiliation that shapes memory and belonging. Who does not fit this space remains isolated—insulated—like ethnic or religious minorities who are confined to real or symbolic enclaves, ghettos, or camps.

Thanks to this peculiar "sea-land conversion," a maritime semantic (rising tides, migration waves, minority submersions, ethnic dispersions, and so on) become popular to describe ethnic relations within and among terrestrial nation-states.[37] These semantic turns were popular at the time of the population exchanges after the First and Second World Wars, when millions of people were displaced to their "new homeland." They are now back in currency because new international migration flows are massively reaching European shores from Africa and Asia. At the same time, the old Mediterranean cultural affiliations and social networks are deconstructed, partitioned, and reshaped according to the "solid" nation-state codes of territoriality.[38] The people of the sea, like mariners, fishermen, and seafarers, do not fit very well in the picture of a "converted" Mediterranean where social relations (identity, citizenship, belonging, e.g.) have to take place only at shore and according to the law of the land. In this framework the sea makes sense only as an extension of state territory, and the law of the sea (i.e., rescuing and landing people in danger) can conflict with the one of the land (i.e., facilitating illegal migration).

I personally consider this sea-land conversion, which shapes the Mediterranean space in terms of "liquid lands and solid seas," as a global trend, and it is quite well illustrated by the changing role of islands in the last centuries.[39] Islands, which were the symbols and means of communication both in ancient times and in the process of European commercial and political expansion, became gradually a metaphor of exile, isolation, and hospitalization.[40] As Godfrey Baldacchino quite effectively claims, in the early modern period islands served as prototypes of idealized polities (utopias), near perfect spaces (with perfect borders!) where an equally near perfect configuration of state and nation could survive and prosper. But later in the modern era islands have been projected as special places where rules of the parent state need not completely apply: whether as export-processing zones, offshore finance centers, detention camps, or nature reserves, islands started to manifest the flexibility and creative governance of states.[41] In this perspective the islands between Europe and Africa, literally located in the middle of the sea, such as Malta and Lampedusa, are privileged sites of "creative" bordering processes. These islands set the stage for both temporary and permanent conditions (i.e., temporary detention and undefined citizenship status) of border crossers and border structures, which shape the frontier-scape. In the islands the maritime frontier can be solidified and turned into land—like area (terrestrified) to be better "managed" by the territorial national states or by other political authorities firmly anchored to the ground. Accordingly, the Mediterranean frontier becomes a place where the relationship between land and sea, that is to say, between a sovereign space and an extraterritorial place, reveals the bio-political contradictions of modern citizenship and the difficult relationship between freedom, human rights, and surveillance. These problems spur a number of interesting research questions that begin to be challenged by fieldwork and research actions, such as the one conducted by Elena Ricci. Ricci applies the theory of sea-land conversion to understand the emergence of a Mediterranean frontier and the social construction of the maritime border between Malta, Italy, and Tunisia.[42] From this standpoint the phenomenon of the "frontier" in the Mediterranean is read as an "emergency," and the meaning of *emergency* here is twofold, as the same etymological lemma says. On one hand, *emergency* (from the Latin verb *emerge*) means to "come to the surface of the water," and on the other one, *emergency* is a "critical situation of grave danger [state of emergency], circumstances, unexpected difficulties."

THE RELATIONAL-MATERIAL CONTEXT OF SEA-LAND MOBILITY AND THE EUROPEAN MACROSPACE

To investigate the dynamics of exchanges and conversions at the southeastern European maritime frontier means to shed light on an emerging macrospatial representation of the European continent. Such representation, I believe, is deeply framed within a larger relational-material context of sea-land mobility. Pamela Ballinger argues that scholars examining efforts to "make a society legible" (to borrow James Scott's phrasing) through the use of technical instruments, such as censuses and maps designed to measure and consolidate clear-cut categorizations of identity, usually focus on top-down directives.[43] Moreover, such instruments are aimed at binding identities with lands in exclusivist ways, reproducing the nation-states' codes of territoriality and leaving the wilderness of the free sea out of the picture.

On the contrary, to overcome the limitations of methodological nationalism and to go beyond a terrestrial bias requires a specific attention to the oceanic imagination. In other words, to treat seawater as a theory machine requires social scientists to focus on the "mobile relations" between sociality and materiality that reciprocally co-constitute each other in time. Consequently, borders between the sea and the land do not fit linear and stable cartographic representations but ought to be reinterpreted as peculiar sites of social and material exchanges that enable cultural transformations. Accordingly, the Mediterranean Sea would neither be understandable only in terms of bridge and connectivity nor simply represented as a littoral periphery of the European landmass.[44] Thus, approaching Europe from the maritime perspective, that is to say from its Mediterranean frontier, responds to two inseparable objectives: one is to "recontinentalize" Europe from its changing social-material edges, while the second is to reconnect the Mediterranean seawater with a macrospatial European representation in which the sea is mostly absent. This approach could eventually engender some productive research actions that explore the wider social implications of a macrospatial representation of Europe.

For this purpose I suggest that scholars should concentrate future research on the analysis of material and imaginary "territorial conversions" of watery spaces at the edge of the European landmass. These conversions are part of ongoing border-making processes that constantly shape the nature of the continent by dislocations and relocations of people, objects, symbols, memories, and so on. Additionally, these conversions are bidirectional as they are enabled by symbolic exchanges between the sea and the land, which on the one hand territorialize the sea and on the other "liquefy" land-borne social structures through maritime semantics. For instance, national cultures are bound by political-administrative pools and thrive on metaphors of submersion, emergence, waves, flows, islands, routes, trajectories, and channels. As a result of sea-land interplay, the European nationally homogenized cultures perform the role of liquid *medium* in a bounded, pool-like territory. So symbolic exchanges and processes of conversion between the maritime and terrestrial spaces have been largely shaping the way nation-states are imagined and materially constructed at Europe's Mediterranean edge. However, a nationally and terrestrially biased approach could never provide a viable macrospatial representation of the European continent as seen from this mobile frontier.

On the contrary, it requires an analysis of the relational and morphogenetic dimensions of the border-making process at the Southern European seashore, its insular and maritime spheres, through the investigation of ongoing dynamics of dislocations, exchanges, and relocations. In this perspective I approach border making at the European southern maritime frontier as a morphogenetic process of dislocations, exchanges, and relocations. Thus, I believe that an understanding of ongoing border-making processes through the analysis of exchanges and conversions between the sea and the land would pave the way for a recontinentalization of Europe. In other words, from the investigation of border making at the maritime edge of the continent, we would come to an original redefinition of Europe's macrospatial identity. This way we would skip the bias of nationalism and terrestrialism to promote a reconceptualization of Europe as a peninsular body surrounded by and exchanging with a larger, relentlessly changing social-material globe.

NOTES

1. Taussig, *Walter Benjamin's Grave*, 99.
2. See Baldacchino, "There Is So Much More to Sea."
3. See Sielen, "Oceans Manifesto."
4. See Helmreich, *Alien Ocean*; Ballinger, "Liquid Borderland"; and Chambers, *Maritime Criticism*, 17.
5. Cocco, "Theoretical Implications."
6. See Wimmer et al., "Methodological Nationalism"; and Chernilo, *Social Theory of the Nation-State*.
7. King, *Black Sea*, 3–5.
8. Favell, "Migration, Mobility and Globaloney," 390, 395, 397.
9. See Horden et al., *Corrupting Sea*; Ballinger, "Lines in the Water"; Gillis, *Islands of the Mind*; Gillis, *Human Shore*; Steinberg, *Social Construction of the Ocean*; Steinberg, "Of Other Seas."
10. See Broeze, "From the Periphery."
11. See Helmreich, *Alien Ocean*.

12. Raban, *Oxford Book of the Sea*; Davis, *Spectacular Nature*; Orlove, *Lines in the Water*.
13. See Vannini et al., "Recontinentalizing Canada."
14. Vannini et al., "Recontinentalizing Canada," 122–24.
15. See Wilson et al. *Border Identities*.
16. See Ivakhiv, "Stoking the Heart."
17. See Topaloglou, "Role and Nature of Borders."
18. See Strassoldo, "Boundaries in Sociological Theory."
19. Ivakhiv, "Stoking the Heart," 2.
20. See Zielonka, "How New Enlarged Borders."
21. See Topaloglou, "Role and Nature."
22. See Wilson et al., "*Border Identities.*"
23. See Green, "Lines, Traces and Tidemarks."
24. See Bakić-Hayden, "Nesting Orientalisms"; Wolff, *Inventing Eastern Europe*.
25. See Green, "Lines, Traces and Tidemarks"; and Luhmann, "Territorial Borders."
26. Bechev and Nicolaidis seems to run this risk claiming that borders/ boundaries/frontiers are "social structures" that define "social relations." Nonetheless, their edited book shows a quite different and more sophisticated picture.
27. See Kaplan, *Questions of Travel*; Deleuze et al., *Nomadology*; and Ingold, *Lines*.
28. See Turner, *Frontier in American History*; Prescott, *Geography of Frontiers*; and Foucher, *Front et frontières*.
29. See Schopflin, *Nations, Identity and Power*.
30. See Simmel, *Über Sociale Differenzierung*.
31. Cocco, "Touring the Frontier," 30.
32. See Öktem, "Ambivalent Sea."
33. Steinberg, *Social Construction of the Ocean*, 61.
34. Cocco, "Performing Maritime Imperial Legacies," 40.
35. See Bianchini, *Le Sfide della modernità*.
36. See Ballinger, "La Frantumazione dello spazio adriatico."
37. See Boeri, "Liquid Europe, Solid Sea"; Cocco, "Adriatic Space of Identities"; and Ballinger, "Adriatic Forum."
38. A fascinating way to show the deconstruction of the trans-maritime Mediterranean networks is to "follow the money." Sarah Green, in a study of the use of gold and Euros in the Greek-Turkish borderland, says: "Some currencies have the capacity to cross borders and to generate both links and separations between peoples and places. For centuries, gold coins had that capacity, and most recently, the Euro was designed to travel across borders without the need for currency conversion. Each, gold coins and the Euro, was linked with very different transnational political

and economic conditions, ones that defined what could be called a certain order of things in the world." "Of Gold and Euros," 167–68.

39. See Schmitt, *Land und Meer*.

40. See Gillis, *Islands of the Mind*.

41. See Baldacchino, *Island Enclaves*.

42. See Ricci, *Il Dramma del mediterraneo*.

43. Ballinger, "Liquid Borderland," 430.

44. Such a paradox between connection and marginalization emerges in the travel and tourism literature, which often celebrates the immobility of the Mediterranean. According to Antonis Liakos, the creation of such a diffused stereotype "has to do with the human body and its relationship to time and space and with changes in the coordinates of the corporeality and in the cultural image of the body. . . . Instead of concealed and covered bodies, the prevalent images are a celebration of the naked body. Thus, Mediterranean immobility has given way to Mediterranean fantasy, a sense of out of time temporality. Mediterranean nostalgia is nostalgia without past. It is the nostalgic yearning for a privatized Garden of Eden."

BIBLIOGRAPHY

Bakić-Hayden, Milica. "Nesting Orientalisms: The Case of Former Yugoslavia." *Slavic Review* 54, no. 4 (1995): 917–31.

Baldacchino, Godfrey. *Island Enclaves: Offshoring, Creative Governance and Subnational Island Jurisdictions*. Montreal: McGill-Queen's University Press, 2010.

———. "There Is So Much More to Sea: The Myriad Aquatic Engagements of Humankind." *ETNOFOOR: Anthropological Journal* 27, no. 2 (2015): 179–84.

Ballinger, Pamela. "Adriatic Forum: A Comment." *Austrian History Yearbook* 42 (2011): 56–63.

———. "La Frantumazione dello spazio Adriatico." In *Immaginare l'adriatico*, edited by Emilio Cocco and Everardo Minardi, 27–44. Milano: Franco Angeli, 2007.

———. "Lines in the Water, Peoples on the Map: Maritime Museums and the Representation of Cultural Boundaries in the Upper Adriatic." *Narodna Umjetnost* 43, no. 1 (2006): 15–39.

———. "Liquid Borderland, Inelastic Sea: Mapping the Eastern Adriatic." In *Shatterzone of Empires: Coexistence and Violence in the German, Habsburg, Russian and Ottoman Borderlands*, edited by Omer Bartov and Edin D. Weitz, 423–37. Bloomington: Indiana University Press, 2013.

Bechev, Dimitri, and Kalypso Nicolaidis. *Mediterranean Frontiers: Borders,*

Conflict and Memory in a Transnational World. London: Tauris Academic Studies, 2010.

Bianchini, Stefano. *Le Sfide della modernità. Idee, politiche e percorsi dell'Europa orientale nel XIX e XX secolo.* Soveria Mannelli: Rubettino Editore, 2009.

Boeri, Stefano. "Liquid Europe, Solid Sea." In *Territories: Builders, Warriors and Other Mythologies,* edited by Anselm Franke, Rafi Segal, and Eyal Weizman. Berlin: Kunst-Werke, 2003.

Broeze, Frank. "From the Periphery to the Mainstream: The Challenge of Australia's Maritime History." *Great Circle* 11, no. 1 (1989): 1–14.

Chambers, Iain. "Maritime Criticism and Lessons from the Sea." *Insights* 3, no. 9 (2010). Accessed September 29, 2010. http://www.dur.ac.uk/ias /insights/volume3/ article9/.

Chernilo, Daniel. *A Social Theory of the Nation-State: The Political Forms of Modernity beyond Methodological Nationalism.* London: Routledge, 2007.

Cocco, Emilio. "The Adriatic Space of Identities." *Narodna Umjetnost: Croatian Journal of Ethnology and Folklore Research* 43, no. 1 (2006): 7–15.

———. "Performing Maritime Imperial Legacies: Tourism and Cosmopolitanism in Odessa and Trieste." *Anthropological Notebooks* 16, no. 1 (2010): 37–57.

———. "Theoretical Implications of Maritime Sociology." *Annals of Marine Sociology* 22 (2014): 5–18.

———. "Touring the Frontier: Reinventing the Eastern Adriatic for Tourism." In *Culture and Society in Tourism Contexts,* Tourism and Social Science Series 17, edited by A. M. Nogués-Pedregal, 25–55. Bingley UK: Emerald Group Publishing Limited, 2012.

Davis, Susan. *Spectacular Nature: Corporate Culture and the Sea World Experience.* Berkeley: University of California Press, 1997.

Deleuze, Gilles, and Félix Guattari. *Nomadology: The War Machine.* New York: Semiotext(e), 1986.

Favell, Adrian. "Migration, Mobility and Globaloney: Metaphors and Rhetoric in the Sociology of Globalization." *Global Networks* 1, no. 4 (2001): 389–98.

Foucher, Michel. *Front et frontières.* Paris: Fayard, 1992.

Gillis, John R. *The Human Shore: Seacoasts in History.* Chicago: University of Chicago Press, 2012.

———. *Islands of the Mind.* New York: Palgrave Macmillan, 2004.

Green, Sarah. "Lines Traces and Tidemarks: Reflections on Forms of Borderli-ness." *Eastbordnet Working Papers* 1, no. 17 (2009). Accessed July 5, 2016. http://www.eastbordnet.org/wiki/Documents/Lines_Traces _Tidemarks_Nicosia_2009_090416.pdf.

————. "Of Gold and Euros: Locating Value on the Greek-Turkish Border." *Etnološka Tribina* 41, no. 34 (2011): 153–68.

Helmreich, Stefan. *Alien Ocean: Anthropological Voyages in Microbial Sea.* Berkeley: University of California Press, 2009.

Horden, Peregrine, and Nicholas Purcell. *The Corrupting Sea: A Study of Mediterranean History.* Oxford: Blackwell, 2010.

Ingold, Tim. *Lines: A Brief History.* London: Routledge, 2007.

Ivakhiv, Adrian. "Stoking the Heart of (a Certain) Europe: Crafting Hybrid Identities in the Ukraine-EU Borderlands." *Spaces of Identities* 6, no. 1 (2006): 11–44.

Kaplan, Caren. *Questions of Travel: Postmodern Discourses of Displacement.* Durham NC: Duke University Press, 1996.

King, Charles. *The Black Sea: A History.* Oxford: Oxford University Press, 2004.

Liakos, Antonis. *What Happened to the Braudelian Mediterranean after Braudel?* Paper presented at the conference Regimes of Historicity and Regimes of Spatiality, CAS, Sofia, Bulgaria, November 20, 2010.

Luhmann, Niklas. "Territorial Borders as System Boundaries." In *Cooperation and Conflict in Border Areas*, edited by Strassoldo Raimondo and Giovanni Delli Zotti, 235–44. Milano: Franco Angeli, 1982.

Öktem, Kerem H. L. "The Ambivalent Sea: Regionalizing the Mediterranean Differently." In *Mediterranean Frontiers*, edited by Dimitar Bechev and Kalypso Nicolaidis, 13–24. London: Tauris Academic Studies, 2010.

Orlove, Benjamin. *Lines in the Water: Nature and Culture in Lake Titicaca.* Berkeley: University of California Press, 2002.

Prescott, J.R.V. *The Geography of Frontiers and Boundaries.* Chicago: Aldine, 1965.

Raban, Jonathan, ed. *The Oxford Book of the Sea.* Oxford: Oxford University Press, 1993.

Ricci, Elena. *Il Dramma del mediterraneo: Malta e Lampedusa, frontiere liquide, confini solidi.* Milano: Meltemi, 2015.

Schmitt, Carl. *Land und Meer.* Stuttgart: Klett-Cotta, 2001.

Schopflin George. *Nations, Identity and Power: The New Politics of Europe.* London: Hurst & Co., 2000.

Simmel, Georg. *Über Sociale Differenzierung.* Leipzig: Duncker & Humblot, 1890.

Sielen, Alan B. "An Oceans Manifesto: The Present Global Crisis." *Fletcher Forum of World Affairs*, 32, no. 1 (Winter 2008): 42–52.

Steinberg, Philip E. *The Social Construction of the Ocean.* Cambridge: Cambridge University Press, 2001.

——. "Of Other Seas: Metaphors and Materialities in Maritime Regions." *Atlantic Studies* 2, no. 10 (2013): 156–69.

Strassoldo, Raimondo. "Boundaries in Sociological Theory—A Reassessment." In *Cooperation and Conflict in Border Areas*, edited by Raimondo Strassoldo and Giovanni Delli Zotti, 245–71. Milano: Franco Angeli, 1982.

Taussig, Michael. *Walter Benjamin's Grave*. Chicago: University of Chicago Press, 2006.

Topaloglou, Lefteris. "The Role and Nature of Borders." COST Action IS0803 Eastbordnet, Working paper, 2009. Accessed July 5, 2016. http://www.eastbordnet.org/working_papers/open/documents/Topaloglou_The_role_and_nature_of_borders_090414.pdf.

Turner, Fredrick Jackson. *The Frontier in American History*. New York: Holt, 1921.

Vannini, Philip, Godfrey Baldacchino, Lorraine Guay, Stephen A. Royle, and Philip E. Steinberg. "Recontinentalizing Canada: Arctic Ice's Liquid Modernity and the Imagining of Canadian Archipelago." *Island Studies* 2, no. 4 (2009): 121–38.

Wilson, Thomas M., and Hastings Donnan. *Border Identities: Nation and State at International Frontiers*. Cambridge: Cambridge University Press, 1998.

Wimmer, Andreas, and Nina Glick Schiller. "Methodological Nationalism and Beyond: Nation-State Building, Migration, and the Social Sciences." *Global Networks* 2, no. 4 (2002): 301–34.

Wolff, Larry. *Inventing Eastern Europe: The Map of Civilization in the Mind of the Enlightenment*. Palo Alto: Stanford University Press, 1994.

Zielonka, Jan. "How New Enlarged Borders Will Reshape the European Union." *Journal of Common Market Studies* 39, no. 3 (2001): 507–36.

POETRY 2 | *Watershed Ways*

With a Hurricane, She Climbs Mountains while She Dreams

PAM USCHUK

When she leans against aspen trunks,
she can hear the storm roaring through
the gold coinage of leaves, a rush
like wind under the ocean, the rattle
of blood in veins big as her arms.

Bark smooth as skin, folded
and elephantine, fit to her ear
like a cool herbal sachet
above 10,000 feet.

Clarified by the wildfire of early fall leaves, sun dogs
leap from peak to high peak, transparent
as stained glass, bioluminescent as breath
passing up through the woody heart.

Rain soaks her dreams of flight, nails all night
wet hawk primaries to their dusky roosts
while Congress debates our skewed history of torture techniques—
which raw beatings to lose, which waterboarding to keep.

All night, her rescue dog snuggles closer to her thigh.
Lightning spikes thunder's huge and terrible mouth
til dawn ravens croak through cloud rags, what
is left of the hurricane from the invisible gulf.

She holds silver sunrise, wafer of nonviolent
hope under her tongue, as ice rain
slicks the bark of aspens in their distant nurseries,
out of reach of news scarring the radio.

The Mighty Mississippi

TWYLA M. HANSEN

All water on Earth is connected. Into the Gulf
flows groundwater, snowmelt and runoff of the Mighty
Mississippi from its vein-rivers and capillary-streams.
The river is the heart, the red pulse of our nation.

The flow of groundwater and snowmelt and runoff
is diked, harnessed, dammed, polluted: it carries our worst.
The river is the heart, the red pulse of our nation,
transporting our goods and grains.

Diked, harnessed, dammed, polluted: it carries our worst
as well as our best. We seem to tolerate it both ways
because we like all those goods and grains.
Yet our industrial worst brings death to the Gulf.

Is this our best, to tolerate the endless ways
humans invent to poison our own nest?
Our industrial worst brings death to the Gulf.
We try to separate our daily lives from the river.

Humans are capable of not poisoning the Mighty
Mississippi, its vein-rivers and capillary-streams.
No longer can we separate our daily lives from the river.
Even schoolchildren know all water on Earth is connected.

Mississippi Delta Lay Down

ANN FISHER-WIRTH

The day lays down
   first summer heat
         as we drive
      from Clarksdale

past cotton silos
   pecan trees
          Baptist churches
      little swamps with

floating trash
   maybe an egret
          one-lane roads
      leading off

into cotton
   or alfalfa fields
          and a yellow
      cropduster

gassing up
   getting ready
         to spray poison

    ≈

My husband tells me
   Dylan's 75 today
         first time I heard him
      Baez pulled his

scrawny ass on stage
    to sing *Blowin' in*
           the Wind maybe
        Hattie Carroll

at the Berkeley
    Folk Music Festival
           where Lightnin'
        Hopkins dragged

a straightback
    wooden chair
           to a single mike
        and in that summer

of snarling dogs
    on the end of chains
           and fire hoses that I'd
        watch every night

on TV and vow
    never never never
           to live in the South
        Hopkins sang

I'm gonna walk with
    the Prince of Peace
           down by the riverside
        down by the riverside

Links

BRENDAN GALVIN

Those zooplankton drifts—
bottom stocks in the great soup
of being—are aggregating now
in places around the bay. Undersea
clouds are thickening with krill
and larval swimmers,
sea butterflies and beings
so small they could travel
in our blood. Radiolarians like
minute satellites are attracting
the spouts that blow images of trees
briefly over water, and even onshore
we catch the sunlit backs of right
whales slipping toward sustenance—
the Right Whale because oil-rich
and slow-going, a floater once
the harpoon found its heart.
A tenth of maybe three hundred
survivors are here now,
socializing and making their
plankton-filtering runs between
Long Point and the Manomet
Hills, on Stellwagen Bank,
and all the way from the Race
to the ocean off the Highland
clay pounds. They do not
recognize shipping lanes or
the concept of hull strike.
On a tanker's bridge, at the wheel

of the *Little Infant,* who sees
the single stunned-water print
that's left when a whale dives,
how it looks as if the surface
were beginning the change to ice?

By the Sea

DAVID LLOYD

We haven't always parked by the sea—
it wasn't chic to sit and gaze at waves
until royalty finished with England's
rusted spas and baths, packed their trunks, and turned
to better-appointed waters. The rest
soon followed. But I think there must be more

than keeping up with titles. And that more
has to do with absence: how the sea
holds up so little—boats, birds, leaves, weeds—a nest
maybe, a bottle, this suspension from wave
to wave. This renewable turning
from what we know too well, the land's

strictures: the stasis we crawled onto, hand
over webbed hand. I love land that's more-
or-less itself, depending how the tide turns,
where life lives or dies in what the sea
leaves behind: where there's no depth, width, pull, waves—
just pools with wind-driven ripples or crests

and forgotten jellyfish. *They're rest-
ing*, a crouching child will say, though the land
will soon dry what rests to rubber. The waves
I watched off Pembroke's placid coast killed more
men than men could count. That's why the sea
drew my mother in only so far: she'd turn

careful, waist-high circles, so the sea turned
and swelled well below her voice; no crest

ignored by her; no suck or swell unseen.
She knew Ocean Grove, Hyannis, England's
honeymooning south coast, where there's always more
of what we want and don't want: rain, wild waves

and wind; tacky shops. But with all that, the waves
insist on ground rules, our vital turning
with the moon's turning. Sand keeps making more
of itself as we unroll towels to rest—
from what, we're not sure. Ourselves? The land
we can't bring ourselves to leave? We walk the sea-

shore beneath the sun, counting waves to rest
our eyes. We want to turn from the land
forever: we want more of that constant sea.

Aubade

WILLIAM LOGAN

It was the whiteness of the whale that above all things appalled me.
—*Moby-Dick*, chapter 42

Starving off the coast of Japan, say,
they took sovereign isolation in sovereign waters.
The slate sky rendered the colors blank,
ripe for the painter of death. Corpses
bobbed to the backwash of tides
like jetsam or flotsam, depending. Nothing
lightened movement toward the love-pull
of the grave, so one would think. Meanwhile
the stands of bamboo wavered like pikemen,
as if to guard against the black ships, hoping
like whalers to barrel home on a crest
and avoid anything with teeth.

River Dolphins

MICHAEL S. BEGNAL

Looking down from the Bluff
upon the Monongahela,
a pod of pink dolphins
visible below the surface,
shifting pink flashes
in the green muddy water
descend from view
and go under
the Birmingham Bridge

   —looking down in winter,
how hard when winter ice forms,
the asphyxiations and communal grief

   —like countries were
   where groups of humans
   amassed for a while—

these mammals, though,
they lit out for oceans
and reemerged, Ages after,
in estuaries and rivers,

we huddle now in Uptown,
they huddle in the murk,
they osmose acid and dissolve solids,
we in our garrets,
   they in their reserves

—yet some summer days
they spout spume
where the glint suns the surface,
and neighborhood girls
crane down for a glimpse of an arc
from certain Boulevard blocks

Sruth Fada Con

BARRY JOHNSTON

I will walk the *Sruth Fada Con,*
Haunt of fox and badger, of
Tamed crags drinking water

From smoked wreaks of turf,
Cutback, exposing the bronzed
Gully, the forgotten Ben Bulben

A jumping hare with a glistened
Tear on the eye, watching the centuries
Chased and harried, Swaddled in wind-cloth;

Its beautiful bone can no longer hide
The surface taken. Neolithic slug,
Weathering seasons by the minute.

Wanting Choughs

TONY CURTIS

The last living thing
to be seen by Mallory in '24
as the mountain squeezed his breath away
was surely a chough,
for they are recorded near the summit
by Norton and, who knows, in '53
may well have been drawn to the biscuits
hurriedly buried by Tensing Norgay,
his Buddhist offering to Everest,
as he and Hillary paused at the peak
for as long as their oxygen would allow.

Those perpetually moving beaks,
Coronation flunkies in the Himalayan abbey,
their bright legs like Elizabethan courtiers,
as Noyce saw them, choughs drawn
to the droppings of the climbers,
their tea leaves, the spillage of their camp.

A chough: that would be a thing indeed,
that would make my year;
but each time I walk our headland
they are nowhere to be seen.
Reported by others, a certain pair
at least, clear against Whitesheet Rock,
but the constant crosses of black
against blue and green
are always for me no more than
the common *Corvus*, crow or raven,
never the red-beaked, red-legged
undisputed primal, heraldic chough.

I've seen them on the island of Skomer,
common enough and close enough
to linger in the lens, strut their flashy stuff—
polished boot-black wings and legs full-gaitered.
But here at Lydstep,
where we scattered my father and mother,
nothing.

There's bullying black-backed gulls, rock pigeons,
once a peregrine's feeding stoop,
launched from its nest scrape in the cliffs,
hunting between Smuggler's Cave and Mother Carey's Kitchen,
but the choughs of Everest and Skomer and elsewhere
are a shape in the mind and not the evening air.

Though I should want them often to appear
for friends and family
and those who never knew me
or ever read a word of mine,
but come to the headland for the sea's green heartbeat
and a sky that goes on forever,
if my ashes were emptied out here.

Double View of the Adirondacks as Reflected over Lake Champlain from Waterfront Park

MAJOR JACKSON

The mountains are at their theater again,
each ridge practicing an oration of scale and crest,
and the sails, performing glides across the lake, complain
for being out-shadowed despite their gracious
bows. Thirteen years in this state, what hasn't occurred?
A cyclone in my spirit led to divorce, four books
gave darkness an echo of control, my slurred
hand finding steadiness by the prop of a page,
and God, my children whom I scarred! Pray they forgive.
My crimes felt mountainous, yet perspective
came with distance, and like those peaks, once keening
beneath biting ice, then felt resurrection in a vestige
of water, unfrozen, cascading and adding to the lake's
depth, such have I come to gauge my own screaming.
The masts tip so far they appear to capsize, keeling
over where every father is a boat on water. The wakes
carry the memory of battles, and the Adirondacks
hold their measure. I am a tributary of something greater.

Portage

ALICE AZURE

She drags her kayak along the portage path
away from chaos to the calm of Basin Pond
where loons dance, cry out their eerie laughs.

She lights candles from Boston to Baden-Baden,
wonders how many it takes for God to respond?
She pulls her kayak along the portage path.

She sailed the seas of Indonesia and St. Barth's,
ferried Stockholm's waters like a vagabond
too far from loons' dance and their eerie laughs.

Widowhood and grief—after his selfish passing—
made plain the importance of carrying on—
pushing her kayak along the portage path.

Basin Pond is deep and calm, her craft
a heavy heave, even with the chaos gone.
Still, loons dance. She joins their eerie laughs.

Florida is lovely in winter; so is La Paz.
But Maine is the place of which she's most fond,
pulling her kayak along its portage path
to where loons dance, cry their welcome laughs.

PART 3 | *Planetary Currents*

The Lariat and the GPS

Cowboys, Cattle Ranching, and Global Agricultural Practices

NANCY S. COOK

For decades scholars in western American studies and ecocriticism celebrated the local and the microregional as an antidote to homogeneous national cultures and later to the deleterious effects of global capitalism. More recently, scholars have cataloged the limitations of an undying romance for the microregional and the local. In *Sense of Place and Sense of Planet* Ursula Heise urges us to move away from an American tradition that valorizes the microspatial, the tradition that celebrates rootedness as the most important value, as perhaps the only means to ecological health. Instead, Heise asks us to acknowledge our connectedness. How might we, she asks, "be able to develop cultural forms of identity and belonging that are commensurate with the rapid growth in political, economic, and social interconnectedness that has characterized the last few decades[?]"[1]

This essay looks at representations of North American ranching communities, a segment of the population in the outback American West best known as über-local, nationalistic, and isolationist. While ranchers may be daunted by exchanging their idea of rootedness in place for a globally engaged sense of identity, such a shift is necessary for their survival. In fact, many ranchers routinely reach across ranch, state, and national borders watching treaties, currencies, diseases, national and international politics from half a world away, because such issues can affect their market and business practices. The problem, then, lies not so much in ranching practice but in the image of ranching in both ranchers' and the public's imagination. The stakes are high: far from sustainable local markets, most ranchers participate in one way or another in globalized commodities markets, yet the representational demands of ranching as cowboy practice ties them to an invented past, making them actors in a living history museum. As such, they are at the mercy of subsidies, policies, and public opinion that value their way of life but don't allow them a place in contemporary life. If those representations turn sour, as they have with the publicity earned by outlaw ranchers such as Cliven Bundy or the Malheur National Wildlife Refuge occupiers, public opinion can turn, taking down a way of life, the ranching practices, and ranches critical to environmental and social health in the outback West and beyond.

Neil Campbell's critical voice is crucial here. Campbell moves beyond the traditional sense of the American West as if it were "some *a priori* order, some given and established reality that 'goes-without-saying' and exists as if independent of experience." Instead, he reenvisions the West as a place of multiplicity and dynamism, increasingly engaged in global as well as local processes, balancing tensions between the rooted and the routed. Critical regionalism, or more properly, "critical regionality," Campbell argues, offers the West

> a different approach valuing the small-scale and local, without sentimentality and nostalgia, [and] would forge a greater social care and communal regionality that attended to how local affects and actions related to and interacted with global interests and decisions; a genuine process of worlding. "Worldings," after all, as Kathleen Stewart argues, are not distant and remote, but part of the attunements and attachments thrown together in the everyday; a multiplicity of trajectories, forces, intensities like a "nexus of worlds" surrounding us all in our intimate connectedness, prismatically refracted and reflected in the lives we live and our various "ways of going on."[2]

In his three books on the West and in his book on critical regionality, Campbell offers strategies for teasing out the presence of the global within the local, for negotiating the tension between near and far, for understanding place-based studies that are engaged with the world outside the microcosm, for understanding the relationships and multiplicity of identities contained in a single descriptor such as *cowboy* or *rancher*.

This essay responds to Heise's and Campbell's calls to put the local in relation to other places, processes, and categories. In order to do so, we need to look at multiple kinds of texts and rhetorics to find boundaries that are concentric, not linear (or arbitrary), whether we are confronting the flow of diseased bison across National Park Service boundaries into states with different livestock regulations and wildlife management policies, making policies about the transportation of diseased cattle across national boundaries under North American Free Trade Agreement (NAFTA) accords, or trading bull semen and seedstock herds around the world. A world of concentric boundaries reveals negotiations between micro and macro that are essential to the future of ranching. Fiction, nonfiction, ranch histories, glossy magazines, trade journals, documents, websites, as well as internet ephemera, together reveal the ways micro and macro are intimately and necessarily entangled. These entanglements complicate political ideologies (and their biological consequences) that insist on the efficacy of boundaries and policies that have global ramifications.

This essay braids information and analysis from two aspects of my life. I am an academic, and I am a Montana rancher working to keep my ranch healthy and financially viable. In each of these lives I am both insider and outsider: a defender and explainer of ranching cultures and practices to my eco-warrior and often vegetarian students; a Democrat, agnostic, intellectual humanist among my Christian, Republican, pragmatist rancher colleagues and neighbors. From this dual perspective I see the complex ways that ranchers fulfill and defy aspects of public perceptions. At a time when literary and popular culture portrays the rancher either as a rapacious beast ("welfare" ranching) or romantic anachronism (cowboy code of honor), much of what is happening in cowboy country is neither.

Within the vast archive of portrayals of western ranching culture and practices, the romantic cowboy prevails. Why? What are the consequences of such a limited vision of this western figure for eco-recovery projects, public policies, writers, and scholars? How might we include the complicating narratives that are currently found outside the mainstream? How might we reframe these textual economies to make a place for creative narratives of conservation and recovery? In order for the business and the lifeway of Northern American ranching to survive in complex national and global communities, our understanding of ranching must extend far beyond the limitations of cowboy culture and embrace the vast technological and economic changes that are already taking place on the range.

There is a revolution on the range—a technological and economic revolution. Ranchers across the North American West are setting aside their lariats and picking up their GPS as they head out on their range. Moreover, many ranchers use cutting-edge technology both on the ranch and in an effort to tell a fact-based conservation story, one with data verifiable by public sector scientists, because they are frustrated by public sector and advocacy groups' inability to read the land as text, much less interpret that text. Peruse the case studies and bibliography of Jim Howell's *For the Love of the Land: Global Case Studies of Grazing in Nature's Image*, and you will find rigorous systems in place on many ranches to measure moisture, dry matter, and plant protein, supported by academic articles in peer-reviewed journals. These testimonials and conservation success stories have largely been confined to trade publications such as the *Stockman Grass Farmer*, the *Drover's Journal*, the *Western Farmer-Stockman*, and the *Western Ag Reporter* or in books published by small presses and marketed to a predominately insider readership.[3]

These stories of globally connected, transnational, technologically sophisticated, and environmentally "green" ranching are by and large limited to audiences primarily in the business. The stories with worldwide circulation remain the romantic, nostalgic ones, with images of ranchers as cowboys. Books, magazines, and photo essay collections present ranching culture as a highly aestheticized lifeway with ranchers, both men and women, intimately connected to the animals and land in their care. These images and texts deploy Old West mythologies to legitimatize contemporary ranching economies, celebrating ranchers as stewards of the land, preservers of open space, and stalwart models of American character. Yet while these publications honor the tradition of men and women on horseback with their stoicism, good husbandry, and deep commitment to place, they also portray them as old-fashioned and anachronistic in an era marked by mobility, urbanity, and technological sophistication. Moreover, cowboy mythologies and culture remain an important American export. While we might send agricultural technologies, cattle hides, and beef around the word, instead of illustrating the details of their production, we show the world a fantasy. Why does an industry deeply involved in the global obscure those relationships in favor of stagings that feature the mythology of the microregion, such as the western family ranch?

Within the United States numerous publications run the gamut from the trade journal's "all cattle and no hat" utilitarian approach to popular magazines that tout an "all hat and no cattle" cowboy lifestyle. This span might begin with the very practical "Big Ag" *Western Livestock Journal*, through trade journals such as the *Stockman Grass Farmer* and the *Drover's Journal* to the more commercial *Range, Western Horseman, American Cowboy,* and *True West,* moving on to the glossy lifestyle magazine *Cowboys and Indians.* We may find a varied and complex set of representations of contemporary ranching life in these periodicals, but the deck has been stacked in favor of cowboy mythologies, wherein men and women (mostly men) are isolated in an outback American West, labor in a kind of handmade world—on horseback, with a faithful cattle dog, but they have no internal combustion engines, solar-powered electric fences, or computers in sight. In these images ranchers are cowboys, confined to a living history museum (a ranch) that is isolated deep inside the boundaries of the interior American West.

The North American cattle business has, in fact, been reaching across ranch, state, and national borders for more than two centuries, and in the twenty-first century U.S. cattle producers watch treaties; state, national, and international policies and laws; currencies and livestock diseases; as well as weather across the continents, looking for signs and shifts that will affect their businesses despite legal and political boundaries. Simultaneously, from the King Ranch's expansion in mid-twentieth century into a global empire, to Ted Turner's hemispheric eco-ranching kingdom in the twenty-first century, to the importation of an entire cattle ranch to Russia, the influence of ranching practices from the American West can be tracked globally.[4] Ranchers manage the microregional ranch while they engage macrospaces, both continental and global. What needs scrutiny and exploration is the relationship between the rhetoric of ranching cultures (the individual ranch, and its subregional variants, from Nevada's buckaroo or Montana's cowboy culture) and the rhetoric of macroregions (global livestock pandemics, multinational corporations, currency fluctuations of trade agreements). We need to take a crucial step in the "worlding" of North American ranching.[5]

The stakes are high. Numbers vary widely, but ranches and rangeland comprise approximately 400 million acres (including public grazing land) in the U.S. West, in addition to significant acreage in western Canada and northern Mexico.[6] If North American ranching enterprises fail economically, the consequences are significant for wildlife, watersheds, ecosystems, open space, regional cultures, and regional and national economies. While some ranchers bury themselves deeper in cowboy and isolationist mythologies, others accept their places as cogs in the industrial commodity beef business. Still others, including those who have banded together as R-CALF (Ranchers-Cattlemen Action Legal Fund), take on multinational corporations while using cowboy mythologies and isolationist trade policies strategically to protect independent cattle producers. In some cases cowboy myths are useful insofar as they create opportunities for ranchers and cattlemen to renegotiate their relationship to multinational corporations, cartels, and global markets. In this respect ranching is a culture that, not unlike the wine industry, relentlessly promotes its own version of "terroir," one in which macrospatial narratives hide within microspatial ones but at a significant cost. The image of the independent and local suggests that viniculturists and ranchers have more power over what they do and where their products go than they actually do.

Ranching cultures in the American West have always already been multinational. In *Two Years before the Mast* (1840) Richard Henry Dana describes the vast ranchos of Alta California and his work tanning hides to prepare them for shipment around the Horn for leather-dependent industries in New England, such as the shoe trade. They would be exchanged for goods—fabric, housewares, and personal items not manufactured in Mexican California. In Dana's account these ranchos were not only fiefdoms unto themselves, but they were also absolutely dependent upon international trade for their survival.[7] Nearly every essential aspect of North American ranch life has been the product of international and transcontinental hybridity—from the importation of cattle breeds from different parts of Europe and the subsequent crossbreeding for subregional adaptation, to the tools used, to the traditions of livestock handling.[8] We know a great deal about the influx of foreign investors and workers into the ranching business in post–Civil War America, but by the early twentieth century a different story, one of isolation, even xenophobia, emerges as dominant in popular culture.

Owen Wister's *The Virginian* (1902) reveals that many ranch workers come from somewhere else, while it also works to offer an adopted nativism against the mores and cultures of the East—the Virginian argues on behalf of a microregional ethic, while Molly Stark, his fiancée, stands on the side of national, even universal values. The microregional ethic appears to win, although upon closer scrutiny *The Virginian* engages with the world beyond the ranch's subregion of Wyoming. *The Virginian* depends upon the narrator's cultural and regional status as an outsider in order to frame the microregion in the first place. The cattle must be transported and sold at points far east of the home ranch, and the Virginian's and Molly's postmarital financial success depends upon engaging beyond the microregion economically, through his coal mine.[9]

For the rest of the twentieth century most popular and middle-brow cultural media portray the American ranch as resolutely in the realm of microregion—isolated from cities, with unique cultural practices, and engaged in work attuned to the particularities of the topography and the environment within its borders. In such representations the world outside generally extends no farther than the small town, the slightly larger market town, or the county seat closest to the ranch. Literature, high- and lowbrow—painting, periodicals, films, and television shows—worked to reinforce the image of the isolated ranch that was its own micro-nation. Think of the map that opened the long-running TV series *Bonanza.*

Celebrating and exploiting the environmental and cultural distinctiveness of ranching in the American West have served economic, cultural, and political interests for years. Ranching in the outback American West sells, whether in the form of dude ranch vacations, films, slick magazines, or coffee-table photo-essay books. These experiences, texts, and images promise an authentic relation to the natural world and portray the romance of physical labor in concert with nature in working landscapes remote from metropolitan areas. In many cases public policy has endorsed this mythology, working to preserve ranching as both business and culture.[10] By the close of the twentieth century the dominant image of ranching included cowboys on horseback riding across spaces that resembled living history museums more than working landscapes in contemporary America.

Many critiques of traditional cowboy and ranch life that have sprung directly from ranching culture—memoirs, essays, and fiction— have been read largely as correctives within an isolationist tradition and rarely for the ways they connect people to communities beyond the ranch and microregion. Reviews of and critical work on Judy Blunt's memoir *Breaking Clean* provide an excellent example.[11] Many of them focus on the isolation of the ranch life she describes. True, the ranches she lived and worked on were a long way from town, but connections to the world beyond the ranch abound, and Blunt's sophisticated awareness of the costs of stubborn, proud isolation make Blunt's memoir complex. Whether it is her family's racist attitudes toward the Native Americans they rarely encounter, or the way Blunt discovers feminism in town, the fluctuations in the cattle market, or the consolidation of working landscapes that she sees everywhere in eastern Montana, Blunt's sense of isolation depends upon connections, allusions to larger frames and concentric boundaries, to make meaning for her readers and herself.

While Blunt sees her neighbors' extraordinary efforts to help get her sick child to town under dangerous weather conditions as a key moment in her book, many readers, especially urban ones, read her text very differently. Her account of the harrowing trip to town shows the ranching community at its best. For Blunt among the significant losses she incurred when she left the ranch and her husband and headed west to college and single motherhood was the loss of this community. Perhaps trained by a vast number of images and narratives of ranching, many readers tended to see the divorce, rather than community ties, as the key in Blunt's memoir. By emphasizing the loss of the marriage rather than the loss of the community, those readers miss a richer, more cosmopolitan reading of Blunt's outback ranch life. Challenging, yes, but not as isolated as we imagine. In a subsequent essay Blunt ponders the changes since she left. In ranch country "the barriers that separate us from the rest of the world are less geographical, now, and more internal—an intentional separation, like a fortress. The ones who defend it most vigorously have grown more rigid and angry over time. A pervasive pessimism."[12] William Kittredge diagnoses them as "Westerners [who] feel protected by distance, like escapees after jailbreak."[13]

Kittredge both honors and critiques life on the ranch kingdom in southeastern Oregon where he was raised and lived until early midlife. Of all the writers who have taken up ranching in the West, Kittredge offers the most sustained and critical analysis. Over his writing career the emphasis has shifted, alternating between clear-eyed celebration and pointed critique. Writing as "Owen Roundtree" with coauthor Steven Krauzer, Kittredge wrote nine "Cord" novels, set in an outback West with cowboy traditions largely unchallenged. His novel, *The Willow Field*, offers thick descriptions of buckaroo life led largely on horseback. But across both his nonfiction and fiction, Kittredge looks back at the isolation, particularly in his childhood, while reminding readers of their connections to the world beyond the boundaries of the enormous MC Ranch.

The MC Ranch, which at one time comprised more than one million acres, was in many ways a world unto itself. Ranch economics, however, depended upon fluctuating world markets, which were affected by war—World War I and World War II in particular. When the ranch turned to large-scale farming, it benefited from federal policies and government money while still being subject to the price swings inherent in commodity agriculture. As a proudly private and family example of Big Ag, Kittredge portrays the consequences of the belief that land ownership affords absolute control over the environment. On the MC Kittredge and his family drained marshland and, in so doing, disrupted the lives of hundreds of thousands of migratory birds. They applied chemicals, including "2,4-D ethyl and malathion and the German World War II nerve gas called parathion," damaging the watershed and the wildlife and compromising their own health.[14] They killed everything that wasn't merchantable—insects, birds, rodents, and coyotes—changing the ecosystem dramatically. The MC Ranch, as Kittredge knew it, came crashing down because of his family's desires and strategies within the larger boundaries of political power, finance, and the vagaries of commodity markets.

Kittredge diagnoses the diseases—personal, economic, and ideological—that brought down the ranching kingdom dreams of his ancestors. In particular he highlights the lingering resistance to change among ranchers, especially concerning the rights of ownership. In *Owning It All* Kittredge writes about the sheltered isolation that insulated his people from the world outside: "When I came home from the Air Force in 1958, I found our backland rich with television from the Great World. But that old attitude from my childhood, the notion that my people live in a separate kingdom where they own it all, secure from the world, is still powerful and troublesome. When people ask me where I am from I still say southeastern Oregon, expecting them to understand my obvious pride."[15] While agricultural practices continue to change, developing a more intimate, at times daily engagement with global practices and markets, there remains a deep divide between the myth-bound ideologies of ranching and the economics of the ranching business itself.

The split between the myth-bound cowboy and working ranch is nowhere more evident than in the difference between David Stoecklein's romantic photographs and the practical publications for ranchers. Stoecklein's photographs depict dust-shrouded cowboys and stalwart cowgirls on horseback celebrating ranching "heritage" versus the trade journals, workshops, schools, and websites that are devoted to progressive, sustainable ranching practices for the twenty-first century. In more than fifty coffee-table books and dozens of calendars at the time of Stoecklein's death, the premodern, handmade, American flag–waving West provides no visual confirmation of the late-twentieth- and early-twenty-first-century business of ranching beyond the photographic apparatus itself.

Kittredge describes the disparity between what people expect coming to the West—"Freedom"—and what it is to live in the West, which involves complexity beyond mythology. "We like to claim the West is a place where you can have a shot at being what you want to be," he writes in "Redneck Secrets." "You can come to terms with yourself. Freedom, in a livable community, is supposed to be the point of things. It's our primary mythology, and it sort of works out, more so if you're white and have some money."[16] The myth brings another wave of "pioneers" to the outback West, "people who come to the country with what seems to be an idea that connection with simplicities will save their lives. Which simplicities are those?" Kittredge asks. "The condescension implicit in the program is staggering. If you want to feel you are being taken lightly, try sitting around while someone tells you how he envies the simplicity of your life."[17]

All over ranch country the disconnect between cowboy mythologies and commodity capitalism feeds the anger that such disparity creates. Tom Field describes the powerlessness faced by ranchers: "Regardless of the products, ranchers function under a commodity pricing structure not all that different from the one faced at the end of the trail drives in the late 1800s. For the uninitiated, commodity selling is akin to playing in a poker game when the other players control the cards and make bets for you. In short, selling cows or yearlings under the conventional auction market system means a rancher is in the undesirable position of being a price-taker, not a price-setter."[18]

Ranchers in the commodity beef business (and most of them are), no matter how far from town, have their prices and profit margins set by multinational corporations, their competition set by trade agreements such as CAFTA, CETA, NAFTA, TPP, and TTIP. Within the

United States subsidies, laws, and policies made by Congress, the EPA, the USDA, as well as the BLM, all constrain ranchers, but the members of these federal entities rarely fully consider the impact of these policies on ranchers. No wonder they are a cranky bunch. As Kittredge notes, "The liberties our people came seeking are more and more constrained, and here in the West, as everywhere, we hate it."[18] So what are we to do? How can one hundred–plus years of representational tradition make room for new stories, for depictions of ranching that emphasize connections, flows, engagements with macrospace? That portray the worlding of ranch life?

One area that is rife with such connections also commits simplification on nearly every page. The anti-ranching and anti-beef books—books such as *Welfare Ranching, Beyond Beef,* or even Ruth Ozeki's marvelous *My Year of Meats*—do a great job connecting American livestock practices to multinational corporations and cartels, while making an urgent plea to halt worldwide environmental degradation that can come with commodity agriculture. These books, however, overstate ranching's complicity with multinational corporations and at the same time conflate ranching with the rest of the beef industry food chain processes, such as feedlot practices and large corporate slaughterhouses. While there are books that don't simplify, they remain under the radar for general readers, unreviewed in the mainstream press, published by small or specialty presses.[19]

Ranching in the American West remains a business, a valuable one for the planet. Years ago farm bureaus in western states routinely offered members agriculture tours all over the world. In the 1970s my dad, a sheep rancher, traveled to Australia and New Zealand, where he saw firsthand why he couldn't successfully compete. Not long after that trip, he sold his sheep and began selling his grass to other graziers. No more death losses, no more heartbreak while he continued to grow healthier land. Graziers of the world unite! When agriculturalists worldwide see what each of them both contributes and destroys, we can move toward an international ethic of environmental care. And when ranchers, farmers, and graziers meet family to family, they just might figure out how to navigate around Big Ag.

As for how the West might be represented in images and in text, Kittredge offers a suggestion: "Try this for openers: the art of a region begins to come mature when it is no longer what we think it should be."[20] The old stories that tie ranching to the handmade world of cowboy fantasy render ranching quaint, a relic of the past, but those stories have little place in the future. Many, if not most of the books and articles that link ranching to business, good stewardship, the health of the land and the eaters (not "consumers") of livestock, inform or advocate, but generally they don't delight. We don't yet have a body of images or texts that counter the Old West myths in a creative, beautiful, or humorous way.

But there are glimpses of what a transnational story of ranching might look like. Ryan Bell, former columnist for *Western Horseman*, Fulbright–National Geographic fellow to rural Russia and Kazakhstan, tells a new kind of story. Bell has written extensively about the exportation of a Montana cattle ranch—Angus breeding stock, cow horses, cowboys, and gear, everything but the land—to Russia. Such a project, Bell's account reveals, involves a lot more than moving livestock. Although cattle were native to the steppes, decades of collective farming followed by post-Soviet policy changes caused massive depletion of cattle herds. The Russian workers had no experience in handling livestock on a large scale, with working to finish a job rather than to finish a shift, and they had no experience with the ethic of care evident in the Montana ranching culture that served as their model.[21] Along with the technologies of ranching, Bell writes, Montana cowboys had to teach a little bit of cowboy culture to the Russian employees of the joint venture Stevenson Sputnik Ranch. But after a few years the Russians had adapted rather than copied Montana ranching culture and practices to suit their needs. Recent videos of cattle ranching ventures in Russia reveal a blending of technological and cultural practices, a new kind of ranching that suits (apparently) the location but looks across national boundaries for best management practices.[22]

When we have representations of ranching that more accurately reflect the ways ranches connect beyond their boundary fences, people in cities and suburbs might learn to care enough to reward stewardship and restoration, thereby helping ranches step outside the domination of Big Ag and the global cartels. When we have popular photos of ranchers repairing machinery in the shop, analyzing profitability on the headquarters computer, locating a temporary fence line with GPS, and walking across the pasture with cattle headed to new grass, then we might allow ranching a place in our transnational imaginary.

NOTES

1. Heise, *Sense of Place and Sense of Planet*, 6.
2. Campbell, *Affective Critical Regionality*, n.p.
3. Books that use case studies and documented science to tell stories of ranching as sustainable, conservation based, and often rehabilitative have appeared with greater frequency in the past few years. As valuable as they are for telling a different kind of story, they are generally published by small or specialty presses, they aren't routinely reviewed in places where they might attract a larger readership, and generally, they neglect the economics of ranching. Examples include books by Denis Hayes and Gail Boyer Hayes, Nicolette Hahn Niman, Judith D. Schwartz, Courtney White, and Todd Wilkinson. Nonfiction books by rancher/writers such as Linda Hasslestrom and Dan O'Brien, while at times addressing the economics of ranching, tend to focus on their ranches as microregions. The few books that negotiate the biology and economics of grazing, on one hand, and the global, on the other, reach only the specialist reader. Jim Howell's excellent book, *For the Love of the Land: Global Case Studies of Grazing in Nature's Image*, is self-published with blurbs from major figures within progressive farming and ranching groups. Of the three blurbs on the back cover, general readers might recognize only Joel Salatin, made a household name by Michael Pollan in *The Omnivore's Dilemma*.
4. See Cypher, *Bob Kleberg*, "Turner Ranches"; and Bell's website and articles.
5. Such a reading practice can only be hinted at here but might include critically reading a popular or literary text from a deeply contextual perspective. What might Ruth Ozeki's *My Year of Meats* look like in the company of Eric Schlosser's *Fast Food Nation* or alongside articles on Somalian meatpackers in small-town southern Alberta? What might emerge if we read David Stocklein's romantic images of American cowboys against a *National Geographic* feature on Kazakh horsemen?
6. See U.S. Department of Agriculture, "National Resources Inventory." I found no single current source for acreage, but extrapolating from various USDA articles online, this estimate is conservative. A 1994 report

claims over 300 million acres of public lands were used for grazing, and the bulk of that is Bureau of Land Management land in the West. Elsewhere a 2002 report claims 587 million acres of grass and rangeland in the United States. The majority of that land would be in the West.

7. Dana, *Two Years before the Mast.*
8. Fussell, *Raising Steaks*, 1–16.
9. See Wister, *Virginian*; Graulich and Tatum, *Reading* The Virginian. Graulich and Tatum's collection offers a model for addressing concentric boundaries and resituating Wister's classic text.
10. Starrs, *Let the Cowboy Ride.*
11. Blunt, *Breaking Clean.*
12. Blunt, "Occupying the Real West," 43.
13. Kittredge, "Next Rodeo," 234.
14. Kittredge, "Leaving the Ranch," 24.
15. Kittredge, "Home," 4.
16. Kittredge, *Who Owns the West*, 37.
17. Field, "Making a Living in the Age of Wal-Mart," 185.
18. Kittredge, "Owning It All," 68.
19. Hayes and Hayes (*Cowed*) are particularly good on the complexities of cattle raising in the Anthropocene.
20. Kittredge, "Doors to Our House," 176.
21. Bell, "Comrade Cowboys."
22. See the winning videos at "The First (and Only) Russian Ranch Video Awards," posted by Ryan T. Bell, April 5, 2016, http://voices .nationalgeographic.com/2016/04/05/the-first-and-only-russian-ranch -video-awards/.

BIBLIOGRAPHY

Bell, Ryan. *Comrade Cowboys.* 2015. Accessed July 4, 2016. http://www .comradecowboys.com.
———. "The First (and Only) Russian Ranch Video Awards." *National Geographic: Voices*, April 5, 2016. Accessed July 4, 2016. http://voices.national geographic.com/2016/04/05/the-first-and-only-russian-ranch-video -awards/.
Blunt, Judy. *Breaking Clean.* New York: Knopf, 2002.
———. "Occupying the Real West." *New Letters* 78, nos. 3–4 (2012): 43.
Campbell, Neil. *Affective Critical Regionality.* London: Rowman & Littlefield International, 2016.
Cypher, John. *Bob Kleberg and the King Ranch: A Worldwide Sea of Grass.* Austin: University of Texas Press, 1996.
Dana, Richard Henry, Jr. *Two Years before the Mast* (1840). *Two Years before the*

Mast and Other Voyages, edited by Thomas Philbrick. New York: Library of
   America, 2005.
Field, Tom. "Making a Living in the Age of Wal-Mart." In *Ranching West of
   the 100th Meridian: Culture, Ecology, and Economics*, edited by Richard L.
   Knight, Wendell C. Gilgert, and Ed Marston, 183–94. Washington DC:
   Island Press, 2002.
Fussell, Betty. *Raising Steaks: The Life and Times of American Beef.* Orlando:
   Harcourt, 2008.
Graulich, Melody, and Stephen Tatum, eds. *Reading* The Virginian *in the New
   West.* Lincoln: University of Nebraska Press, 2003.
Hasselstrom, Linda M. *Between Grass and Sky: Where I Live and Work.* Reno:
   University of Nevada Press, 2005.
Hayes, Denis, and Gail Boyer Hayes. *Cowed: The Hidden Impact of 93 Million
   Cows on America's Health, Economy, Politics, Culture, and Environment.* New
   York: Norton, 2015.
Heise, Ursula K. *Sense of Place and Sense of Planet: The Environmental Imagina-
   tion of the Global.* New York: Oxford University Press, 2008.
Howell, Jim. *For the Love of the Land: Global Case Studies of Grazing in Nature's
   Image.* North Charleston SC: Booksurge Publishing, 2008.
Kittredge, William. "Doors to Our House." *Owning It All: Essays*, 165–79.
   Saint Paul MN: Graywolf Press, 1987.
———. "Home." *Owning It All: Essays*, 3–19. Saint Paul MN: Graywolf Press,
   1987.
———. "Leaving the Ranch." *Taking Care: Thoughts on Storytelling and Belief*,
   13–31. Minneapolis: Milkweed, 1999.
———. "The Next Rodeo." *The Next Rodeo: New and Selected Essays*, 225–40.
   Saint Paul MN: Graywolf Press, 2007.
———. "Owning It All." *Owning It All: Essays*, 55–71. Saint Paul MN: Graywolf
   Press, 1987.
———. "Redneck Secrets." *The Next Rodeo: New and Selected Essays*, 113–23.
   Saint Paul MN: Graywolf Press, 2007.
———. "White People in Paradise." *The Next Rodeo: New and Selected Essays*,
   159–82. Saint Paul MN: Graywolf Press, 2007.
———. *Who Owns the West?* San Francisco: Mercury House, 1996.
Niman, Nicolette Hahn. *Defending Beef: The Case for Sustainable Meat Produc-
   tion.* White River Junction VT: Chelsea Green Publishing, 2014.
O'Brien, Dan. *Buffalo for the Broken Heart: Restoring Life to a Black Hills Ranch.*
   New York: Random House, 2001.
Ozeki, Ruth. *My Year of Meats.* New York: Viking, 1998.
Pollan, Michael. *The Omnivore's Dilemma: A Natural History of Four Meals.* New
   York: Penguin, 2006.

Schlosser, Eric. *Fast Food Nation: The Dark Side of the All-American Meal.* New York: Houghton Mifflin, 2001.

Schwartz, Judith D. *Cows Save the Planet.* White River Junction VT: Chelsea Green Publishing, 2013.

Starrs, Paul F. *Let the Cowboy Ride: Cattle Ranching in the American West.* Baltimore: Johns Hopkins University Press, 1998.

Thomas, Heather Smith. *Storey's Guide to Raising Beef Cattle.* North Adams MA: Storey Books, 1998.

"Turner Ranches." *Ted Turner Enterprises.* 2015. Accessed July 4, 2016.http:// www.tedturner.com/turner-ranches/.

U.S. Department of Agriculture. "National Resources Inventory Rangeland Resource Assessment." Natural Resources Conservation Service. Washington DC, 2014. Accessed November 20, 2015. http://www.nrcs .usda.gov/wps/portal/nrcs/detail/ national/technical/nra/nri/?cid= stelprdb1253602.

White, Courtney. *The Age of Consequences: A Chronicle of Concern and Hope.* Berkeley CA: Counterpoint, 2015.

———. *Revolution on the Range: The Rise of the New Ranch in the American West.* Washington DC: Island Press, 2008.

Wilkinson, Todd. *Last Stand: Ted Turner's Quest to Save a Troubled Planet.* Guilford CT: Lyons Press, 2013.

Wister, Owen. *The Virginian* (1902). New York: Penguin, 1988.

Life on the Western Edge of It All

Conceptions of Place in Tess Gallagher's Lough Arrow Poems

DRUCILLA WALL

Lough Arrow, in County Sligo, Ireland, holds the evening light brightly in the days just past midsummer. Night will not wrap the water until nearly eleven. I am listening to the water lapping while I stand at the slipway across the road from the home of my sister-in-law, Susan Frazer Wall, her husband, Michael Wall, and their three sons. Michael is my husband's youngest brother and also his godson; their youngest son, Oliver, is also his godson. Michael and Susan have welcomed us every summer for years. I never tire of their company, hearing the news over dinner of what the boys are doing or how the hens are outsmarting the foxes or how Susan's brother is coming to save the hay from their back field. Susan's family has lived here for generations. Their shared life expands along the shore of Lough Arrow to include Susan's extended family, and the Ballindoon area at this side of Lough Arrow plays an important part in the stories and events that form our sense of the world and its way of revealing meaning to us human inhabitants. I have enjoyed walking with Susan through the farmlands and hearing details of local history no book contains.

One time we walked a grassy, hillside pasture overlooking the lake. Softened shapes of furrows striped the width of it, broken by occasional low gorse or heather, and the air held a glistening of moisture, repeated and multiplied more heavily on the ground. The grass leaned with the wind in lush shades of green, and I was startled with delight as tiny frogs began to leap across our path. They were plentiful and unafraid. One let me pick it up in my hand. Darker than the grass and perfectly formed like a living amphibian jewel, the little frog seemed to be communicating the unsettling beauty and sacred presence of the place, although I could not have put that thought into words at the time. It paused in the center of my upturned palm, then leapt away among a mass of yellow flowers. To our left a whitethorn tree grew alone and, although not tall, had a tough, thick trunk and branches that had long withstood wild weather. Susan told me that the lingering furrows told the story of the people who had been lost in the Great Famine of the nineteenth century, the worst year of it still called "Black '47." The work of their hands remained imprinted on the meadows here in the shadowy swales. And the whitethorn tree was never disturbed, perhaps because of its association with the fairies or perhaps because in some now forgotten time an infant may have been buried under its shelter. We walked back down to Lough Arrow's shore, where her house faces the west, and I felt how truly the beauty of this place is shot through with a measure of sadness and that all the life of it that has ever been beats at once in the present, as if time holds no linear reality.

My youngest nephew, Oliver, who is about six years old, shakes me from my meditation and trots past me onto the short concrete dock that extends along the edge of the lake, for easy fishing or mooring of boats. He sits and runs a stick through the clear water where I cannot miss seeing him, and I am drawn to sit with him.

"You know, this is the best time of day for catching fish," he explains, "but you are too late for the mayfly. But there could be good trout, say, over there in the reeds or even bigger fish out in the deep water."

"How big could they get?" I ask, hoping for something outrageous. "Like, could there be a fish as big as a dog?"

"If you are talking about our dog, then there definitely are loads of fish bigger than a Jack Russell. Look way out as far as you can. That water is really cold and dark. I'd say there'd be fish out by the island that no one has ever seen and so big and so deep that they'd be bigger than a small whale." The lake goes down hundreds of feet in places, so Oliver may be right.

We pause to think about that. I recall that this is Yeats country. The Lake Isle of Innisfree, setting for his Thoreau-inspired poem, could be any of the wooded islands dotted on Lough Arrow or the neighboring lakes. The striking mountain, Ben Bulben, is not far away, as is Drumcliff Church and grounds, where Yeats is buried. Closer, the ancient tomb of Queen Medhbh crowns Knocknarea with an imposing cairn and hidden Neolithic passage grave. Stone circles, dolmens, and other smaller passage tombs are clustered at Carrowmore and Carrowkeel, just a short way down the road. We are near the Atlantic coast with expansive beaches. Limestone dominates the geology of the area, and such numerous underground springs and rivers carve their ways, emerging at their caprice, that no one bothers to try to count them all. And then there is the matter of the ley lines—the invisible energy lines that some people believe run through Sligo's sacred sites to connect with other key places as far away as the pyramids of Egypt. Michael told me that once we reached the top of Knocknarea, on that day we all climbed it together, that I would feel a clarity of mind and spirit and a burst of energy because of the special nature of the place. He was right. If it hadn't been raining sideways in a strong wind, I would not have wanted to climb back down. It felt so exhilarating.

I turn to Oliver. He has gone over to the gravel bank and is trying to skip stones on the calm water, shimmering silver in the late twilight. This is his home, and like home everywhere, it has an intimate and ordinary reality that he owns as much as he owns his heart. The mysteries of limestone and poets and ancient queens matter little when one is skipping stones. We walk back to the house and settle in for the evening.

A neighbor who is American like me and has a cottage nearby comes to visit from time to time, Susan mentions to me, and asks if I have ever heard of her. I might have heard of her because she is a writer and I am a writer, and we are both American. This sounds doubtful to me, but who knows. Her name is Tess Gallagher, she tells me. I go to my handbag and pull out a book I have brought along: *Midnight Lantern*, a poetry collection by Tess Gallagher.

In the intervening three years I have delved into Gallagher's work and her engagement with the place we both love. We may meet in person for the first time next summer, if the timing of our visits allow, and I feel that through her poems of place Gallagher appreciates something subtle that I, too, have noticed and found reflected in unexpected ways in her Lough Arrow poems. There is a westward gaze, perhaps more accurately a sense of many-layered meanings in living in the West of Ireland, of living on the edges of things—of the land where it meets the power of the Atlantic; of the banks of Lough Arrow where the Ballindoon townland looks westward to the cold depths and the limestone heights; of the natural world with its small wild creatures claiming their place in the human-dominated agricultural landscape; of the world of the living itself because to the west one finds *Tír na nÓg*, the land of eternal youth, the land of the dead.

Tess Gallagher is a poet of many Wests—the American Pacific Northwest, where she grew up; the West of Ireland at Ballindoon by Lough Arrow, where she has lived part of the year for decades; and the West of the spirit and of the dead, a place just off the physical grid. To inhabit any of Gallagher's Wests is to feel what it means to be on the western edge of things, a coastal feeling that gazes farther west to the cold ocean waves or wind-carved mountaintops at the horizon. She has long employed the idea of a rhizomatic, multivalent roughness of the rocky, westernmost edge of the United States, Europe, and that border between this world and possible others that both call to us and frighten.

Gallagher does not set out self-consciously to write poems of the West but, rather, situates the material of the poems in the complex implications of the western edge of things. Although she has poems engaging the Pacific Northwest of the United States and elsewhere, those set in Lough Arrow in County Sligo offer the common ground of place known to us both, and that intrigues me the most.

The theoretical concept of multiple Wests continues to be explored and developed in western American studies, and I would like to offer one road into how those explorations apply to the sense of place in the West of Ireland. Neil Campbell considers the American context as it reaches out into the larger world when he ponders how we might "think differently about the American West, to decentralize and dislocate the ways it has so often been considered . . . so that we might see westness as part of a larger system of discourse, beyond the national imaginary, pointing in many directions at once."[1]

The many-layered nature of human engagement with place—our ways of being and our seeking of full beingness in place—is not new, but the recognition of how we might understand and theorize it is the province of poets in unique ways. Gallagher presents the action of thought processes in the particularity of Lough Arrow in poetic form that engages place without explaining it into submission. For an outsider writing about an Irish setting, this involves a delicate artistic balance. In comparison to Campbell's idea, the Irish language term for the lore of place, *dinnseanchas*, provides an even more finely tuned idea of the deep mapping involved in Gallagher's poems of place at Lough Arrow. *Dinnseanchas* (pronounced *deen-shan-na-cus*) embraces a totality of topography, history, geology, animal life, nonhuman spirit beings, and human impact on a place—all the living and the dead in a nonlinear simultaneity of presence. The term has the sense of containing the story of the place in that the story is the heartbeat, the very spirit and life of the place. In his groundbreaking book *Writing the Irish West*, Eamonn Wall examines how this concept is at play in the works of a number of West of Ireland writers, including Tim Robinson, who is well-known for his deep mapping work in the area not far south of Lough Arrow.[2]

At the start of the last section of her new and selected collection of poetry *Midnight Lantern*, Tess Gallagher quotes Vincent Van Gogh: "The earth has been thought to be flat . . . science has proved that the earth is round . . . they persist these days in believing that life is flat and runs from birth to death. However, life, too, is probably round."[3] The section is titled "Signatures" and holds a concentration of poems set in Ballindoon, Lough Arrow, and areas nearby. I say "set," but that is not adequate to describe the Irishness of the poems. They engage combinations of place, people, and an ultimate elusiveness of meaning that permeates the concept of that nonlinear roundness of life, alongside the simultaneous sense of living on the edge of everything in the West—both precarious and experienced in the closeness of worlds thought of as separate in other places. Animals, neighbors, weather, the lake, the mountains, and, of course, the dead percolate through ordinary life, challenging the poet to do them justice in all their complexity.

Gallagher comes to this edge-of-everything sensibility from her earliest years, no doubt. She grew up in Port Angeles, Washington, in the American Pacific Northwest, to a logging family that struggled at times to make a go of it. She has mentioned in various interviews that as a child she enjoyed the freedom to roam the landscape both there and at her grandmother's place in the woods of the Missouri Ozarks. The unpeopled places of the wild woods of her American childhood might well have grounded Gallagher in a sense of the mystery and of the sacred that makes itself known in quiet, liminal space. N. Scott Momaday discusses this sensibility in *The Man Made of Words*, stating, "Sacred ground is in some way earned. . . . The mind does not comprehend it; it is at last to be recognized and acknowledged in the heart and soul. . . . The sacred is not a discipline. It is dimension beyond the ordinary and beyond the mechanics of analysis."[4] Place and all its aspects matter to Gallagher, and poetry offers the means to approach the edges hidden in place that allow glimpses of this sacred quality of being.

Gallagher studied with Theodore Roethke, has degrees from the University of Washington and the Iowa Writer's Workshop. She has taught in many places over the years, including the University of Montana, University of Arizona, and Whitman College. She has published short story collections and numerous books of poetry. A quick Google search will reveal a long list of accomplishments. She was instrumental in the publication of the original versions of the short stories by her late husband, Raymond Carver, which had been severely and controversially edited by his publisher. Gallagher has suffered loss of loved ones and is a cancer survivor herself. She divides her residence between Port Angeles and Lough Arrow, where she has spent much time over the past thirty years, long enough to gain some intimacy with the place and people.

In her explorations of the nonlinear edges of life and art, Gallagher has added works of collaboration to her individual pieces. This also fits her living on the western edge of things, in that she reaches toward other worldviews, other minds, other art forms, through collaboration. Gazing west at the edge of a continent or at the edge of Ireland's West, it seems natural enough to wonder what is out there. Who is out there? How might I make contact? How can we make something meaningful of these world's edges, these Wests, these places close to *Tír na nÓg*, to the vast Pacific, to the frightening, dark Sublime that fellow American poet Wallace Stevens saw in a postcard from which arose his famous poem "The Irish Cliffs of Moher"? Gallagher is not a timid poet. Her aesthetic is more intimate, free ranging, with a humility that is more comfortable with the diction of everyday language than Stevens's Modernist approach.

And of course, if one travels far enough west, one arrives in the East. Like fellow Northwest poet Gary Snyder, Gallagher employs some Japanese poetic influences and certain Buddhist worldviews. Snyder's idea that Buddhism calls for a complete conscious inhabiting of the natural world, including acceptance of its complex web of interconnected realities, is reflected in Gallagher's own expression of that idea in the Lough Arrow poems. In keeping with the concept of intersecting, multiple sites of meaning in the natural world, Gallagher has created collaborative works with Jakucho Setouchi, a Japanese Buddhist nun; translations of Romanian poet Liana Ursu; plays and screenplays with her late husband, Raymond Carver; free-ranging jazzlike poems with Lawrence Matsuda; and other works with her partner, painter, and native of Ballindoon, Josie Gray. The give-and-take of collaboration is not unlike Gallagher's relationship to the land in the Lough Arrow poems. Gallagher states in a 2014 interview: "I have always been fascinated by reciprocality—that is, the way one thing happens and then responsiveness gets going that would never have occurred without that initial stimulation."[5] This is another piece of Gallagher's aesthetic, grown from the edge of things. Again that reaching into the West, that sometimes brings one to the East, in that roundness of life of the Van Gogh quote.

Taking a closer look at the particular landscapes of Gallagher's childhood and those she encountered later in the West of Ireland, we can see the lush intimacy of the land itself, something that colors her poetry. The relatively mild climate, the high rainfall and lush wooded world of the Pacific Northwest, do not lend themselves to harsh sublimities but, rather, to something more akin to a conversation at the table in a kitchen or pub. Not that there are no dangers; it's just that one can know the dangers and make peace with them, like knowing where the bears live and how to respect their place without wanting to control or kill them.

The landscape at Lough Arrow has its dangers too, as Gallagher describes in the poem "Perished," about the accidental drowning of four men gone fishing. Lough Arrow is a V-shaped valley carved by the glaciers, and a black-surfaced, windswept place when you get away from the shore. But also the country has been shaped by intense human agriculture and habitation over thousands of years, so any wildness is mitigated into a nearly human form. Her treatment of such wild animals as a badger in "Brushing Fate" or a group of snails in "Walking on Annaugh Loy" shows this. Gallagher writes some of her most moving poems when dealing with loss, grief, and the burden of going on with life, something with which she has perhaps almost too much experience. She combines this unblinking yet elegiac stance with what has been articulated by Momaday in *The Way to Rainy Mountain*: "In his life a man ought to concentrate his mind on the remembered earth. He ought to give himself up to a particular landscape . . . to look at it from as many angles as he can, to wonder about it, to dwell upon it."[6] For Gallagher the angles of Lough Arrow include the layers of people's stories—the lives and the deaths and their intersections with the land.

In "Red Perch" Gallagher plays the poem against its epigraph from Paul Durcan, "But for the red perch in the black stream / my life has been nothing," using repetition of parts of it as a touchstone for the thin border that separates us from our neighbors who have died and entered the *Tír na nÓg* to the west of everything. The speaker recalls the girl who forty years ago came to her writer's caravan parked in the field of a Lough Arrow family. Yvonne. She loved poetry and was full of innocent yearnings after the stuff of life. The poem begins with an anchoring to place, including one of the most beautiful, ancient, and important Neolithic passage grave sites in the world:

Low fog-bloom of morning across the islands
of Lough Arrow below Carrowkeel
and the passage graves. I'm full circle
to my runaway coach of the sixties.[7]

Further recalling, the speaker contrasts the girl's eager life to the
poet's then-husband, a young pilot in the Vietnam War, using the
word *strafing* in reference to the violence that he would never com-
pletely survive. Gallagher is naming the dead, calling them, as the
poem continues. The girl becomes a young woman, and dies of can-
cer only one year into her happy marriage. In a touch of the ghostly
that feels Irish to me, Gallagher's third stanza reveals:

her letter discovered after her death, telling me in first glow
she had met her love. The great luck accomplished,
she wanted me to know.

The ending stanza takes the story, along with the implied relation-
ship between the women—one still living—one step further into a
mythic place. A small bird, a coal tit, takes center stage. The bird

pecks every morning
at my windows until I come.
It's her, I think,
wanting in. . . .
day after day, the bird returns,
we don't call her name, but
like air after flight,
she is there.[8]

The play on the word *morning*, time of day and, with one letter
changed, a state of mind, is just one of the ripples radiating into
the other-worldly West that is the edge of loss. The idea of a haunt-
ing that is not unwelcome, that is tactile in the pecking of the bird,
that brings an accepted and familiar sense of pain in its grief, is
reflected in that kitchen table rhythm of language.

In further dealings with poetry of loss and mourning, Gallagher centers her poem "Perished" on the figure of a young man bound for America from Lough Arrow. He and his three friends fish well and celebrate their catch but never return to shore. The connection to the old story of youth forced to emigrate from home to America resonates throughout Irish American writing, of course, but this particular view incorporates the primordial power of the lake itself, a nod to the Famine in the date of the incident, 1848, and its accompanying aftermath of sound in the storm winds that remain to this day. The chant-like quality of the seanachie can be heard in the lines, melded with the more direct conversational tone of the American voice. The epigraph is Stevie Smith's line "not waving but drowning."

One minute they were laughing,
The next they were drowning.
Three of them farmers, and Charlton
Slated for good-byes to America.
But he made no good-byes and never would be
found, for the lake takes a drink
Any way it can, and four good men, careless
On a Sabbath make a party
. . . .
One minute they were laughing,
The next they were drowning.

Charlton alone floats deep,
. . . .
Stayed endless with water, transformed
By the general mind of all who carry him now
As a voice inside the wind.[9]

In her treatment of those who have died too soon, Gallagher seeks an intimacy that is both affectionate in its appreciation of their part in the collective life of Lough Arrow and coolly accepting of their loss. Gallagher furthers her practice of Momaday's idea of dwelling deeply in a place by linking the human presence with the animals, especially those animals undervalued or even hated by many of their human neighbors. In "Brushing Fate" she captures the many layers of implication that surround avoiding hitting a badger on the road at night. And in "Walking on Annaugh Loy" fanciful musing about the adventurous lives of snails in the back garden turn out to be about much more than these humble creatures.

The badger in "Brushing Fate" is spared by a quick application of the car's brake:

> Badger does not so much as glance, as if his errand in the
>   night could not
> have been broken by any force, its current so strong,
> bearing him and us
> away from that hollowed-out
> moment, cave of never, in which life is
> everlasting and renewed by simply going on past averted
>   calamity.

Gallagher links this to her telling her partner, Josie, about her first husband, who returned from Vietnam but not unscathed, as one would have hoped. They have a simple evening meal. The badger is the linchpin who

> let us have again the freezing stars
> of an Irish morning.
> And in the starkness
> of lost love, could you see me
> afresh, Josie, and hesitate crucially,
> for him you never knew.[10]

The poem is dedicated to Lawrence Gallagher and Josie Gray. I like to think all badgers share that dedication as well. The natural world of the wild, even diminished as it is in Ireland, holds a strong and meaningful presence in this poem and many others, demonstrating Gallagher's belonging in both the writing traditions of the Irish and American Wests.

The setting for the snails of "Walking on Annaugh Loy" includes the fields adjacent to Lough Arrow, places farmed by families for generations, but the snails have farmed there for far longer. As ground-dwelling animals, nocturnal in their activities, they are often associated with death. Not the sort of creature most of us would want to curl up with on a cold night. But they are part of the Irish collective being that Gallagher explores, not unlike certain Native American concepts of the interconnectedness of all things. The question indirectly asked and answered in this poem is what do the snails tell us, what do they offer to teach us. The lessons are revealed through a juxtaposition of human conversation and snail beingness. In stanza 4:

> My friend and I talk news: a government eviction
> . . . .
> lives once turned to the good suddenly loosed again
> . . . .
> prison, drugs, or suicide.
> so unlike the noiseless ascent of snails clinging to my roof slates.

Dreams come into the poem, and the last stanza answers with:

> Since snails got into my head
> I am sleeping somewhere dark under bridges,
> And neither rain nor stars gleam romantic.
> For snails have, no doubt, had hard lessons
> From an inhospitable world. Thus
> those houses that are their backs.[11]

The snails are described always on the edge of things, as precariously making their way as the humans who live metaphorically on the edges of life. The snails persevere better, have adapted better.

And my little nephew has grown taller since our moments by the slipway, better at skipping stones, and good company for Tess Gallagher, just as he has been for me on my short walks to the lake dock. Oliver, bright and sociable, has made his way into a Gallagher poem and enjoys the same careful attention and wonder as all the inhabitants of Ballindoon. In "Oliver" she writes:

> He appears like a genie
> in my sun-shattered kitchen,
> . . . .
> Croissants are just coming out
> of the oven. His timing exact.

They have their tea and treats, and the speaker in the poem notes the energy and unselfconscious loudness of the boy's voice as he regales her with whatever is happening in his child's world. And the poem turns at her thought "But I've grown old." And we step over an edge, into the realm of mythic time, at an ancient spring where Oliver merges with those who have gone there before:

> How did he learn to imagine
> the strange, exact gift—that
> shadowed errand to Sruthlinn
> Spring, kneeling there to pick
> Watercress to be left in a plastic
> bag at my door?

The last stanza completes the connection of real boy layered with other-worldly wisdom:

> And the young letting the old
> know, that memory is that other
> seeping green that melds
> each moment to silence until
> it reappears as something else.[12]

The spring is an apt image. Springs feed Lough Arrow, while other springs offer a green, mossy source for cress, and others carve the mountains on high or sustain the tiny frogs in otherwise dry fields.

Gallagher understands the slow and covert processes of the limestone and water-fed expanses at Ballindoon. In harmony with that, she does not apply her aesthetic directly and explicitly but, rather, indirectly through narrative and contemplative poetry. Her work resists easy categorization, which is much to its credit. However, the common threads of life lived in close awareness of place in a West on the edge of things, where one can never really leave the edge and know the mystery, is present in the Sligo poems. The nonlinear roundness of life well experienced and observed from that western edge resonates throughout the work, especially in intersections with the hard lessons of loss and grief. In a 1988 interview Gallagher describes her approach to poetry: "I like some mystery, and I like to blur, sometimes, the way in which I arrived at a mood in a poem, so that my development might not be linear. I'll have little grottoes, sometimes, signals that not everything can be known. I don't do that just to be oblique. But to preserve the secret from which the poem emanates."[13] Lough Arrow in Sligo is a good place for a poet with such ideas. Knocknarea, sacred mountain crowned with the cairn of Queen Medhbh, looks down upon Lough Arrow, with its Yeatsian lake isles, fathomless depths, and haunted winds. The fields yield rich hay, and sometimes tiny frogs leap from nowhere on hills high above any seen water source. The Labby Rock of legend is near. Occasionally, a strange small black-barked tree juts from an otherwise mowed field, hinting at a private burial, too sacred for any articulated headstone. Des's country pub, the only one for miles, collects everyone to watch the World Cup or while away an evening. And badgers, snails, and their human neighbors, the living and the dead, look into the West, as we join them in Tess Gallagher's poems.

NOTES

1. Campbell, *Rhizomatic West*, 41.
2. Wall, *Writing the Irish West.*
3. Gallagher, *Midnight Lantern*, 273.
4. Momaday, *Man Made of Words*, 114.
5. Bancroft, "For Poet Tess Gallagher."
6. Momaday, *Way to Rainy Mountain*, 45.
7. Gallagher, "Red Perch," *Midnight Lantern*, 277.

8. Gallagher, "Red Perch," *Midnight Lantern*, 277.

9. Gallagher, "Perished," *Midnight Lantern*, 282.

10. Gallagher, "Brushing Fate," *Midnight Lantern*, 286–87.

11. Gallagher, "Walking on Annaugh Loy," *Midnight Lantern*, 306–8.

12. Gallagher, "Oliver."

13. Gallagher, "Interview," 42.

BIBLIOGRAPHY

Bancroft, Colette. "For Poet Tess Gallagher, Creativity Grows from Collaboration." *Tampa Bay Times*. April 15, 2014. Accessed July 4, 2016. http://www.tampabay.com/features/ books/for-poet-tess-gallagher-creativity -grows-from-collaboration/2175217.

Campbell, Neil. *The Rhizomatic West: Representing the American West in a Transnational, Global, Media Age*. Lincoln: University of Nebraska Press, 2008.

Gallagher, Tess. "An Interview with Tess Gallagher." By Penelope Moffett. *Poets and Writers* (July–August 1988). Posted July 19, 2010. Accessed July 4, 2016. http://www.pw.org/content/an_interview_with_tess_gallagher ?cmnt_all=1.

———. *Midnight Lantern: New and Selected Poems*. Minneapolis: Graywolf Press, 2011.

———. "Oliver." *Narrative Magazine* (Spring 2016). Accessed July 4, 2016. http://www.narrativemagazine.com/ issues/spring-2016/poetry/oliver -tess-gallagher.

Momaday, N. Scott. *The Man Made of Words: Essays, Stories, Passages*. New York: St. Martin's, 1997.

———. *The Way to Rainy Mountain*. New York: Ecco Press, 1995.

Wall, Eamonn. *Writing the Irish West: Ecologies and Traditions*. Notre Dame IN: University of Notre Dame Press, 2011.

Return to Finland, Robert Creeley, Continental Drift

EAMONN WALL

On my next-to-last day in Finland, I set out for Ekenäs, a town of fifteen thousand people, ninety-six kilometers southwest of Helsinki. Six months earlier, in the Christmas Day edition of the *New York Times*, I had read that "more than 80 percent of the residents of Ekenäs speak Swedish" and that Swedish speakers constitute about 5 percent of the population of the country as a whole. Since 1917, when Finland secured its independence from Russia, the rights of the Swedish minority, a much larger minority at that time than today, have been guaranteed in the constitution. Finland, like Ireland, has two national languages, and the relationship between the majority and minority languages is as tangled in one country as it is in the other; despite their respective legal statuses, both minority languages are under pressure and in decline. They should not be, but they are. In the Helsinki train station I asked for a ticket to Ekenäs and when I looked at it noticed that it read "Tammisaari." Before I could question the clerk, she said, a little too proudly I felt, "It's Tammisaari in Finnish."

The previous few days had been spent attending an academic conference, so I felt the need to escape from the city. Also, I thought that walking in the fresh air would allow those things that were racing around my head to settle into thoughts. I had come to Finland to speak on the American poet William Stafford at a conference at the University of Helsinki, to seek traces of another American poet—Robert Creeley—who had lived in Helsinki for a short time in the 1980s and who had written both memorably and bitterly about his experiences there, and because I'd enjoyed an earlier visit so much. A few months before undertaking this trip I had become an American citizen, so this journey, my first as an American passport holder, had some aspect of the landmark or novelty about it. I had not given it much thought beforehand, but the fact of my now being an American citizen affected, in odd and subtle ways, how I thought of myself. Though I lived in the same house and went to the same office each day, I was aware of some new and intangible sense of belonging—a degree of ownership, though one that did not bestow entitlement. At the same time my loyalties were divided—two countries, two continents—though my firmest sense of place continued to tie me to the smaller and more intimate spaces of neighborhood and town rather than to more abstract ideas of nations. At another level, and a deeper one, I knew that no such division existed: people and culture connect America to Ireland and Finland. In the literary sphere Ireland and the United States are interdependent. Our writers feed off theirs and vice versa. This week in Finland, more than ever, I belonged to both ours and theirs. For me writing is local and continental rather than national.

Ekenäs was the farthest I had traveled from my Helsinki base and therefore, I thought, a likely location for taking stock on this journey I had undertaken and my new persona as an American. I felt something of what the Finnish writer Pentti Saarikoski felt when he arrived in Dublin on Bloomsday in 1982: "This is journey's end, I sit in my room at the Ormond in Dublin, gazing out at Anna Livia and the seagulls circling above and the row of houses on the far side. Or not journey's end, it's just that I have been sitting here before, looking out this way."[1] Saarikoski reminds us that it is foolish to think that we can sit on a bed, stop the clock, and, idly almost, take stock. It is a waste of time to imagine that what did not work before can be made to succeed the second time round. Though becoming an American citizen had clarified things by squaring the reality of where I had lived for twenty-five years with the travel document I bore, it also, as I was often reminded on this visit to Helsinki, led to confusion because no one I spoke to believed, or wanted to accept, that I was an American. In fact, I myself was surprised that the immigration officer at the airport did not raise his eyes suspiciously after I presented him with my passport for inspection on my arrival in Finland.

Two months earlier I had been seated in a room at the convention center in Austin, Texas, to hear panelists at the annual Association of Writers and Writing Programs (AWP) conference speak in memory of the poet Robert Creeley, who had recently passed away. Over the decades, though hardly systematically, I had read and reread Creeley's work, the poems and essays in particular. One of my favorites is "The Rhythm":

It is all a rhythm,
from the shutting
door, to the window
opening,

the seasons, the sun's
light, the moon,
the oceans, the
growing of things.[2]

This poem exhibits a concise and sharp view of the human condition, one formed in the cold, late-Puritan New England shade and warmed under the sun in Majorca, California, and New Mexico. His wit had been refined by Black Mountain and the post–World War II counterculture. In Creeley's work the line of Emily Dickinson is engaged with the poetics of Pound, Olson, Williams, and others and with the philosophy of thinkers as varied as Gurdjieff and Wittgenstein. Beneath a surface that appears simple, almost simplistic perhaps, and casual, there lurk strenuous questionings and hard efforts at engagement with humans and their ideas.

Reading Creeley's poems and essays, one is brought into the heart of the poetry debates that took place in the United States in the decades after World War II and which resound today—between a formalist poetic model and a more "projective" structure, to use the term that Creeley coined. Writing from Bolinas in 1974, Creeley states his position:

Like many of my contemporaries I felt myself obliged to be an explicit craftsman so as to have defense against the authoritative poetry of my youth—whose persons I'd like now not to recall just that it's taken me so long to forget them. So, from that initial, crotchety purview, I've continued, finding and choosing as heroes men and women who must at this point be familiar to anyone who has read me at all: Williams, Pound, H.D., Stein, Zukofsky, Olson, Duncan, Levertov, Ginsberg, Dorn, Bunting, Wieners, McClure, Whalen, Snyder, Berrigan—and so on, being those I can almost see out the window if I look. Put more simply, there's been a way of doing things which found company with others, and in that company one has found a particular life of insistent and sustaining kind.[3]

I am drawn to Creeley's mixture of independence, resistance, and belonging. Working as a poet for over forty years, I continue to be guided by his passionate intelligence. He has provided me with a means of escaping—a ladder raised to my bedroom window—from the rather rigid poetic practices and injunctions that were so prevalent in the Irish literary scene of my youth. At the same time, and this is what his detractors often fail to notice, Creeley's work, as Arthur Ford points out, is technically complex and never quite as projective as it appears.[4] William Stafford's work, as I tried to point out rather hopelessly at the conference, while seemingly casual technically, is also rooted in tradition with the depth of thought matched by a more latent gravity of style. An advantage of being a writer and scholar is that when one is engaged with the work of the latter, one is forced to read very patiently, to slow down, to adjust one's consciousness so that the poem or story under consideration begins to glow and give off something of its spirit and mechanism. Today we are tempted to read a poem as we might scan a text message; the demands of scholarship, on the other hand, force us into another continuum of space and time. As was the case in the old days, we learn to write from imitation.

Over the years I have wondered about Creeley in Placitas, New Mexico, Creeley in Bolinas, California, where Richard Brautigan also lived, and imagined what fun it must all have been with so many writers gathered for weekends of sport. Unfortunately, I never got to meet Creeley or hear him read, except on tape and video. Much of the final phase of Creeley's life was spent in Buffalo, representing a return to the cold North, one from all accounts he found amenable. I'd had a teacher once who had been a student of Creeley in Buffalo, who venerated him, and who railed against Helen Vendler for omitting Creeley from her Oxford anthology of American poetry: he said that there could be no anthology of American poetry without Creeley. Hearing him say this, I had gone back to the poems. Later I came across Thom Gunn's review of the *Collected Poems* in which he noted that Creeley's "language has never fit in with the official current notions of the poetic"; even though he finds the language to be "neutral," at the same time Gunn finds the poetry to be "powerful and persuasive."[5]

Interestingly enough, Gunn enumerates the similarities between the "rhetorical flatness" of Creeley's poetry and the verse of such early Elizabethans as Barnaby Googe, a further indication of the literary rootedness of post-1945 American poets in the English tradition (syntax and diction in particular), all of which is so apparent in the work of Olson, Stafford, Duncan, and Berryman. It is interesting to note how aspects of Elizabethan English are encoded in contemporary American poetry. Gunn notes Creeley's dogged belief in the narrow, personal world and finds his best work to be "fresh and clean."[6] Exploring his poetics from within, Gunn describes the projective elements in the work—the breaths and emphatic endings, the degree to which so much is qualified and made more complex by Creeley's use of punctuation—and he explores "the recurrent term of *stumbling* for his poetic procedure":

My luck
is your gift,
my melodious
breath, my stumbling.[7]

"If one stumbles," Gunn notes, "led or pushed by impulse, one stumbles into the unforeseen, the accidental. Even so, the accidental may have its patterns."[8] To come across Creeley for the first time is exciting and challenging. Like Thom Gunn, I was moved by Creeley's work and remain so, while at the same time, on first reading, I was perplexed by its line, diction, and syntax. Initially, I could describe neither his points nor his poetics, not even to myself.

My presence that day in a room in Texas to hear Creeley's friends and admirers speak was no accident, or mere stumbling: a stumbling occurred when I discovered that Creeley had held the Bicentennial Chair in American Studies at the University of Helsinki in 1988–89. At the anniversary banquet celebrating the creation of this position, which I attended as one of the conference participants on my second visit to the city, I looked across the room toward the table where many of the holders of this chair were seated. In the center of this group of scholars was one creative writer—N. Scott Momaday, the great Kiowa writer—and I felt a rare privilege to be in the same room as the author of *House Made of Dawn* and other works. When the meal had ended, the last speeches had been delivered, and while the group tiredly exited, I lingered a moment as I made my departure, resting my two hands on the back of the chair on which Momaday had sat to give thanks to him, in my own way, for the generosity of spirit displayed in his books. I might have approached him that evening, but I thought better of it, seeing that he was surrounded by many professors, a majority of this group being political scientists. I would have liked to have seen Robert Creeley seated beside Momaday at the table of the honorees, two writers babbling about the lives and the scrapes they had managed to survive both at home and abroad. Though his books remain, Creeley's image had disappeared.

Creeley's "Autobiography" is appended to Tom Clark's study of the poet's work and is dated Helsinki, Finland, March 23, 1989.[9] At a kind of journey's end in Dublin, Pentti Saarikoski did not manage to gain the hoped-for insight because, he felt, "one should not return to places associated with cherished memories."[10] For Creeley, a long way from home, at a kind of journey's end and in a new place, Helsinki provided imaginative opportunities, both in poetry and prose. Helsinki does not figure greatly in the "Autobiography"—there's a brief account of a meeting with Claes Andersson, poet member of Finland's parliament and, near the end, a description of what is visible from his apartment window—though I have a sense, or perhaps I just imagine it, that the prose takes some elements of its shape from the city.

The early part of the autobiography is written in a complex, highly punctuated prose style, as is the case in many of his poems. This short autobiography, its very compactness in keeping with the modus operandi behind the poetry, teems with personal and literary history and is underlined by apology, description, and revision: "When young I'd written Olson with almost pious exclamation: 'Form is never more than an extension of content.' Now I might say equally, 'Content is never more than an extension of form.'"[11] One can only wonder the degree to which the tone, timbre, and thoughts present in the autobiography are the result of Creeley's presence in Helsinki. For example, to what extent can we say that the poet's memory of his early life in New England has somehow been filtered through the view from his Helsinki apartment window? When I returned to Helsinki having read the autobiography, I noted the marks Creeley had made on the city and remembered how at the beginning Creeley had teased out his own childhood, while at the end, in Helsinki, he had explored that of his children, who had been sent out merrily onto the streets to walk to school. Helsinki, I conjectured, was where past, present, and future aligned for Robert Creeley.

The Helsinki poems are gathered in *Windows* (1990) and comprise the collection's sixth and final section, titled "Helsinki Window."[12] The starting point is the view from his apartment:

Old sky freshened with cloud bulk
slides over frame of window the
shadings of softened greys a light
of air up out of this dense high
structured enclosure of buildings
top or pushed up flat of bricked roof
frame I love *I love* the safety of
small world this door frame back
of me the panes of simple glass yet

airy up sweep of birch trees sit in
flat below all designation declaration
here as clouds move so simply away.[13]

Like the window, bricks, and sky, the parts of the sequence are
shaped as rectangular frames that contain aspects of what is visible,
and the voice of the speaker, each forming a Black Mountain, pro-
jective verse "field." The window is the field. Helsinki, for Creeley, is
personified by its sky—"I can watch, from this window, an insistent
height of sky that has been all this past fall and winter a companion
to my being here, and a subtle, unaggressive information of where,
in fact, it is"—which can be both a field itself on which words can be
transcribed and, at its outer edges, the place where one begins and
departs: "There is a broken-record tone of necessity in that it keeps
coming back to the beginning of the proposition, that there was
someone to begin with, and that something therefore followed."[14]
On the level of metaphor the window serves Creeley perfectly as it
is pliable and can be made to suggest so much: our limited view of
the world, the small shape of the poem contrasted with the world's
complex contortions, the fact that the viewer is always himself on
display, and the reality that nothing outside is fixed, that all is sub-
ject to change, that one's children walk along the streets to the city
tram stop in preparation for the walk into their own independent
lives. The room where Creeley writes is the body, "the someone to
begin with," the windows his eyes on the world.

Interviewed by Charles Bernstein, who spoke on the memorial
panel to Creeley at the AWP conference in Austin, Creeley noted
that "the light in Finland was just mind-blowing, whether it was in
the diminution of it towards the center of the year, in the winter. But,
equally, this vatic light that would then come back at the edge of sum-
mer."[15] In Finland I too had noticed the light. One morning sailing
out from Helsinki toward Tallinn, I observed how the light was simi-
lar to Irish light and, as a result, how much the rhythms of my mind
and body are rooted in the North. I understood that I am of this
light, this clear cold space. That morning I experienced the deepest
feelings of ecstasy and belonging: to Finland, Ireland, and America.

In the summer of 1996, seven years later, Creeley made a return visit to Helsinki to read at the Helsinki Festival. In another essay sizing up both trips, he noted how much more satisfactory his second had been compared to the first. The occasion of his reading he described as being "one of those golden moments for a poet, when he or she can say or do nothing wrongly, when the audience will secure and sustain the music it has come to hear."[16] Because it was summer, "people were so instantly handsome, their movement lithe, sensuous, confident. It was lovely. No place I came to seemed apart from its spell."[17] His Fulbright visit had ended before summer began and throughout served to reinforce Creeley's "impatience and displacement" and made him feel "more isolated than ever."[18] At the root of his unhappiness was the winter. The temperatures seemed to hover around freezing (unseasonably mild for Finland) so that the ice rinks never froze enough for his kids to skate in anything better than slush, and he decried the shortness of winter days in the far North. Certainly, *kaamos*, the dark-blue glow of the polar night, was not for him: "The days, of course, had grown ironically to only a few hours of light, and now the night's blackness prevailed for hours and hours on end. We rose in the dark, and by mid-afternoon it was dark again. Why did we get up at all?"[19]

Everything in the North is transformed by summer—from the moods and faces of the inhabitants to the landscapes that define us all. Creeley's complaints in winter and rejoicings in summer seem Irish to me; even the freakish winter weather he experienced in Finland is a dead ringer for the damp Irish winter through which one is often cold and dispirited. Creeley's unhappiness on his Fulbright year is further explained by his poor physical state on arrival: "I arrived with both feet crippled from a recent operation to free the joints of my big toes on either foot, locked as they'd been with arthritis. So, together with patient family attending, I was wheeled out of the airport, into a car, then taken to what was to be our home in Helsinki, a generously provided apartment just up from the Forum and the railroad station."[20] Clearly, given his condition, he had chosen the wrong year to winter in Finland. His attitude to the weather is underlined by, or even explained by, his claim to "being part Irish myself."[21] Of course, this harsh tone is diluted later when he speaks in hindsight to Bernstein. It was only later, from reading Daniel Tobin's scholarship, that I began to understand how Irish Creeley actually was, how connected we were:

> Then, when at last I was twenty-one,
> my mother finally told me
> indeed the name *Creeley* was Irish—
>
> and heavens opened, birds sang,
> and the trees and ladies spoke
> with wondrous voices. The power of the glory
> of poetry—was at last mine.[22]

I had loved Creeley's work long before learning of his connection to Ireland, and this new knowledge did not make me feel that I should admire him even more. I suppose, out of a loyalty to American poetry, I bristled at the romantic notion that Creeley pushed connecting Ireland to the essence of verse. On the other hand, I liked how things came together, how language formed continents and tied continents together.

The hours of working on poems in his apartment and the window through which Creeley looked outside and which gave the volume of poems its title are both described: "I wrote at odd times of the day and night in the small study just off the kitchen. It's one window faced out to the apartment block's inner courtyard."[23] He notes that his teaching assignment at the university was a "farce," finds that Finns, the great poet Paavo Haavikko included, do not consider American writing to be of much interest, and makes so many trips outside of the country, including several returns to the United States, that one wonders if he had been living in Finland at all. The poets he finds common ground with in Finland write in Swedish. Except for the celebration of summer in Helsinki and the notes he provides on his own working routine as a poet, the essay is embittered in tone. Even so, given my own sad experience of trying to explain Stafford's vision at the conference (in the same building where Creeley had taught), I am heartened by his account of how difficult he found it to get Levertov's and Olson's ideas and poetics across to his students at the University of Helsinki; at the same time I read "Coming Home" with misgivings. About the Finns' attitude to American writing, Creeley is wrong. In my experience Finns appreciate American writing and are in awe of American literary achievement, and the Renvall Institute at the University of Helsinki is a warm space for the American writer. Wandering around Helsinki's streets, stepping in and out of cathedrals, churches, cafés, and bars, I felt none of the loathing that Creeley expresses. On the contrary, I was blissfully happy way up north in the light. I was home.

In *Self Portrait* the Irish poet Patrick Kavanagh writes about going away and returning home, seeing them as two modes of simplicity: "There are two kinds of simplicity, the simplicity of going away and the simplicity of return. The last is the ultimate in sophistication. In the final simplicity we don't care whether we appear foolish or not. We talk of things that earlier would embarrass. We are satisfied with being ourselves, however small."[24] Kavanagh is describing the transformation that took place in his outlook on life and poetry while he was recovering from lung cancer, a shift that produced a remarkable synthesis in his work. More generally, he implies that the journey garners for the traveler a newfound confidence that allows him or her to be veiled behind the mask of experience on returning home. For Creeley, who quotes this passage in his essay on Kavanagh, the going away from America (after surgery) was not simple: it was literally a stumbling.

His return to America from his Fulbright, given the hostility he often felt in Finland and his sense that neither he nor his literature was taken seriously by the Finns, was simple: it was a return to what was known, to a place where he had prestige. I wonder why he felt the Finns were so reluctant to praise American writing. Was it because Creeley sought their affirmation too eagerly? Or because America seemed to lead at everything else—business, technology, medicine, space exploration, film—could it be that the Finns were reluctant to assent to the fact that America was also the leader of literature? If so, what was left for the rest of the world? For Creeley the final simplicity was his return trip: he enjoyed good weather and was feted as a poet. Kavanagh has written that "real technique is a spiritual quality, a condition of mind, or an ability to invoke a particular condition of mind," qualities both Creeley and Kavanagh possessed in abundance.[25] Retreating to the United States from Helsinki for a second time, I recall Italo Calvino's maxim: "The city exists and it has a simple secret: it knows only departures, not returns."[26] It defines my return more than it does Creeley's, his being closer to what Kavanagh describes. Landing at JFK, I stood in the shorter of the two lines in front of a sign that read: U.S. CITIZENS. Handing over my passport at the desk, I was aware of my own multiple sense of belonging: I am home on two continents, stumbling into languages—oral, written, connected.

NOTES

1. Saarikoski, *Edge of Europe*, 160.
2. Creeley, *Selected Poems*, 90.
3. Creeley, *Was That a Real Poem*, 100.
4. Ford, *Creeley*.
5. Gunn, *Shelf Life*, 87.
6. Gunn, *Shelf Life*, 91.
7. Gunn, *Shelf Life*, 88.
8. Gunn, *Shelf Life*, 88–89.
9. Clark, *Robert Creeley*, 122–44.
10. Saarikoski, *Edge of Europe*, 161.
11. Clark, *Robert Creeley*, 142.
12. Creeley, *Windows*, 117–50.
13. Creeley, *Windows*, 136.
14. Clark, *Robert Creeley*, 143–44.
15. Creeley, *Just in Time*, 31.
16. Creeley, "Coming Home," 38.
17. Creeley, "Coming Home," 37–38.
18. Creeley, "Coming Home," 35.
19. Creeley, "Coming Home," 35.
20. Creeley, "Coming Home," 31.
21. Creeley, "Coming Home," 31.
22. Tobin, *Irish American Poetry*; Creeley, "Theresa's Friends," 139.
23. Creeley, "Coming Home," 36.
24. Kavanagh, *Poet's Country*, 314.

25. Kavanagh, *Poet's Country*, 278.
26. Calvino, *Invisible Cities*, 56.

BIBLIOGRAPHY

Calvino, Italo. *Invisible Cities*. Translated by William Weaver. San Diego: Harcourt, 1974.

Clark, Tom. *Robert Creeley and the Genius of the American Commonplace*. New York: New Directions, 1993.

Creeley, Robert. "Coming Home." *Books from Finland* 1 (1997): 30–37.

———. *Just in Time: Poems, 1984–1994*. New York: New Directions, 2001.

———. *Selected Poems*. Berkeley: University of California Press, 1991.

———. "Theresa's Friends." *So There: Poems, 1976–83*, 139. New York: New Directions, 1998.

———. *Was That a Real Poem and Other Essays*. Edited by Donald Allen. Bolinas CA: Four Seasons Foundation, 1979.

———. *Windows*. New York: New Directions, 1990.

Ford, Arthur. *Robert Creeley*. Boston: Twayne, 1978.

Gunn, Thom. *Shelf Life: Essays, Memoirs and an Interview*. London: Faber & Faber, 1994.

Kavanagh, Patrick. *A Poet's Country: Selected Prose*. Edited by Antoinette Quinn. Dublin: Lilliput Press, 2003.

Saarikoski, Pentti. *The Edge of Europe: A Kinetic Image*. Translated by Anselm Hollo. South Bend IN: Action Books, 2007.

Tobin, Daniel. *Irish American Poetry from the Eighteenth Century to the Present*. South Bend IN: University of Notre Dame Press, 2007.

Excerpts from COSMOGRAPHY

Re-Minding Our Place in the Universe

JOEL WEISHAUS

Tracing the human imagination back to the animal, vegetable, and mineral domains and forward to where "great Orion, the Pleiades, and Sirius become speaking acquaintances,"[1] in the twentieth century, Pythagoras's *kosmos* metamorphosed from "to arrange in a beautiful order" into a science that designs experiments to test its theories in a process that collapses mysteries into measurements and subtracts daemonic ciphers as if metaphysical gossip.

Even the Muses, who for centuries inspired artists to see deeply what is revealed before them, have become an actionable at-a-distance pastiche of marketable clones.

Does consciousness deploy billions of neurons and synapses only to endow an expanding universe with a limited imagination?

Creativity is the art of balancing on the edge of the bottomless pit from which the Sibil's auguring fumes are rising. However, unlike the theistic Prophets, artists can breathe deeply without falling in.

COSMOGRAPHY is a five-year Digital Literary Art project that reflects the universe archetypically. Inscribed as a journal, its tropes include invaginations: fragments of texts exhumed from literature's corpus and transplanted into the body of a text, interrupting its continuity, disrupting its literal meaning; and it superimposes images and animations that initiate various degrees of interpretation. These texts and images offer an art living "on the earth with a cosmic sense, but living on the earth."[2]

The project consists of seven planets, plus the sun, the moon, and Incognita, a body that can only be imagined circling Earth in pre-Copernican orbit because it is on Earth that we observe and decode a universe hurrying away from us. That Earth revolves around the sun has been confirmed by astronomers for over five hundred years.

On the other hand, art is to me the rueful expression of what is not yet, and can never be, conclusive.

COSMOGRAPHY's full design, which includes my trope of "invagination," photography, and animations, is available online.[3]

1. Waters, Frank. *Mountain Dialogues* (Athens OH: Swallow Press, 1981). 77.
2. White, Kenneth. "Elements of Geopoetics," *Edinburgh Review* 88 (1992): 167.
3. Weishaus, Joel. *Cosmography: Re-Minding Our Place in the Universe,* http://www.cddc.vt.edu/host/weishaus/Cosmography/intro.htm.

SUN

2.

I leave before dawn, the trail already warm as the sun rises to enlighten me. But I am too old, too clever: my bones already chill the earth.

A slight breeze rustles the grass; a yellow flower chimes in: "Vincent was a writer with a radiant force whose words tasted of turpentine."

Fiery tongues personify a sun, one among billions. Yet only *its* sparks leap into the darkness where our ancestors are dancing in circles.

radiant force: G. Mayer, quoted in R. Huyghe, "Color and the Expression of Interior Time in Western Art," *Color Symbolism: Eranos Excerpts* (Zurich, 1977).

5.

I had almost forgotten where I was, my thoughts wayfaring to
   painted caves and giant standing stones.
Then a narrow path appeared, verged with a florid landscape of
   wildly golden poppies, and I saw how California is "cobbled
   together from the rest of the world."
Far west of here, beyond hazy strings of islands and oil-sucking
   rigs, one dark morning Amaterasu, the Sun Goddess,
      was born in the luminous Iris
      of her father's left eye.

cobbled together: J. McPhee, *Assembling California* (New York, 1994).
Amaterasu: "The Sun goddess' father, Izanagi (Male-Who-Invites) has just

come back from the underworld. He had gone there to fetch his wife, Izanami (Female-Who-Invites), who died giving birth to the fire god. He failed to bring her back. But because he has been to a polluted land he must purify himself. Entering a river for the purification . . . Izanagi purifies his left eye and gives birth to the Sun Goddess, Amaterasu." H. Kawai, *Dreams, Myths and Fairy Tales in Japan* (Einsiedein, 1995).

Iris: The Greek goddess personified as a rainbow. She is a messenger of the gods, traveling between the darkness of Hades and the bright world above. Besides controlling the diameter of the pupil's admission of light, the iris gives the eye its color.

12.

Begin in darkness, picking your way along the path, relying more on memory map than flashlight's narrow beam. The moon is setting; the sun, as if drawn on the same string, has not yet reached the horizon. The old gods assume the myths of ascent and descent, while art is before and after.

Sun lights the dangling roots of a tree half-embedded atop an eroding cliff. If it rains hard again, tree will slide into a raging river below.

Rocks and plants appear immersed together in early morning meditation.

What is and what is not walk in the tracks of a bobcat's four separated pads. A fifth in the middle like a fox's heart-shaped center.

on the same string: "The Chumash believed the sun to be a very powerful anthropomorphic being who dwelt in the Upper World in a quartz crystal house along with his two daughters. He was a widower and extremely old. . . . Carrying a torch which was the sun, he made a daily trip across the sky, following a cord which stretched around the world. If the cord were to break he would fall into the Middle World below." T. Hudson and E. Underhay, *Crystals in the Sky: An Intellectual Odyssey Involving Chumash Astronomy, Cosmology and Rock Art* (Santa Barbara, 1978).

a fox's heart-shaped center: "Cosmologically, the heart was the Sun, center of the world." D. Cosgrove, "Apollo's Eye: A Cultural Geography of the Globe," Hettner Lecture, June 2005.

MOON

3.

"Even when I was a boy I could never walk in a woods without feeling that at any moment I might find before me somebody or something I had long looked for without knowing what I looked for."

In Wills Canyon an old woman bent beneath a large backpack hurried past me. Later I learned she was Dorothy Wordsworth, Bill's sister, of whom Sam Coleridge wrote, "If you expected to see a pretty woman you would think her ordinary; if you expected to see an ordinary woman you'd think her pretty!" I would add: She could write remarkable lines like "The moon shone like herrings in the water," even in midst of a drought!

"There's water down there?" I asked the Water Company man.

"Yes," he said, with an amused smile.

"Where'd it come from?"

He shook his head and turned back to repairing the pump.

This morning rocks with "fine white lines, fine as the wrinkles in an old lady's face," breathe heavy and slow, one breath every one hundred million or so years.

Even when I was a boy: W. B. Yeats, *The Celtic Twilight: Faerie and Folklore* (London, 1902).

If you expected: S. Coleridge, June 1797, quoted by M. Moorman, ed., *Journals of Dorothy Wordsworth* (Oxford, 1971).

The moon shone: D. Wordsworth, *Grasmere Journal*, October 31, 1800.

fine white lines: N. Mailer, *Of a Fire on the Moon* (Boston, 1970).

one hundred million or so years: "Some of the distinctive rock deposit evidence seen by LRO (Lunar Reconnaissance Orbiter) could be as young as a hundred million years, right around the time of the dinosaurs on Earth. . . . Previously, it was thought that all volcanic activity on the Moon ended a billion years ago." B. A. Parnell, "Throw Out the Geology Books—Volcanoes Were Erupting on the Moon Just 100 Million Years Ago," *Forbes*, October 13, 2014.

9.

Sun Face, Moon Face, gods and goddesses swapping masks. On this path brains diminish, fewer neurons connect, technology begins

to think for itself. Lurking in shadows, untamed beings prepare to
take our place.

> History is (after all)
>> fresh tracks circling
>>> a muddy pond

Sun Face, Moon Face: "In the Scripture of Buddha Names it says that Sun
Face Buddha lives for eighteen hundred years, while Moon Face Buddha
enters extinction after a day and a night. But what about your own Sun
Face Buddha, Moon Face Buddha? Is it something long or short? How
do you understand it? Set your eyes on the absolutely inextricable within
yourself." Tenkei Denson (1648–1735), in *Secrets of the Blue Cliff Record*, ed.
T. Cleary (Boston 2002).

untamed beings: "The tree of life is a twisted, tangled, pulsing entity with
roots and branches meeting underground and in midair to form eccentric
new fruits and hybrids." L. Margulis, *Symbiotic Planet* (Amherst MA, 1998).

17.

As a student planted the tree from which he took his name, Bashō
asked himself, "How am I doing? Let me answer, 'in lonely pov-
erty' . . . but no one responds." While walking Japan's backroads
and paths, Bashō would conjure his forerunners, engaging them
in "conversations between a 'ghost and a ghost to be.'" Was he won-
dering if his poems would weather the moon's deathless gaze? In
Bashō's wake generations would see "the glow of the song as vividly
as if they were running along great lighted pathways."

Bashō: Matsuo Bashō (1644–94) was born Matsuo Kinsaku in Ueno, Iga
Province. In 1681 a pupil of his transplanted a banana (bashō) tree by the
poet's small hut.

How am I doing: D. L. Barnhill, *Bashō's Journey: The Literary Prose of Matsuo
Bashō* (Albany NY, 2005).

conversations: R. Macfarlane, *The Old Ways: A Journey on Foot* (New York, 2012).

moon's deathless gaze:
> her face—
> old woman weeps alone,
> moon her only companion.
>> (Bashō, from "An Account of the Moon at Mount Obasute in Sarashina")

the glow of the song: MacFarlane, *Old Ways*. He is actually speaking "of certain Aboriginal Australian dream-runners who were exceptionally fluent in the Songlines, and whose knowledge allowed them to move across the land at great speed in the dark."

SATURN

2.

In a predawn haze I walk through a valley reaping dust and onto a ridge of the mountain surrounding it, leap over the corpus callosum, and open a path on the other side of my mind.

Since leaving my childhood's flat gray streets, I have lived in exile. How did I get here? How can I live anywhere else? How marvelous it is to be old and see a hawk with keen eyes land on a branch nearby.

reaping dust: Roman god of winter harvest, Saturn has been called the Grim Reaper.

flat streets: "During the Renaissance-in-alchemy, the art of memory, and astrology-thick-crusted things, things gray and dull, wintry, or living in isolated places, belonged to Saturn." J. Hillman, "Back to Beyond: On Cosmology," in *Archetypal Process*, ed. D. R. Griffin (Evanston IL, 1989).

How can I live anywhere else: Thus, "The slow westward motion of more than I am." C. Olson, Maximus to Gloucester, letter 27.

8.

Rain pelting the roof tonight recalls the sound of sand scouring the lid of my father's coffin. The year before, as he swam in the timeless depths of alzheimeric sleep, I kissed his forehead and whispered *Good-bye*, another rosy dawn rising over Florida's shell-strewn beaches.

One year later, a blustery rainstorm pelting New Mexico's high desert, I read on a mesa's cold brow:

What am I to myself
that must be remembered
insisted upon
so often?

timeless depths: "At the end of the story Cronus-Saturn, with his last transformation, seems to go beyond time, thereby disclosing the full meaning of his process." A. Vitale, "The Archetype of Saturn or the Transformation of the Father," in *Fathers and Mothers*, ed. P. Berry (Dallas, 1990).

What am I to myself: R. Creeley, from "The Rain."

9.

> So many times I thought
> this is the place where my spine will bond
> with the roots of trees
> *then I'd move*
> To where it was sometimes wetter,
> now hotter, always sowing
> the groundless illusion of place.

Late September on the cusp of dawn. Walking past an early AA meeting seen through an open door, across the street a woman is standing in the bright-lit doorway of a storefront gym. The Mexican restaurant's neon sign blinks OPEN in red. A pack of horsepowered headlights turns onto the town's main street; while veiled in shadows, a horse patiently waits for his morning feed. Across the valley two coyotes call to each other, giving voice to the one incalculable place.

where my spine will bond: "All around me, my fellow-men are new grafting their vines and dwelling in flourishing arbors; while I am forever pruning mine, till it becomes but a stump. Yet in this pruning I will persist; I will not add, I will diminish; I will trim myself down to the standard of what is unchangeably true. Day by day will drop off my redundancies; ere long I shall have stripped my ribs; when I die they will but bury my spine." H. Melville, *Mardi, and a Voyage Thither* (New York, 1849).

groundless illusion: "Yet as I lingered in that landscape, I noticed something else happening, something that did not belong simply to the order of space as sheer extension. This was my momentary camp itself, the place I created on the modest mountain where I pitched my tent, built a fire, talked with friends, and gazed out on the landscape itself." E. S. Casey, "Smooth Spaces and Rough-Edged Places: The Hidden History of Place," *Review of Metaphysics* (December 1997).

POETRY 3 | *Planetary Currents*

Asking Why

MARJORIE SAISER

When I sit up to read
in the yellow of the lamp,
the blackest of beautiful black
filling the corners of windows,
I hear the quail.
Not a melody
but one lone note.
She has only one
and she doesn't care
if I hear it. She lies low
in the laurel, as if she queries
the universe in some
ancient language. It's not
the elegant owl who
speaks for me. It's the
one-note of the quail,
a question rising
like a flag in the dark.

The Dark Sky Reserve

HEID E. ERDRICH

Say what you will, silent lake
wimpy shimmer of clouds
shrugging a blueness, a blank slate
non-verbal pre-verbal verb-less breathless expectation
Jet trails uncross the air
so sky no more hatches
plans to own itself
       it owns itself
       reservation by mistake
reserved for our escape
because it is sky, because it is space.

Ornithological Perspectives

WALTER BARGEN
for Tom Carlough

Waking in a strange bed, I'd forgotten magpies
                              until this morning.
Beyond the window, one flies over the weathered picket fence,
                              black-white
staccato wing beat: moonlit cloud against night sky,
snow-streaked shadowed mountain,
                     manic-depressive,
winged declaration of disunion.
The long-tailed bird perches
                     in a bare cottonwood,
on the far side of the creek.

        ≈

Cold sentinels along Kansas dirt roads,
                     stone fence posts
subdivide the vast curve of horizon.
                         Nothing
like the Pacific's stoic statues
              facing centuries of hypnotic waves,
                         their heavy volcanic
brows softening to blank stares,
              having seen it all, all over again.
From corner post
to corner post at the shores of salty prairie
                     tall grasses surf the wind.

        ≈

Immigrant claims of ancestors:
                         a stretched, four-starred
steel rusting toward the future, stone posts
                         grooved by wire
that wind never tires tuning
                         to an infinite low moan,
a tireless sea-voice to an ear sinking in dust.

          ≈

The unpolished granite
                         at the limits of homesteads,
far fields, dry gulches, smoky hills,
                         a foundation of grassy outlines,
clumps of jonquils, and rotting wheel spokes.
                         Rectangular, upright,
chest-high squared limestone slabs,
                                   these high plains
scarred by a single tree and magpie,
                         slowly flying over dry seas.

Spiritus Mundi

GREG DELANTY

"What's the substance called, that incognito element
   in soda, fast food and so much more we scoff
making us crave more? A kind of consumer tapeworm,
   shades of the stuff of myth, akin to what Erysichthon,
who, on hacking sacred trees, is possessed by Famine,
   devouring all about him till finally he turns on his own flesh;
the Hungry Ghosts, their giraffe necks so narrow
   they can't get enough down to fill their bellies,
or that psychedelic vision of the insatiable spirit
   lodged in King Cork, eating the province out of house
and home. (You may have felt it yourselves, the growl
   in the belly.) These lesser known myths can't wait
on the wings any longer, have come into their own.
   They jostle each other as they take center stage."

Strange

ALIKI BARNSTONE

Strange spring of extremes:
   a Mother's Day walk, shedding sleeves,
and overnight, a drop
   of forty degrees;
a picnic of cold vegetables and fruit
   that made us sigh (delicious delight)
gave way to a taste
   for a meal of soup.

Still, my Blue-Eyed Grass opened
   in a storm whose thrashing spread
Oak leaf and Sweet Gumball tree trash
   on the haul we newly spread
on mulched beds, and seedlings
   took a beating from hail the size
of lima beans and peas,
   yet rose again.

I haven't consulted a graph to help me in my belief
   yet grasp the climate chaos
goes beyond the joke—"Don't like the weather?
   wait five minutes."
Hot poisons pushed an Arctic vortex south,
   then blew past, blew on
and a thaw came too soon, then whirled
   in another freeze.

I complain: "My Butterfly Bush died
   that for years gave nectar
for such colorful fluttering joy."

The garden shop owner replies
grimly: "It was a strange winter."
   I shake my head: "Too many extremes."
I buy a new bush, but not with ease,
   and pray it didn't grow from treated seeds

and the flowers won't dose the honeybees
   with nerve destroyers. I think it strange to ask
and despair any of us can keep track
   of the chain that supplies our need.

Killer Butterfly

WALTER BARGEN

I keep coming back to the story of the mountain lion,
fourth largest cat on the planet after tigers,
the tawny beast of the African veldt,
and something that roars in my sleep.
The quiet creature moved into a rich Boulder suburb,
where a man jumped onto the lion's back
when he saw its prey to be his daughter's cat.
He dragged it back into the yard by the tail
as it tried to escape, held it in a head lock,
attempting to free the tabby with his other hand.
A massive hind paw swatted the man across the cheek.
Suddenly aware of not one but four clawed fists he let go.

For months now, going out at night,
taking the compost to the garden,
retrieving an armload of firewood,
searching out stars, a sky to escape into,
I've thought of them, looked for their green eyes
reflecting the flashlight beam back at me,
crouched there in the high weeds,
behind the garden fence, or perched
on a low oak branch, these lions come
to nightly prey on me.

Behind the house across the suburban street,
the lion returned to kill a mule deer. The neighbors
gathered at the kitchen window, drinking wine,
watching days of bloody feasting, a mother
and two half-grown kittens. Only when the lion crouched
in an open garage, stalking a woman unloading groceries,

the woman jumping back in the car and blowing
the horn as if her life depended on it,
did the lion run off and hasn't returned.
Across the creek from my house in the next county,
road kill turns out to be a young mountain lion.
First confirmed sighting in a hundred years.

Now I'm told the woman who sits at the front desk,
receptionist from four to five each afternoon,
is afraid of butterflies. Outside the warehouse,
the air is haphazardly pasted with the orange
and black papery wings of a migration
that stretches from Canada to Mexico
though there are fewer and fewer each year,
and now mostly gone into the pesticides of Monsanto.
In the Sierra Madres each winter, there are trees
that turn into butterflies and in spring fall
back to earth as trees. Yesterday, I found
a monarch in the gutter, touched by a passing car,
its wings caught in a final stroke of flight.
I happen to place it in the small flowerpot
on the counter that holds a philodendron hostage.
At any moment, I'll hear the cries of a receptionist
devoured by a brilliantly winged wound.

When the Body

LINDA HOGAN

When the body wishes to speak, she will
reach into the night and pull back the rapture of this growing root
which has little faith in the other planets of the universe, knowing
only one, by the bulbs of the feet, their branching of toes. But the feet
have walked with the bones of their ancestors over long trails
leaving behind the roots of forests. They walk on the ghosts
of all that has gone before them, not just plant, but animal, human,
the bones of even the ones who left their horses to drink at the
spring running through earth's mortal body which has much to tell
about what happened that day.

When the body wishes to speak from the hands, it tells
of how it pulled children back from death and remembered every detail,
washing the children's bodies, legs, bellies, the delicate lips of the
    girl child,
the vulnerable testicles of the son,
the future of my people who brought themselves out of the river
in a spring freeze. That is only part of the story of hands
that touched the future.

This all started so simply, just a body with so much to say,
one with the hum of life in the ears
in a quiet room,
one of the root growing, finding a way through stone,
one not remembering nights with men and guns,
nor the ragged tresses and broken bones of my body.

I should go back to the hands with a thumb that makes us human,
except other creatures use tools and lift things to themselves,
intelligent all, like the crows here, one making a cast of earth clay

for the broken wing of its loved one and remaining
until it healed, broke through the clay, then flew away.
I will do that one day,
heal and fly, because a human can make no claims
better than any other, especially without wings, only hands.
Think of the willows
that were made into a fence then rooted and leafed,
tearing off the wires as they grew.
A human throws off the bonds if it can, if it tries, if it's possible,
the body so finely a miracle of its own, created of the elements
of anything that has lived on earth where everything that was
still is.

What I Keep

LINDA HOGAN

Once we had mountains
and you took them down.

It was enchanted before,
with the song of golden winds
of pollens from flowers
you also removed, as if it were gold
you searched for. We gave you our labor.
We gave you our food, our sleeping mats.
You slept a year before we sent you away
with burning arrows and your fat ran across earth.

You took the plants on ships
away from our beautiful woods
from the forest,
you took them back to strange lands
already destroyed.
Then you needed our lands,
our labor,
and more of you
always arriving,
until you took our homes
while we still lived inside them.
You took the birds, the rookeries of beautiful waters,
feathers for hats
made from animals of this land
and all the time you lost,
so much even
a young woman had to lead the way
for your fame.

You need us now,
so I give to you
my knowledge, my mind, my stone soup.
But to myself, for myself
I keep my soul.
Your god, your people
will never take it.

War Memorial

KATHERINE SONIAT

The day they put you back in the hospital ward,
you told the janitor how to be in five places at once
but only after he'd discovered you invented the plastic
garbage bag, so everyone at the nurse's station thought
you a millionaire and me the prettiest woman this side
of the toilet down the hall—because you said so
and they liked you, and I liked them.

In the parking lot that morning I held a blend of carrot juice to
    the sun,
and the man in the next car whispered to his wife, she must be
    European—
something suspect in the smoothed carrots, ginger, and celery
spun with light.
                    But let's go back to the lure of those five places
you took off for with your ochre robes flowing. Haunts as
    inexplicable
as the ancient fox koan is, and will remain. At night, you try to
    show me
what's wrong. "Like this" you manage, palms gliding past one
    another.
"Split line," your next attempt.   Never-meeting-hands, the gesture

that nails it—
single bird wing   the mind out of sync
                      out on a
limb

Bulk

DANIEL TOBIN

Far off in the unsayable distances
Beyond effect and cause, our own vast
Membrane no bigger than a nanochip
In the still vaster assemblages, the bulk
Hunkers, endless stack, infinite sum,
Barnacle lashed to the whale of itself
Cruising to no home, nowhere near here
Where on the far side of the stockade fence
Between facing yards our neighbor ventures
Outside her house, a screen door slamming shut,
Then smoker's cough on the guttering porch
Glimpsed between weathered gray slats,
Or wondered at through a passing veil of leaves
From the deck above: her hoard, her detritus.
How long since we'd heard her husband died?
For years on weekends his music blared.
Saddened for her, but not alone in being
Glad for the quiet, we worried our respects
Across the gulf of our differing lives,
And kept that quiet when her daughter's shouts
Echoed outside the peeling clapboards
To please stop, she was pleading, her drinking.
Years since, the quiet has settled in,
Her presence signaled by her clotted hacks,
Insistent, massing. She moves among them,
The unused tables, haphazard chairs,
Scattered playthings on grassless ground,
The dog-less doghouse, and at the lot's edge,
Wedged in by growth, monumental, moored
To nothing but its own floored gravity,

A delivery truck, mottled gray, rust-worn,
No sign of what goods it once had carried,
Windows fogged with grit, the ancient wheel still,
As if somehow it has always been here,
Always will be, while the satellite lens
Pulls back, panoptical, into its ken
With the blown weight of every receding thing.

All Hallows' Eve, County Mayo

JOAN MCBREEN

i.m. Jane Kenyon

Although late October sun brightens the morning,
flowers and grass are doomed. Yesterday
leaves came down around me from arches of trees
over the road near Cong. I remembered that you, Jane,
once wrote: *diminishing light contributes to our sense
of loss.* I bring in the last of the sweet pea and peonies,

check the small, hard tomatoes in the greenhouse,
plant a few spring bulbs, and remember you, too,
my lost father, as I look again at the sepia photograph

of you, aged six, in a sailor suit, your head almost
on your sister's shoulder, your hands joined.

As the Diamond

TESS GALLAGHER
for Medbh McGuckian

is bound by light, so are we
breath-bound into our
shining. But for that, the stone
of us would gray us past silence
into some deeper, earned
neglect. I wore a diamond once,

like a crown to a finger, but its
flash and imperial glance had
belonged to the mother
of the beloved and would not
accept my stolen ways. Giving it
back was like trying to give back
love, or give back a mother

when her worth quenched
even the beauty of the garden
she'd left behind. Still, I am
over-attracted to the shade she
designed under the largest
evergreen, planting in formation
the stalwart deer-proof lilies

and striped hostas, those whose
petals can leach light from a cloaked
star. Why here? I ask and swing
the mattock into parched
ground, loving the weight of its dull
thud and having to claw my way
down to something gentle—as with

an Irish-moment when you realize
you will never be let in except by
holding silence so it turns
back on itself—the power of the unsaid,
an ultimate compression,
so exceeding language you banish
vast libraries with a glance away

into my hearth where blackest coal
noiselessly witnesses two word-smiths
toiling in broad daylight
by firelight, in the glow of after-flame,
where my presence to your presence
is a humming out of which
the cottage midwife reappears

to recount the particularities
of each parish birth and we are thus
reborn in sparks of *first-breaths*
that ring us like a fairy fort, protecting
our held-in-light, until some
force-of-heart stuns us again
into stumbled speech and we agree

to the hostage-taking each word requires
of us, strung like that across the brow
of someone else's shadow-moment.
So it is when a reader opens the poem's
in-breathing, that which we took care
not to press too fully upon them
for fear of extinguishing its outlaw
vagabonding with freedom's
quarrelsome uptake.

The Burden of Theology

KELLY CHERRY

It was the burden of theology
to reconcile human love with death
but now theology has failed to do
what it was meant to do and in its place
we have the nihilism of savagery,
the cynicism of the ruthless rich,
the flagrant brutalization of girls and women,
a planet hopelessly in disrepair.

What can we do? Not turn back. The past
is past and irredeemable, a river
racing downstream, white water rapids none
can navigate. The former gods are old
and tired, they walk with canes, their backs hunched,
their eyesight fading, hearing failing, knees
like ladders that collapsed when we weren't looking.
Nor are there new ones who will rescue us.

I do not mean that we can stand in for
the gods of yesterday. I mean that all
of us together can make a difference
no god could or would make. But trust is necessary
to re-envision human life, and trust
is what we lack. So are we doomed to die
and die out? It seems so. We must not fool ourselves.
The future's here. It will not last for long.

A Line from Dogen

WALTER BARGEN

These clocks are useless.
　　They only measure themselves:
　　　　early, late, later still.

How long can they go on chanting
　　this one tick before you walk
　　　　out the door.

Room upon room
　　you continue on uncertain.
　　　　What is it you hope to find?

Calendars can't keep track
　　of the days.
　　　　Vast seasons come and go.

You follow the geese
　　that follow the stars.
　　　　Departure and arrival unspeakable.

Knowing, an illusion.
　　Not knowing, ignorance.
　　　　We measure the timeless.

Where do we turn?
　　Where do we turn?
　　　　Into the turning.

Contributors

JESS ALLEN is an aerial dancer, ecological performer, and walking artist from Aberystwyth, Wales. She is currently working toward a doctorate in walking and talking in rural landscapes as eco-activist arts practice at the University of Manchester. She uses walking to create unexpected performative encounters in unusual locations. Originally a biologist, she gained her first PhD degree from Aberystwyth before retraining in contemporary dance.

ALICE AZURE'S recent poetry appears in *Dawnland Voices 2.0, Yellow Medicine Review, Cream City Review, About Place Journal,* and *Dawnland Voices: An Anthology of Indigenous Writing from New England* (2014) . Her books include *In Mi'kmaq Country: Selected Poems and Stories* (2007), *Games of Transformation* (2012), *Along Came a Spider* (2011), and *Worn Cities* (2014), which received recognition for Chapbook of 2015 by Wordcraft Circle of Native Writers and Storytellers. Her Mi'kmaq heritage is rooted in the Kespu'kwitk District of Nova Scotia.

WALTER BARGEN has published eighteen books of poetry. His most recent books are *Days Like This Are Necessary: New and Selected Poems* (2009), *Endearing Ruins* (2012), *Trouble behind Glass Doors* (2013), *Quixotic* (2014), and *Gone West* (2014). He was the first poet laureate of Missouri (2008–9). His poems, essays, and stories have appeared in over 150 magazines.

ALIKI BARNSTONE, poet laureate of Missouri, is a translator, critic, editor, and visual artist. Author of seven books of poetry, most recently, *Bright Body* (2011); *Dear God Dear, Dr. Heartbreak: New and Selected Poems* (2009); and a chapbook, *Winter, with Child* (2015). Awards include a Senior Fulbright Fellowship in Greece, the Silver Pen Award from the Nevada Writers Hall of Fame, a Pennsylvania Council on the Arts Literature Fellowship, and a residency at the Anderson Center at Tower View. She is professor of English and creative writing at the University of Missouri.

MICHAEL S. BEGNAL'S books include *Future Blues* (2012), *Ancestor Worship* (2007), and a chapbook, *The Muddy Banks* (2016). His work appears in numerous journals and anthologies and has been nominated for a Pushcart Prize. He has an MFA from North Carolina State University and teaches at Ball State University.

ANDREA BENASSI received a PhD degree in anthropology in 2014 from La Sapienza University of Rome. He has done fieldwork and research in Southeast Asia (Laos and Indonesia) and worked as an anthropologist in Baltistan (Pakistan) for ISIAO (Italian Institute for Africa and Orient) for environmental and heritage promotion projects. In Italy he works as an ethno-anthropological expert about intangible cultural heritage, global policies, and museography. His research focus is on the perception of landscapes and nature in relationship to the emergence of a new aesthetic in the Anthropocene.

KIMBERLY BLAESER, Anishinaabe poet, photographer, and scholar, is the author of three poetry collections—*Apprenticed to Justice* (2007), *Absentee Indians and Other Poems* (2002), and *Trailing You* (1994). A professor at University of Wisconsin-Milwaukee and the Wisconsin Poet Laureate, she teaches creative writing and Native American literature. Her scholarly monograph, *Gerald Vizenor: Writing in the Oral Tradition*, was the first native-authored book-length study of an Indigenous author. Blaeser is editor of *Traces in Blood, Bone, and Stone: Contemporary Ojibwe Poetry* (2006) and *Stories Migrating Home: A Collection of Anishinaabe Prose* (1999). Her poetry, short fiction, and essays have been widely anthologized, and selections of her poetry have also been translated into several languages, including Spanish, Norwegian, Indonesian, Hungarian, and French. Blaeser is an editorial board member for the American Indian Lives series of University of Nebraska Press and for the Native American Series of Michigan State University Press and has served on the advisory board for the Sequoyah Research Center and Native American Press Archives and on the Poetry Fellowship Panel for the National Endowment of the Arts. She is involved in collaborative creative and scholarly endeavors, most recently with the Crow Commons. Among her current projects is an art chapbook of her picto-poems and ekphrastic poetry, *Ancient Light.*

DAVID BRANNAN'S poems have been published in two chapbooks and a scattering of magazines from Blue Canary Press as well as in other publications such as the *Shepherd-Express, Nobody Quarterly, Burdock, Beloit Poetry Journal,* and *Asphodel Madness.* He lives in Milwaukee where he works in Bottlehouse B of the former Schlitz brewery as an international academic credential evaluator.

CHRISTINE CASSON, scholar/writer-in-residence at Emerson College, is the author of *After the First World* (2008), a book of poems. Her work has appeared in numerous journals and anthologies, including *Agenda* (England), *Stand* (England), the *Dalhousie Review, DoubleTake, Natural Bridge, Alabama Literary Review, Fashioned Pleasures* (2005), *Never Before* (2005), and *Conversation Pieces* (2007). She has also published critical essays on the work of Leslie Marmon Silko, Linda Hogan, and Robert Penn Warren.

KELLY CHERRY is the author of twenty-five books, ten chapbooks, and two translations of classical drama. Her most recent book is *Quartet for J. Robert Oppenheimer: A Poem* (2017). Cherry is a former poet laureate of Virginia and member of Poets Corner, Cathedral Church of St. John the Divine, New York City. She was the first recipient of the Hanes Poetry Prize from the Fellowship of Southern Writers and has received awards from the National Endowment for the Arts, U.S. Information Agency, and the Rockefeller Foundation as well as the Bradley Lifetime Award and Weinstein Award, among other distinctions. Her work appears in prize anthologies. Cherry is Eudora Welty Professor Emerita of English and Evjue-Bascom Professor in the Humanities, University of Wisconsin–Madison.

EMILIO COCCO is a sociologist with an international background and an interdisciplinary approach to cross-sectorial domains such as cultural memories, tourism and mobility, identity making, and political communication. A specialist in the emerging field of maritime sociology, he is the author of *Sociologia oceanica* (2015) and coauthor, with Fabiana Dimpflmeier, of *I confini nel mare / Borders in the Sea* (2015). Dr. Cocco teaches at the University of Teramo and at the American University of Rome.

NANCY S. COOK is professor of English at the University of Montana Missoula. Her publications include work on the language of U.S. water policy, on ranching, on Montana writers, and on authenticity in western American writing. She is a past president of the Western Literature Association. Currently she is at work on a book-length study of twentieth-century U.S. ranching cultures.

NESSA CRONIN is lecturer in Irish Studies, Centre for Irish Studies, National University of Ireland–Galway. She has published widely on various aspects of Irish cultural geography and literary geographies and is coeditor of *Anáil an Bhéil Bheo: Orality and Modern Irish Culture* (2009). She is currently writing a monograph on governmentality, cartography, and the making of Irish colonial space and is coeditor of the volume *Lifeworlds: Space, Place and Irish Culture* (2017).

TONY CURTIS is emeritus professor of poetry at the University of South Wales. He is the author and editor of over forty books, most recently *Poems Selected and New: From the Fortunate Isles* (2016), *Selected Stories: Some Kind of Immortality* (2017), and a memoir, *My Life with Dylan Thomas* (2014). He is a fellow of the Royal Society for Literature.

GREG DELANTY is poet-in-residence at St. Michael's College, Vermont. His latest book of poems is *The Greek Anthology, Book XVII* (England, 2012), released in the United States as *Book Seventeen* (2015). He is the lead poet in the anthology *So Little Time: A World in Climate Crisis* (2014). His poems are widely anthologized, including in the *Norton Introduction to Poetry*, the *Field Day Anthology of Irish Writing*, *American Poets of the New Century*, *20th Century Irish Poems*, and *Contemporary Poets of New England*. Delanty has received numerous awards, most recently a Guggenheim for poetry.

FABIANA DIMPFLMEIER earned her doctorate in cultural anthropology at La Sapienza University of Rome and currently is an independent researcher specializing in nineteenth- and early-twentieth-century history of anthropology. Her research interests include travel writing, maritime anthropology, regionalism, and nation building in connection with the representation of otherness. Most recently, she has coedited *Lamberto Loria e la ragnatela dei suoi significati* (2014); coauthored *I confini nel mare. Alterità e identità nei diari della Marina italiana sull'oceano* (2016) (winner of the De Cia Prize); and authored the volume *Nelle mille patrie insulari. Etnografia di Lamberto Loria nella Nuova Guinea britannica* (2017).

ELIZABETH DODD is a university distinguished professor of English at Kansas State University. She is the author of three collections of essays and two of poetry, most recently *Horizon's Lens: My Time on the Turning World* (2012). She is the nonfiction editor for *Terrain. org: An Online Journal of the Built + Natural Environments.*

SUSAN MILLAR DUMARS has published four collections with Salmon Poetry, the most recent of which, *Bone Fire*, appeared in 2016. She published a book of short stories, *Lights in the Distance*, in 2010 and is currently at work on a second story collection. Born in Philadelphia, Susan lives in Galway, Ireland, where she and her husband, Kevin Higgins, have coordinated the Over the Edge reading series since 2003. She is the editor of the 2013 anthology *Over the Edge: The First Ten Years.*

DAWN DUPLER'S poetry and fiction can be found in *Natural Bridge, Chiron Review, Whiskey Island Magazine, Blue Earth Review*, and other literary journals and anthologies. She is one of the 2015 recipients of the James Nash Award of the St. Louis Poetry Center and first place poetry winner of the 2013 Columbia Chapter of the Missouri Writers' Guild. Her nonfiction book *St. Louis in the Civil War* was published in 2014. Dupler spent her early career as an engineer in product development, working for several Fortune 500 companies.

HEID E. ERDRICH is a member of the Turtle Mountain Band of Ojibwe. Her poetry collections include *Cell Traffic: New and Selected Poems* (2012); *National Monuments* (2008), winner of the Minnesota Book Award; and *The Mother's Tongue* (2005), part of Salt Publishing's award-winning Earthworks series. With Laura Tohe she coedited the anthology *Sister Nations: Native American Women on Community* (2002). She is at work on an edited collection titled *New Poets of Native Nations.* Her work appears in numerous anthologies, including the *Anthology of Contemporary American Poetry* (2014). Erdrich teaches in the low-residency MFA creative writing program of Augsburg College. She is curator of Ephemera at the New Museum for Archaic Media.

ANN FISHER-WIRTH'S fourth book of poems is *Dream Cabinet* (2012). With Laura-Gray Street she coedited the groundbreaking *Eco-*

poetry Anthology (2013). Her current project is a collaborative poetry-photography book manuscript and museum exhibition, *Mississippi*, with Maude Schuyler Clay. A fellow of the Black Earth Institute, she has published widely and received numerous awards for her work. She teaches at the University of Mississippi, where she also directs the Environmental Studies minor.

TESS GALLAGHER'S ninth volume of poetry is *Midnight Lantern: New and Selected Poems* (2011) published in the United States and England. *Boogie-Woogie Crisscross*, a collaboration with Lawrence Matsuda, appeared in 2016. Other poetry includes *Dear Ghosts* (2008), *Moon Crossing Bridge* (1992), and *Amplitude* (1987). *The Man from Kenvara: Selected Stories* was published in 2009. *Barnacle Soup—Stories from the West of Ireland* (2007) is a collaboration with the Sligo storyteller and painter Josie Gray. Gallagher spearheaded the publication of Raymond Carver's *Beginners* in Library of America's complete collection of his stories. Many of her new poems are set at Lough Arrow in County Sligo in the West of Ireland.

BRENDAN GALVIN is the author of eighteen collections of poems. *Habitat: New and Selected Poems* 1965–2005 (2005) was a finalist for the National Book Award. *Egg Island Almanac* (2017) was a Crab Orchard series prizewinner. His awards include a Guggenheim Fellowship, two National Endowment for the Arts fellowships, the Sotheby Prize (Arvon Foundation), the Iowa Poetry Prize, and Poetry's Levinson Prize, the first O. B. Hardison Jr. Poetry Prize (Folger Shakespeare Library), the Charity Randall Citation (International Poetry Forum), the *Sewanee Review*'s Aiken Taylor Award in Modern American Poetry, and the Boatwright Prize (*Shenandoah*).

TWYLA M. HANSEN is Nebraska's state poet and codirector of the website *Poetry from the Plains: A Nebraska Perspective*. Her newest book of poetry is *Rock•Tree•Bird*, (2017), and she has six previous books, including Nebraska Book Award winners *Dirt Songs: A Plains Duet* (2011) and *Potato Soup* (2001), named as one of the 150 Notable Nebraska Books. Her writing has been published in *Broadkill Review, Canary, Midwest Quarterly, Organization & Environment, Prairie Fire Newspaper, Prairie Schooner, Nebraska Poetry: A*

Sesquicentennial Anthology 1867–2017, Poetry Out Loud Anthology, The Encyclopedia of the Great Plains, and the Writer's Almanac. Her work has also been filmed by NET Nebraska.

MICHAEL HEFFERNAN'S *The Night-Watchman's Daughter* was published in 2016. He has taught poetry at the University of Arkansas–Fayetteville since 1986. His other books include *To the Wreakers of Havoc* (1984), *Love's Answer* (1994), *The Night Breeze Off the Ocean* (2005), *At the Bureau of Divine Music* (2011), and *Walking Distance* (2013). He has won three fellowships from the National Endowment for the Arts.

LINDA HOGAN is a Native American (Chickasaw) poet, novelist, essayist, and environmentalist. Hogan's poetry collections include *Seeing through the Sun* (1985), which won the American Book Award from the Before Columbus Foundation; *Savings* (1988); *The Book of Medicines,* a National Book Critics Circle Award finalist (1993); and *Rounding the Human Corners* (2008). She has published nonfiction works such as *Dwellings: A Spiritual History of the Living World* (1995), *The Woman Who Watches over the World: A Native Memoir* (2001), and, with Brenda Peterson, *Sighting: The Gray Whales' Mysterious Journey* (2002). A recipient of grants from the National Endowment for the Arts and the Guggenheim Foundation for her fiction, Hogan's novels include *Mean Spirit* (1990), *Solar Storms* (1995), *Power* (1998), and *People of the Whale: A Novel* (2008).

MAJOR JACKSON is the author of four collections of poetry, most recently *Roll Deep* (2015). He teaches at the University of Vermont as the Richard Dennis University Professor in the Department of English.

BARRY JOHNSTON was born in County Monaghan, Ireland, and he is employed as a community development worker in Belfast, Northern Ireland. He has recorded and published two music CDs and is currently working on a collection of short stories. Barry has previously attained a master's degree in Ethics, Culture and Global Change from the National University of Ireland–Galway. He currently volunteers with several environmental conservationist groups in Northern Ireland.

DAVID LLOYD is the author of nine books, including three poetry collections: *Warriors* (2012), *The Gospel According to Frank* (2009), and

The Everyday Apocalypse (2002). In 2000 he received the Poetry Society of America's Robert H. Winner Memorial Award. In 2001 he was a Fulbright Distinguished Scholar-in-Residence at Bangor University. His poems have appeared in numerous magazines, including *Crab Orchard Review*, *DoubleTake*, and *Planet*. He directs the Creative Writing Program at Le Moyne College in Syracuse, New York.

WILLIAM LOGAN is the author of ten volumes of poetry and six books of essays and reviews. *The Undiscovered Country* received the 2005 National Book Critics Circle Award in Criticism. He has also received the inaugural Randall Jarrell Award in Poetry Criticism and the Aiken Taylor Award in Modern American Poetry. His most recent book of criticism, *Guilty Knowledge, Guilty Pleasure*, appeared in 2014. *Rift of Light*, a new book of poems, was published in 2017.

TOM LYNCH is an English professor at the University of Nebraska–Lincoln, where he teaches ecocriticism and place-based approaches to literature. He edits the journal *Western American Literature*. He is the author of *Xerophilia: Ecocritical Explorations in Southwestern Literature* (2008). Along with Cheryll Glotfelty and Karla Armbruster, he coedited *The Bioregional Imagination: Literature, Ecology, Place* (2012). And with Susan N. Maher he coedited *Artifacts and Illuminations: Critical Essays on Loren Eiseley* (2012). He is a contributing author to SueEllen Campbell's *The Face of the Earth: Natural Landscapes, Science, and Culture* (2011). Most recently he coedited *Natural Treasures of the Great Plains: An Ecological Perspective* (2015).

HARMON MAHER for the last thirty-two years has been at the University of Nebraska–Omaha as a professor of geology, with stints as department chair and interim associate vice chancellor for research and creative activity. His geologic field research has been focused on the Southern Appalachians, the Great Plains, and the Arctic archipelago of Svalbard (a Norwegian protectorate and a place he is particularly fond of). Related publications include over forty scholarly contributions in journals and coauthorship of *The Roadside Geology of Nebraska* (2002), a layperson's guide to the geology of the state.

SUSAN NARAMORE MAHER is professor of English and dean of the College of Liberal Arts at the University of Minnesota Duluth. She has published widely on the literature of the American and Canadian Wests, with particular focuses on creative nonfiction, environmental writing, and Willa Cather. Coeditor of *Coming into McPhee Country* (2003) and *Artifacts and Illuminations: Critical Essays on Loren Eiseley* (2012), Dr. Maher's most recent study is *Deep Map Country: Literary Cartography of the Great Plains* (2014).

JOAN MCBREEN is from Sligo, Ireland, and now divides her time between Tuam and Renvyle, County Galway. Her most recent poetry collection is *Heather Island* (2009). In 2014 she produced a CD, *The Mountain Ash in Connemara*, with composer Glen Austin and the RTE Contempo String Quartet. A broadside, "The Mountain Ash," a collaboration with graphic artist Margaret Irwin West, appeared in 2015. She is working on a new collection of poetry, "The Stone Jug." Her anthologies *The White Page-Twentieth-Century Irish Women Poets* (1999) and *The Watchful Heart: A New Generation of Irish Poets* (2009) are soon to be reprinted.

BRONWYN PREECE lives off the grid, in a solar- and waterwheel-powered house on Lasqueti Island, Canada. She is an improvisational site-sensitive performer, community applied theater practitioner, author and poet, butoh dancer, walking and visual eARThist, and the pioneer of earthBODYment. Her work interrogates the tiers of our imbricated relationships with place/self/other and the nexuses of our own (imposed) dichotomies. She has published in *Canadian Theatre Review, Phenomenology and Practice, Trumpeter: Journal of Ecosophy, Contemporary Theatre Review, Theatre Journal, Journal of Somatic and Dance Practices*, and *Choreographic Practices*. She is also the author of *Gulf Islands Alphabet* (2012), *In the Spirit of Homebirth* (2015), and *Off-the-Grid Kid* (2015).

BERNARD QUETCHENBACH is a professor in the Department of English, Philosophy, and Modern Languages at Montana State University Billings, where he teaches courses in writing and literature. His poems, essays, articles, and reviews have appeared in a variety of books, journals, and anthologies; his work has recently been published in an essay collection *Accidental Gravity* (2017) and in the anthologies *Unearthing Paradise* (2016), *Birdsong* (2016), *Animals and the Environment* (2015), and *Trash Animals* (2013) as well as the journals *Poecology, Stone Canoe,* and *ISLE.*

ALBERTO RÍOS, Arizona's inaugural poet laureate and a chancellor of the Academy of American Poets, was born in Nogales, Arizona, on the Mexico-Arizona border, and he has written from that geographic and sociological perspective through five decades. His eleven collections of poetry include, most recently, *A Small Story about the Sky* (2015) and *The Smallest Muscle in the Human Body* (2002), a finalist for the National Book Award. He has also written three short story collections and a memoir about growing up on the Mexican border, *Capirotada* (1999). Ríos is the host of the PBS program *Books & Co.* and has taught at Arizona State University since 1982.

MARJORIE SAISER has received the Little Bluestem Award, the WILLA Literary Award, and four Nebraska Book Awards. Her poems have been published in *Prairie Schooner, Nimrod, RHINO, Burntdistrict, Cimarron Review, Writer's Almanac, The Fourth River, Chattahoochee Review, PoetryMagazine.com,* and *American Life in Poetry.* She coedited *Times of Sorrow / Times of Grace* (2002), a collection of writing by women on the Great Plains, as well as *Road Trip* (2009), which features interviews with writers. Saiser is the author of three chapbooks and five full-length books, including *I Have Nothing to Say about Fire* (2016).

KATHERINE SONIAT'S *The Goodbye Animals* (2014) won the *Turtle Island Quarterly* Chapbook Prize. *The Swing Girl* won Best Collection of 2011 by the Poetry Council of North Carolina, and *A Shared Life: Poems* (1993) was awarded the Iowa Poetry Prize and a Virginia Prize for Poetry. *Notes of Departure* (1986) received the Camden Poetry Prize (Walt Whitman Center for the Arts and Humanities). Her most recent volume is *Bright Stranger* (2016). She lives in Asheville, North Carolina, and teaches in the Great Smokies Writers' Program at the University of North Carolina–Asheville.

MARY SWANDER is the poet laureate of Iowa and the executive director of AgArts, a nonprofit designed to imagine and promote healthy food systems through the arts. Swander holds dual citizenship in Ireland and the United States and has written extensively of life on the land and the sea in both cultures. Her latest book is *The Sunnyside* (2015), about Amish attitudes toward death. Currently, she is touring two plays: *Map of My Kingdom,* on farmland succession, and *Vang,* a drama about immigrant farmers from Mexico, Sudan, Laos, and the Netherlands.

DANIEL TOBIN is the author of seven books of poems, *Where the World Is Made* (1998), *Double Life* (2004), *The Narrows* (2005), *Second Things* (2008), *Belated Heavens* (2010) (winner of the Massachusetts Book Award in Poetry), *The Net* (2014), and the book-length poem *From Nothing* (2016), along with the critical studies *Passage to the Center* (1998) and *Awake in America: On Irish-American Poetry* (2011). He is the editor of *The Book of Irish American Poetry from the Eighteenth Century to the Present* (2007), *Light in Hand: Selected Early Poems of Lola Ridge* (2007), *Poet's Work, Poet's Play* (2008), and *The Collected Early Poems of Lola Ridge* (2017). His awards include fellowships from the National Endowment for the Arts and the John Simon Guggenheim Foundation.

COLM TÓIBÍN, from Enniscorthy, County Wexford, Ireland, is one of the anglophone world's most celebrated authors. Writing across many genres, his works include novels such as *The Master* (2004), *Brooklyn* (2009), and *House of Names* (2017); a nonfiction collection *New Ways to Kill Your Mother* (2012); and a short story collection *The Empty Family* (2010). The major motion picture based on *Brooklyn* (2015) received critical acclaim and a best picture Academy Award nomination.

PAMELA USCHUK is the author of numerous books of poems, including *Blood Flower* (2014), *Wild in the Plaza of Memory* (2012), *Crazy Love: New Poems* (2009), *Finding Peaches in the Desert* (2000), *One Legged Dancer* (2012), *Scattered Risks* (2005), nominated by *Ploughshares* for the Zacharias Poetry Award and for a Pulitzer Prize, and *Without the Comfort of Stars: New and Selected Poems* (2007). Uschuk's work has been widely translated and has appeared in over 250 journals and anthologies. Awards include the Struga International Poetry Prize, the Dorothy Daniels Writing Award from the National League of American PEN Women, the 2001 Literature Award from the Tucson/Pima Arts Council for *Finding Peaches in the Desert*, and the King's English Prize. Uschuk is editor-in-chief of the literary magazine *Cutthroat, A Journal of the Arts* and is a professor of creative writing who teaches courses at the Poetry Center at the University of Arizona.

RICK VAN NOY is the author of *Surveying the Interior: Literary Cartographers and the Sense of Place* (2003) and *A Natural Sense of Wonder: Connecting Kids with Nature through the Seasons* (2008), which won the Reed Award for Outstanding Writing on the Southern Environment. His work has appeared in *Orion, Blue Ridge Country, Appalachian Voices, Watershed,* and elsewhere. He is at work on a book about Southeast communities and climate change. He is a professor of English and environmental literature at Radford University and lives in the New River Valley of Virginia's Blue Ridge Mountains.

DRUCILLA WALL'S book of poetry is *The Geese at the Gates* (2011). Her second collection of poems and essays is forthcoming from Salmon Poetry. Individual poems, scholarly essays, and stories appear in numerous literary journals and are anthologized in *Red Lamp, Black Piano: The Caca Mills Anthology; The People Who Stayed: Southeastern Indian Writing after Removal; Eating Fire, Tasting Blood: Breaking the Great Silence of the American Indian Holocaust;* and *True West: Authenticity and the American West.* She teaches American and Native American literature and essay writing at the University of Missouri–St. Louis.

EAMONN WALL has published numerous volumes of poems and scholarship. His recent publications include *Junction City: Poems 1990–2015* (2015) and *Writing the Irish West: Ecologies and Traditions* (2011). In addition to his various books, Eamonn Wall has published essays, articles, and reviews in such publications as the *Irish Times,* the *Chicago Tribune,* the *Washington Post,* and *New Hibernia Review.* His work has appeared in various anthologies, including *Ireland through Its Writers* (2000) and *The Book of Irish-American Poetry from the 18th Century to the Present* (2008). Eamonn Wall teaches at the University of Missouri–St. Louis as the Smurfit-Stone Corporation Professor in Irish Studies.

JOEL WEISHAUS'S *Feels Like Home Again: Collected Poems* was published in 2014. As an editor, translator, or coauthor, he has published five books and more than forty book reviews, essays, and critiques. Weishaus has been an adjunct curator at the University of New Mexico's Fine Arts Museum, Albuquerque, and a writer in residence at UNM's Center for Southwest Research. He was visiting faculty at Portland State University's English Department, 2003–9 and a visiting scholar at the University of California–Santa Barbara, 2011–12. He is presently artist-in-residence at Pacifica Graduate Institute, Carpinteria, California, where he counsels students on creativity and scholarship.

O. ALAN WELTZIEN, professor of English at the University of Montana Western, has published dozens of articles and authored, edited, or coedited nine books, most recently *Exceptional Mountains: A Cultural History of the Pacific Northwest Volcanoes* (2016) and *Rembrandt in the Stairwell* (2016), his third book of poetry. Weltzien has had two Fulbright fellowships and one UM Missoula International Faculty Award. He teaches a range of American, western American, and Montana literature courses as well as courses in environmental writing. He still skis in winter and hikes and scrambles peaks in summer, and he's still drawn to volcanoes anywhere.